The key ring was in the ignition and the switch remained in the on position. The gearshift was in drive. And the dashboard clock had stopped at 1:50 . . .

When workers finally popped the trunk, they saw a badly decomposed body and were overwhelmed by the smell of rotten flesh . . .

The corpse was nude from the waist down. Her panties and pantyhose were missing and her skirt and white lace slip were pushed above her navel over her chest. There was a shell casing from a .22-caliber bullet in the cuff of her coat . . .

Her jewelry was still intact. On her right hand she wore a gold ring with a cobalt blue stone surrounded by diamonds; a Baume and Mercier watch and a gold linked bracelet adorned her left hand. Around her [illegible] a religious medal . . .

It was Satu[illegible] body had been at the b[illegible] for nine months.

D0835098

BLIND JUSTICE

A Murder, a Scandal, and a Brother's Search to Avenge His Sister's Death

EDIE AND RAY GIBSON
and Randall Turner

ST. MARTIN'S PAPERBACKS

NOTE: If you purchased this book without a cover you should be aware that this book is stolen property. It was reported as 'unsold and destroyed' to the publisher, and neither the author nor the publisher has received any payment for this 'stripped book'.

BLIND JUSTICE

Copyright © 1991 by Edie and Ray Gibson and Randall Turner.
Excerpt from *Fair Game* copyright © 1992 by Bernard DuClos.

Cover photographs by *Star-Herald*.

All rights reserved. No part of this book may be used or reproduced in any manner whatsoever without written permission except in the case of brief quotations embodied in critical articles or reviews. For information, address St. Martin's Press, 175 Fifth Avenue, New York, N.Y. 10010.

Library of Congress Catalog Card Number: 91-20654

ISBN: 0-312-92866-1

Printed in the United States of America

St. Martin's Press hardcover edition/November 1991
St. Martin's Paperbacks edition/October 1992

10 9 8 7 6 5 4 3 2 1

Authors' Note

While much of the dialogue in this book is taken directly from court transcripts and police reports, there are certain instances where it has been reconstructed through interviews with the principals of the story.

Because of the lengthy time lapse and other unique circumstances surrounding the investigations into the murder of Dianne Masters, there are many conflicting statements by witnesses and others interviewed over the years by authorities. Where such conflicts exist, the authors have sought to provide the version which in their opinion is the most plausible.

Every attempt was made to interview all of the principals involved in this case. In some instances, relevant individuals declined.

The names of the major characters in the book have not been changed. Some persons, though, agreed to be interviewed only on the condition that their real identities be concealed. The authors agreed to abide by their request in order to preserve their privacy. Any similarities between the following fictitious names used and those of living persons is coincidental: Gretchen Connell, Bénédicte Kagy, Jane Jerrold, Teri Swanson, Jessica (Jim Koscielniak's daughter), and Bull (nickname of bar owner).

Acknowledgments

This book could not have been completed were it not for the assistance the authors received from a wide variety of individuals. They graciously shared with us their knowledge and their time.

The book was the idea of Randy Turner. To help him launch the project, Rick Hawley proved to be invaluable. Originally, Thomas Burton was to be the coauthor, but when he left the *Chicago Tribune* to join the staff of the *Wall Street Journal*, he learned that he would not be able to finish the task. Many of the hours he had spent on the book are reflected in the following pages.

Several of Ray Gibson's colleagues at the *Chicago Tribune* provided guidance and insight based on their coverage of the story. They include Maurice Possley and William Gaines as well as former staffers John Camper and Dean Baquet. Others who helped us are *Chicago Sun-Times* reporters Chuck Neubauer and Ray Hanania.

We particularly appreciate the efforts of Donna Hurley. A true friend of Dianne Masters, she clipped news stories for us, shared insights into Dianne's life, and offered encouragement along the way.

We are grateful, too, to Diane Olson. Her faith in us never wavered and she was always ready to listen.

Finally, our thanks to the Federal Bureau of Investigation for arranging interviews with agents Larry Damron, Ivan Harris, and David Parker.

Chapter One

March 16, 1982

DIANNE Masters pulled her yellow-and-white Cadillac Coupe de Ville into the parking lot of the Ethan Allen furniture store. When she saw that her lover, Jim Koscielniak, was waiting for her as planned, she quickly got out of her car, locked the door, and jumped into his Pontiac. He greeted her with a wide grin and a lingering kiss that promised an afternoon of amorous pleasure.

Dianne found herself starting to relax. Being with Jim revitalized her spirit. For a few brief hours, she would forget the bitter divorce and custody battle that loomed ahead.

They drove to the La Grange Motel, one of several budget hostelries the couple frequented, which was less than a quarter mile away. It was in Countryside, one of Chicago's southwestern suburbs, along a bustling thoroughfare teeming with shopping centers and fast-food eateries.

A towering sign advertised WEEKLY RATES. The property boasted a small swimming pool, a reminder of the La Grange's heyday, when it catered to guests traveling along the nearby famous Route 66. Now it was one of those insipid places that were cloned across America. Those seeking ambience and luxurious amenities went elsewhere.

Jim parked his red Phoenix directly in front of the door to their room. As soon as they were inside, Dianne double-locked the doors and drew both sets of drapes.

She and Jim embraced, gazing longingly at each other. Theirs was the union the thirty-five-year old Dianne had unsuccessfully sought in her marriage. She had found a soul mate and for the first time in years, her self-doubts had vanished.

She was continuously amazed by their relationship. Admittedly, he was not Robert Redford. Jim's hazel eyes were hidden behind a pair of rectangular-shaped, tortoise shell glasses, and his brown hair, flecked with gray, covered his ears. At five feet eleven inches and 190 pounds, he was stockily built.

Jim, an economics professor, resembled a cuddly teddy bear, and Dianne delighted in his body. Just an accidental touch of elbows could elicit in her a sensual response that she had forgotten existed. She and her husband Alan had slept apart for years and she was overjoyed that someone finally wanted her. Jim had reaffirmed her sexuality. And he was an imaginative and considerate partner in bed.

Jim reached out and drew her into his arms. He felt so lucky that Dianne loved him. She was every man's fantasy. The all-American girl—petite, blond hair, sparkling emerald-green eyes, flawless skin, white teeth, and a trim figure that looked as good in blue jeans as it did in haute couture.

His mouth covered her half-parted lips and her tongue teased his. Jim enjoyed the feel of her hands gently kneading his shoulders as they made their way up to the nape of his neck and became entangled in his hair. Their kisses became more urgent, a consuming fire of sensations.

Dianne unbuttoned Jim's shirt and he helped her take off her skirt and blouse. Their clothes fell to the floor and they moved toward the bed to make love. It had been like this for two and a half months now. Their trysts provided her with the sexual excitement of which she had been bereft for years. "I love our passion," Dianne had told her lover. "Once you flip my switch, I'm yours."

But sex was just a part of their relationship. She and Jim had fallen in love.

It was easy, though, for men to fall in love with Dianne Masters. Many had. She was not only pretty, she was wealthy. The quintessential upper-middle-class suburban housewife. Poised. Articulate. Athletic. Elegantly clad in designer labels and jewelry worth thousands of dollars. Yet money had never brought her the happiness she felt with Jim.

He had known her for two and a half years before their affair began. He had first seen Dianne when she was running as a trustee for the Moraine Valley Community College board and had sought the endorsement of the teachers union. She didn't receive it, but she had captivated Jim.

Dazzled by Dianne's self-confidence, he had telephoned her an hour later. He told Dianne how impressed he was by her presentation but that unfortunately, others had not shared his opinion.

Despite the lack of faculty support, Dianne still won the election. She and Jim, who was divorced, saw each other regularly. Because he was the union's vice president, he frequently attended board meetings. Ensconced in a front row seat, he found himself admiring Dianne's svelte figure. "I used to look at her legs," he admitted later. "I didn't mean to, but I couldn't help myself."

They'd chat during the recess or after the session. When she was on campus, she occasionally stopped in at his office to use his phone. Both brought their children to the numerous school functions, and Dianne's daughter Anndra and Jim's daughter Jessica became friends. While the girls talked, the parents compared notes about their offspring.

In the fall of 1981, they started having coffee together at school and he began socializing with the board members after their meetings. Jim and Dianne discovered that they shared many interests. "We loved knowledge and learning. Culture and book fairs. And we both liked to sleep until noon," he recalls.

Their conversations, however, had veered to a more personal level. Dianne was now confiding in him and her unhappy marriage was foremost on her mind. She wanted to leave her husband, Alan Masters, because they had nothing in common and they were sexually incompatible.

Jim and Dianne also discussed their aspirations for the future. For instance, both wanted a baby boy to complete their family.

The more time Jim and Dianne spent together, the more they realized that their friendship was entering a new stage. Jim did not want to be responsible for the breakup of a marriage, though. He'd been attracted to Dianne from the onset. But as soon as he learned Dianne was married, he had resisted the urge to ask her out. Nonetheless, he found Dianne irresistible.

At a Christmas party for the college staff, they decided to begin their affair in earnest. Dianne and Jim left the festivities and went to a motel. Their first lovemaking session unnerved them. Neither had anticipated the depth of their feelings for each other.

Jim initially thought they were going to have a fling. But the relationship turned serious faster than either of them had imagined. They realized that two souls had met, that each had found a kindred spirit. Dianne told Jim that it had been inevitable that the two would fall in love. She wanted to spend the rest of her life with him.

As the relationship blossomed, Dianne recognized that she had to end her marriage. She hired an attorney, announced her intentions to Alan, and was now waiting for the divorce papers to be filed in court. She told Jim that she wanted the divorce to become finalized as quickly as possible.

She tried to see him whenever she could. Being together helped preserve her sanity. They went out to lunch, to dinner, and to the movies.

One Sunday afternoon, Jim took her to see *On Golden Pond*, and she was deeply affected by the film. She sat there and cried. She and Jim hugged. "I want to grow old with you," she told him.

"Let's go to my house and talk," he suggested to Dianne.

Jim, who was unpretentious, had continued to live in Calumet City, a blue-collar suburb on Chicago's south side, where he had grown up. After his divorce, he returned to his parents' bungalow and was content to stay there.

When Dianne walked into Jim's house, she immediately felt comfortable. It was familiar and reminded her of her own childhood. She, too, had grown up in a Polish home, in the working-class suburb of Franklin Park. Unlike Jim, she had not been happy with her family's life-style. She had desperately sought wealth and all its accoutrements.

To attain her goal, she had reconciled herself to being a man's possession. For thirteen years, Dianne was showered with gifts—furs, jewels, unlimited spending money, a summer home on the shores of Lake Michigan, and a condo in Florida. She had everything she desired. Except love.

Since the birth of her four-year-old daughter Anndra, Dianne had undergone a metamorphosis and had come to understand what truly was important to her. She would tell friends that she knew she was bought and paid for and she was ashamed at the significance she had placed on materialism. She told Jim that real existence meant more than status. And that money couldn't buy the most important thing in life: love.

Now Dianne wanted roots, a family life. So she again embraced the traditional values that had been instilled in her as a young girl. She also had returned to the Catholic church.

Jim had hoped that his parents would be at home after the movie; he was anxious to introduce them to Dianne. But they were out. Dianne ultimately met Jim's mother on the telephone.

Dianne would call Jim's house and often talk to his mother. Usually their exchanges were brief, but sometimes they turned into hour-long chats. Dianne, who was typically blunt, on one occasion told Jim's mother that she was married, she was getting divorced, and that she was having an affair with Jim. She asked Mrs. Koscielniak her opinion of such activities. Dianne's forthrightness impressed Jim's mother. The more the women talked, the more Mrs. Koscielniak grew to like Dianne.

So did Jim's daughter Jessica. When the three of them were together, Jim would sit back and watch Dianne and Jessica gab. They seemed to be genuinely fond of each other. Jim was the happiest he had been in his life.

Yet Dianne worried that Jessica might feel jealous or cheated because she had to share her father with someone else. To make her feel special, Dianne sometimes gave Jim a small gift for his daughter, like a book of Shel Silverstein's poetry or a giant cookie.

It was of paramount importance to her that she establish a good rapport with Jessica because she and Jim were planning to live together after her divorce was finalized. Though she loved her sprawling ranch-style house with its swimming pool in the backyard, she was not certain that she would receive it as part of the settlement. Nor was she convinced that she could afford its upkeep if she did get the house.

So she toured the models at Oak Hills Country Club Village, a luxury condominium complex in Palos Heights. The subdivision had its own nine-hole golf course, pro shop, large swimming pool, clubhouse, and restaurant on the premises. Dianne told Jim that she thought she and Anndra could be happy there.

She and Jim looked at the two-bedroom floor plan but decided to go into the more expensive three-bedroom model. That way, Anndra and Jessica could have their own bedrooms. Dianne realized that her life-style was going to change drastically. No longer would she be able to automatically use her charge cards and spend money frivolously.

She and Jim discussed finances. Dianne earned a small salary working three days a week as the office manager in the Chicago campaign headquarters of the Democratic candidate for secretary of state, Jerome Cosentino. And in the fall, she was going to be employed full time. Yet her wages would not be enough to support her and Anndra.

She joked that Jim's income wouldn't even pay for what she had spent annually on jewelry.

"Do you know how poor you are going to be?" he asked.

"I have all my clothes," she replied. "I don't need to buy any clothes and I have all the jewelry that I will need for the rest of my life . . . I don't want to be poor, but it isn't important to be rich, either," she told him.

Sharing a life together was all that mattered to her. Dianne knew that her situation was testing Jim's patience and understanding as well as her own. The hours they spent together were never enough. "If only we had time," she would say.

Lacking the luxury of seeing each other regularly, they often exchanged cards and letters, sharing their innermost thoughts. Late at night, when Dianne was alone in bed, she often reread Jim's notes. They helped to sustain her.

Soon, though, her problems with Alan would be resolved. For nearly two and a half months, they had locked horns in a turbulent battle of wills over the pending divorce. In many ways, it was typical of the warfare that occurs during the breakup of any marriage. There was verbal sparring over who would gain custody of their four-year-old daughter and continuous quarreling over who would end up with the couple's home.

Alan, a powerful criminal and divorce attorney, was accustomed to employing whatever tactics that were necessary to beat his opponents, and he constantly harangued and harassed Dianne. One minute he was begging her to stay, promising her anything she desired if only she would reconsider her decision. When she refused, he vowed that he would never let her gain custody of Anndra.

A reconciliation, however, was out of the question. "The one thing I have to do through this process," Dianne told her lawyer, Gretchen Connell, "is be true to myself. I would not be true to myself if I even pretended that we could reconcile, even if it would help Alan come to understand this."

Over the years, Dianne had written him dozens of letters begging him to change their superficial relationship and make her a part of his life. In response, he made hollow promises and continued to ignore her pleas.

The divorce was playing havoc with her emotions. Once, when Dianne inadvertently fell asleep and stayed out all night with Jim, she was terrified. She thought it would bolster Alan's chances for custody, and she was filled with remorse.

She lamented her behavior to her attorney, who told Dianne that she needed the companionship of someone who cared for her while she was going through the divorce. To prove to her client that she had not damaged her case, Gretchen cross-examined Dianne about Alan's conduct during their marriage.

"Did he ever stay out all night?" she inquired.

"Constantly," Dianne replied.

"Did he ever not return home until the wee hours of the morning?"

"Regularly."

Gretchen then emphasized that her staying out one night had not created a problem. Dianne, however, was unable to eat or sleep. She spent entire nights vomiting, which in part was due to the flare-up of her ulcer. Her psychiatrist, whom she had seen periodically over the years, prescribed Dalmane, a powerful tranquilizer, and Tagamet for her stomach.

Since meeting Jim, there would be no turning back. No longer would Dianne allow Alan to manipulate her as he had done in the past. When the couple was having one of their frequent feuds, Alan might snatch Dianne's jewelry from her. When his anger dissipated, the jewels would magically reappear, perhaps along with a new bauble. Then, as a conciliatory gesture, he might whisk her away for a holiday.

This time she would have the upper hand. Dianne rented safe-deposit boxes at two financial institutions. In one, she placed $200,000 in jewelry, on the advice of her attorney.

"Get them out of the house, because if you don't get them out of the house, they will be gone," Gretchen warned. "They will disappear and you'll never know where they went."

At another bank, Dianne stored something far more important. In that box, she placed a variety of documents. "They will be my door to freedom," she told her friends.

Chapter Two

March 18, 1982

DIANNE sat at her dining room table sipping her breakfast, a cup of herb tea. Depression overwhelmed her.

Normally she would be seeing Jim this evening, but she had already extracted a promise from him that he would not attend tonight's college board meeting. Dianne's attorney had advised her to be as discreet as possible until the filing of the divorce papers was a fait accompli. That was still four days away—an eternity to Dianne.

She was particularly edgy this morning. She hated to belabor her troubles to friends, but unburdening herself to a sympathetic listener was an anodyne.

She called her hairdresser, Doug Snow, who during the past two years had become one of her confidantes. "I'd like to talk to you," she said.

Thinking Dianne was concerned with her hair, he replied, "Just stop in."

Within twenty-five minutes she arrived at the Erika Hair Styling Salon in Orland Park. It was on one of the suburb's main streets, in a strip shopping center where small businesses, including a carryout chicken joint, a convenience store, and hot dog stand prevailed.

Doug's wizardry as a hairdresser had brought him a loyal, affluent clientele. He was popular with his customers. Adept at the art of flattery, the tall, thin blond had an outgoing personality and a keen sense of humor. He knew when to talk and he knew when to listen.

Gossip swirled around him daily. The women sat at his station and revealed their intimate secrets. Doug heard about their affairs, their spats with their spouses, and their problems with their children.

He greeted Dianne at the front door. She pulled him back into the salon, where he had a private space, away from the prying ears of other customers.

Dianne visited the salon at least three times a month for haircuts and Doug's magical touch with hair coloring. Occasionally, even if she didn't have an appointment, they went out to lunch.

She had told him in the past about the pending divorce, but now she confessed that she was very nervous. Her lawyer was filing the divorce papers on Monday and Alan had been taking some medicine that made him act irrational.

Doug advised her that if she was that concerned, she should take Anndra, leave until the papers are served, and tell her brother where she was.

When Dianne rejected his idea, he promised to have lunch with her on Monday after he returned from his weekend trip to New York. He would have her hairpiece ready then, too, he said. He was taking it with him so that his friends could help him put it together for her.

After leaving the salon, Dianne felt better. Chicago was experiencing one of those rare March days when the skies were blue, the sun was bright, and the temperature soared into the fifties. On the way home, she stopped at the local garden center and picked up a twenty-pound bag of compost. She had noticed that the first bulbs of the season were starting to sprout and break through the topsoil, and the springlike weather made her anxious to tend her garden.

Dianne had enjoyed working in the yard and had spent thousands of hours there. She had converted a shed near the swimming pool into a small garden center, where she started new plants, flowers, and herbs.

The yard had lacked flora of any kind when they moved in and she had devotedly started a garden of herbs and wildflowers in a rainbow of colors that, when in bloom, resembled a meadow. She felt content when working in the soil and seeing the fruits of her labors.

But upon arriving home, it dawned on her that any work in the yard would be for naught. The divorce would mean that the house probably would be sold and the proceeds divided between Alan and her. Dianne loved her home in unincorporated Palos Park, a southwestern suburb twenty-two miles from downtown Chicago, which initially was inhabited by farmers. When they bought the place, she imagined that she would never leave it.

Years ago, the county, to preserve the locale's bucolic charm, had purchased portions of land that included towering oaks and maples as well as patches of prairie. Sod farms and corn crops continued to separate the large residences that were scattered among the main roadways, which were devoid of sidewalks and alleys. The open space and sylvan setting had become highly coveted among home buyers.

The Masters were among the area's early pioneers. They bought the rambling, three-bedroom ranch, ensconced on one and a half acres, in 1976, and Dianne quickly put her imprint upon it. She and an interior designer devoted endless hours to transforming it into her dream house. The eclectic-style furniture was accented with a mélange of paintings, objets d'art, and Dianne's collection of cat and Irish setter figurines. Throughout the house, pillows, samplers, and a large bell pull showcased her exquisite needlepoint and embroidery work.

Her haven was the sunroom, which looked out over the backyard. She had decorated it in hues of cobalt blue and lime green and myriad plants. She frequently curled up on one of the matching floral-print loveseats, surrounded by her three dogs—Caleb, a yellow Labrador retriever, Duff, a chocolate Lab, and Rusty, an Irish setter—and spent hours reading.

There was so much of herself in the house that when Dianne thought about moving, she started to cry. She was still sobbing when she called her brother and sister-in-law, Randy and Kathy Turner.

"I just realized I won't be able to stay," Dianne told Kathy. "I was walking in the backyard and you know all the things

I've done back here. You know I can't keep the house. I'm going to have to give all this up,'' she lamented.

Kathy was worried about Dianne. She had watched Dianne deteriorate physically since asking for the divorce. She and Randy kept reiterating that Dianne had to learn to control her emotions—that Alan was trying to manipulate her mind and her body—but their counsel was to no avail. When Dianne visited the Turners the week before for dinner, she looked exhausted.

After talking to Kathy, Dianne started preparing Alan's dinner. He had returned home after their separation in early February, for his leave-taking had been traumatic for four-year-old Anndra. Although Alan had agreed to move out while Anndra and Dianne visited Randy and Kathy, instead he waited until they returned home, then purposely packed his suitcases in front of the child. Anndra had scolded her mother, telling Dianne it was her fault that her father was leaving.

Dianne tried to explain that she and Alan were no longer happy together and that his presence caused Dianne's stomach problems. But her speech did not stop the little girl's tears and Alan's action was effective theater in the emotional play for their child.

After two weeks, he pleaded with Dianne to let him move back into the house, saying that his psychiatrist recommended that he remain at home for one month while he continued therapy. He promised that he would then move elsewhere, but he never did.

Gretchen had doubted Alan's sincerity from the onset. She told Dianne not to trust him. She knew he would continue to wage his psychological warfare on the homefront and she worried whether her client could withstand his unrelenting pressure to thwart the divorce.

Dianne's mood vacillated as she stood at the kitchen counter peeling apples for Alan's Waldorf salad. She enjoyed cooking. It was therapy for her, like working in the garden, and she liked to experiment with new recipes.

Growing up in a Polish home, she was taught how to prepare the various cuts of red meat, thick gravy, and potatoes that were served almost nightly during her childhood. But concerned with nutrition and Alan's burgeoning weight problem, she frequently prepared lighter fare, such as pasta salads, chicken, and fish.

She mixed the bananas, walnuts, apples, celery, and mayonnaise together and placed the concoction in the refrigerator, which was adorned with her massive collection of magnets. Because of the college board meeting, Dianne decided to let Alan broil a steak for dinner, which she had defrosted for him. It was 5:30 P.M. when she began getting ready for the meeting.

Dianne believed in dressing for success. That night she selected from her gigantic wardrobe a brown suit and brown silk blouse. She donned a matching set of bra and panties and put on her pantyhose. She sat at her vanity to begin her usual forty-five minutes of primping. There was blusher and eye shadow to apply, followed by lipstick.

By the time Alan arrived home at about 6:30, she was dressed. She was just adding her accessories—two gold bracelets, her Baume and Merciere watch, a necklace, and a green-and-gold-print scarf—as he walked through the door. She looked radiant.

Fifteen minutes later, Dianne was ready to depart. She took a dark-blue raincoat out of the front closet and Alan helped her slip into it. He kissed her softly on the cheek, which surprised Dianne. She grabbed her purse, a briefcase filled with notes for the board meeting, and her big brass key ring that held the two car keys, the two house keys, and the key to the home's alarm system. She got into her Cadillac Coup de Ville bearing the vanity license plate DGM 19 and a rather distinctive paint job—a yellow top and white body—then pulled out of the driveway onto Wolf Road.

The trip to the Moraine Valley Community College took only about twelve minutes. The meeting started precisely at 7:30, but Dianne wanted to arrive early to chat with the other board members.

Serving as an elected trustee, a nonpaying position, for nearly three years had given Dianne a new career path. Armed with an IQ of 147 and a bachelor's degree in English and psychology, no job had ever captivated her interest before this one.

But the college board was different. It was continually challenging, and in the process, she discovered that politics intrigued her. She became the Democratic committeewoman of Palos Township and even began to envision running for the state legislature in the not-too-distant future.

Back in the 1960s, community colleges like Moraine, a nondescript, two-story enclave, were viewed as a low-cost alternative for those who either couldn't afford or didn't have the grade point average to attend a four-year institution. Students would spend two years in the community college system, which enabled them, in most instances, to complete their degrees at larger schools.

But a decade later, community colleges assumed another role. Now they also were serving as a liberal arts center for the area, offering a plethora of nondegree classes and activities. While the college had an enrollment of 5,841 full-time students, there were actually 11,642 people on campus.

The state was giving millions of dollars in funding to these colleges. Suburban Democrats were the first to perceive that these schools could become fairly substantial political power bases, and they used the community colleges to dole out jobs and contracts to their friends and campaign donors. Moraine was no exception.

Tonight's session would be fairly anticlimactic. The board's big business had occurred two and a half weeks earlier at a special board meeting when it named a new college president. Dianne, the board's vice chairperson, had headed the search committee. Still, the renewal of the lease for the Crisis Center for South Suburbia was on the agenda.

As the shelter's founder and first president, it had been a focal point of her life since she started the twenty-four-hour hotline for victims of domestic violence right in her own kitchen. For nearly eighteen months, there it remained, until the center, which began as a project of the South Suburban Chapter of the American Association of University Women, found quarters.

When Dianne wasn't manning the phones, she was cajoling businesspeople for funding. An official in nearby Stickney had once turned down her request for a $5,000 donation to the center, contending that his community took care of their own and didn't need any such service from outsiders. So when a woman from the town called the crisis center's hotline at 2 A.M., Dianne politely asked her to call the town official. She assured the woman that he would gladly take her call, despite the late hour.

The next morning, he called Dianne. "Don't you ever do that again, you bitch," he said, adding that a check for the crisis center was on its way.

Dianne had arranged for the crisis center, now three and a half years old, to occupy an old farmhouse owned by the college and annually pay $1 rent. The renewal of its lease was unanimously approved by the seven-member board.

At about 10:30 P.M., as the meeting was ending, Dianne called home. It was customary for her to give Anndra a good-night kiss over the phone, but she had already fallen asleep. Instead she briefly talked to Alan.

Minutes later, the board adjourned. Normally the members congregated at a local pub near the college, Artie G's. Tonight, however, everyone opted for the Village Courtyard.

The board members, an administrator, a humanities professor, and the school's publicist traveled in a procession of cars to the restaurant on 123d Street in Palos Park. The Village Courtyard was a U-shaped brick building that was set back from the dimly lit thoroughfare.

The restaurant stood in the center and was flanked on each side by small shops. Its interior was enhanced by a skylight, creating an open, airy ambience bathed in sunshine during the day. Attesting to this solar power was a towering tree growing right in the middle of the restaurant.

The group headed toward the bar off the main dining room, where a small band provided music. They pulled the tables together to make conversing easier. Dianne sat at one table with board member Patricia Fleming on her right and Mary Nelson, the college's director of public information on her left.

For the next two hours, Dianne seemed in good spirits. She sipped several glasses of chablis, chatted especially with Pat, one of her closest friends, and danced.

By 12:30 A.M., the group began breaking up. Among the first

to depart was Pat Fleming, humanities professor Genevieve Capstaff, and board member Lee Harris, who carpooled with Dianne to the city three days a week to their respective jobs. Before he left, they arranged for her to pick him up the following morning.

"Well, Harris, I suppose you'd like to have a ride downtown tomorrow?" Dianne asked.

"Certainly," Harris replied.

"I'll be by about 8:15," she said.

The evening ended forty minutes later. The remainder of the group—Dianne; Robert Van Raes, a school administrator; fellow school board member Blas Olivares; and Mary Nelson—conversed as they headed toward the parking lot.

Dianne inquired whether Mary could help her sell tickets to a fund-raiser for Cosentino.

"Drop some off in my office in the morning and I'll see what I can do," Mary promised.

As they arrived at the door, Mary stopped. "I just remembered, I won't be in my office first thing in the morning," she told Dianne. "I have to go to a conference downstate in Normal. Just leave them with my secretary."

"Okay, I'll drop them off and talk to you later," Dianne replied.

Robert Van Raes, who was parked in front of the restaurant next to Dianne, walked her to her car. He watched as Dianne got into the Caddy, started the engine, and backed out of the space.

She was now just an eight-minute drive from home. All she had to do was head west along 123d Street, a dark, two-lane thoroughfare lined with trees and residences, until she reached Wolf Road, about four miles away, and then turn left.

As Dianne pulled out of the Courtyard's parking lot, she never saw the maroon station wagon that was following her.

CHAPTER THREE

March 19, 1982

ALAN Masters was an early riser. A workaholic, he was anxious to get to his law office, and today was no different. Without an alarm, he had arisen at 6:30 A.M.

He and Dianne had spent most of their married life sleeping apart. Alan's bedroom was on the opposite side of the house from hers, so Dianne, who was a night owl and liked to sleep late, would not be disturbed.

Seeing that Alan was stirring, Dianne's three dogs sprang to life and wanted to go outside. He had never been particularly enthralled with them or the six cats that roamed the house.

Dianne had turned their home into a mini animal shelter, which he barely tolerated. Most of the creatures were strays who became her coddled pets. Dianne was so fond of one of her first dogs, Baron, that she had commissioned a portrait of the Irish setter, which was prominently displayed over the fireplace in the living room.

Alan went into the small kitchen overlooking the front yard and made himself breakfast. Dianne's Cadillac was not in the driveway. His Eldorado blocked the entrance to the two-car garage, but Dianne rarely used it because it was crammed with junk and Alan's coveted Corvette.

He had gone to bed shortly after her call the night before. After a board meeting, Dianne usually stayed out until the wee hours of the morning, and he would be sleeping soundly when she arrived home.

Dianne's bedroom, decorated in sunshine yellow accented

by lavender and white, was reminiscent of a Victorian lady's. A resplendence of lace was everywhere. On her dresser were some of her cherished pictures of her family and on the walls were some of her favorite paintings, including one of her and Anndra. The spacious room held twin beds, a chaise lounge, and matching armoires, with her vanity sandwiched in between. The bed was undisturbed.

Down the hall was Anndra's room. Alan noted with satisfaction that his daughter was still asleep.

He phoned Burton Odelson, the chairman of the college board and a prominent attorney in the Chicago area. He was also Dianne's mentor and a close friend.

Since her election as a trustee, she had been under Burt's tutelage. They had planned that within a year, after they had accomplished their agenda, Dianne would replace him as the board's new chairman.

Burt was likely to know if Dianne had spent the night with her lover.

"I saw her at the board meeting; then I went home," Burt said sleepily. "I didn't go out afterward."

"Is she at Koscielniak's?" Alan asked.

"I have absolutely no idea."

Burt had been the one Alan had turned to weeks earlier when Dianne had not returned home from a previous board meeting. Burt had then been awakened by a 6 A.M. phone call from the distraught husband.

Thrust in the middle once more, Burt immediately called Jim, who said he hadn't seen Dianne the previous night.

"Look," said Burt, "don't lie to me."

But Jim swore he was telling the truth.

A few minutes later, Jim's phone rang again. This time the caller who was actually Alan Masters, asked for Joe Goodfriend.

"There's no one here by that name," Jim replied.

"I'm sorry," said Alan, who abruptly hung up.

He then began phoning Dianne's other friends. There were Patricia and Robert Casey, with whom the Masters socialized frequently. Pat and Dianne had met selling real estate back in the 1970s and sometimes vacationed together. Bob owned a company that built dome homes, and Alan was not only an investor in his firm, but also his best friend and his attorney.

"Dianne didn't come home last night," he told them. "Do you know where she is?"

The couple had no idea.

Next was Pat Fleming; the women were supposed to have had dinner together after the meeting.

Pat did not know where Dianne was, either. She said she had last seen Dianne at the Village Courtyard restaurant, where they had a few drinks with the other board members.

Alan then called the campaign office where Dianne worked. Although the office wouldn't open for several hours, he left a message for his wife on the answering machine.

"Dianne, where are you? Please come home," he entreated.

Alan also phoned one of his closest associates, a high-ranking official in the Cook County Sheriff's Department. Lt. James Keating was the commander of the criminal intelligence unit. The men had known each other for twenty-five years and had developed a relationship that transcended that of attorney and police officer. They had become confidantes and business associates.

Dianne was missing, Alan explained. What should he do? The veteran cop told Alan not to call the police yet. Most departments wouldn't take a missing persons report for twenty-four hours.

Donna Davis, the family's maid, arrived at the Masters' home at 7:30 A.M. She pulled her car into the driveway alongside Alan's Eldorado and, with her own key, she let herself into the house. In the dining room, she was surprised to find Alan sitting at the table having breakfast with Anndra. Generally he was gone before she arrived.

He asked his daughter to go to her room while he talked to Donna. Alan quickly told her that Dianne had not come home last night and that he was very worried. Anndra would remain at home today rather than attend preschool, he said.

Alan needed something to occupy his mind while he waited for news of Dianne, so he immediately left for his law office. He had built a successful practice over the years in Summit, a grimy southwestern suburb of Chicago, sandwiched between smokestack industries and the world's largest ponds of raw sewage.

One of the area's most renowned attorneys, specializing in drunk driving and criminal cases, Alan's clientele was not the sophisticated, pin-striped suit variety. Instead he served primarily blue-collar workers who got pinched by the police coming home drunk from a neighborhood tavern, and suburban cops who needed his expertise to prevent their wives from getting everything in a divorce.

A sign hanging in his office window proclaimed THE LAW WORKS. And he knew precisely how it operated.

He had learned how the wheels of justice turned in Chicago's courts and that they frequently were greased with dollar bills. His tentacles stretched throughout the system. He adroitly distributed payoffs to judges, who would then rule in his favor, while police officers who pocketed the cash would misplace paperwork or change their testimony to exonerate his client.

These judges and cops were also among Alan's circle of friends. He was their guru. They sought his counsel, attended the couple's lavish parties, watched pornographic movies in his basement, and went to the fights with him. He so ingratiated himself with the lawmen that some of the cops even did odd jobs around the Masters' house.

To the world, Alan displayed the facade of a wealthy, powerful attorney. He had an unquenchable thirst for the status symbols that were synonymous with success: fast cars, boats, the latest gadgetry, and above all, a beautiful woman.

And for thirteen years, Dianne was his most prized possession. Alan loved to show her off. The admiring glances that Dianne received from men and women alike massaged his inflated ego.

His own slovenly appearance did nothing to enhance his image. At five feet ten inches tall, he often tipped the scale beyond 250 pounds. He was always dieting and had a closet full of suits in graduated sizes to accommodate his frequently changing physique. He wore an ill-fitting toupee that caused snickers whenever he was outdoors. In even the slightest breeze, the hairpiece glided across his head like an Olympic skater practicing figure eights.

Without a shirt, Alan was almost a grotesque figure. Extremely hairy, he resembled a barrel-chested gorilla. Despite his girth, he possessed tremendous upper-body strength. He had played football in high school and he'd remained incredibly strong. It was said that he could bring a man to his knees simply by shaking his hand. But how he maintained such power was a mystery; he led a virtually sedentary life, shunning any type of physical activity.

At about 8 A.M., the Masters' phone rang and the maid answered it. It was Lee Harris, the college board member with whom Dianne had agreed to share a ride to work.

"Is Dianne there?" he asked.

"No, she's not," Donna replied.

"She was supposed to give me a ride downtown this morning," Lee explained. "She's not here yet. Has she left?"

"No," Donna said. "Dianne didn't come home last night."

Throughout the morning, Alan called the maid about a half dozen times, asking whether she had heard anything about Dianne or if Dianne had come home yet. But there was no word.

When Alan arrived home shortly before noon, he dismissed the maid and phoned Jim Keating at the police station. Alan told him that Dianne was still missing and that he had called some of her friends in an effort to locate her. Keating suggested that he contact the Cook County Sheriff's Department, the agency responsible for the unincorporated suburbs where the Masters lived.

At 12:30 P.M., Alan kept an appointment with the couple's marriage counselor. He and Dianne had been attending weekly sessions with a psychiatrist for more than a year and a half in hopes of resolving their differences.

From the earliest days of their marriage, Dianne had consistently complained to Alan that he was a workaholic and did not spend enough time with his family. She also was upset that he was overweight, cared little about his physical appearance, and was disinterested in sex. Frustrated with her husband's indifference to the situation, Dianne took matters into her own hands. She asked her therapist to recommend a professional who could help the couple.

After announcing that she was getting a divorce, Dianne wanted to stop going to the counselor, but Alan begged her to accompany him. In recent weeks, he finally elucidated what steps he would take to reconcile their marriage. Dianne had heard Alan repeat the same promises numerous times in the past. She remained steadfast in her desire to divorce him.

After meeting with the psychiatrist, Alan called Randy and Kathy Turner. Dianne had sought refuge before at her brother and sister-in-law's home in the northwestern suburbs, and during one of the couple's separations, she and Anndra had stayed there for nearly a week.

Kathy and her two-year-old son had just returned home from a neighborhood play group when Alan called.

"Have you seen Dianne?" he inquired calmly.

"No, why?" Kathy replied.

"Well, because she didn't come home last night," he explained.

"You haven't seen her at all or heard from her?"

"No," Alan said, trying to end the conversation.

"Well, have you called the police?"

"They're here already," he said.

Official police records indicate that Alan phoned the Cook County Sheriff's Police at 2:30 P.M. and reported Dianne missing. The radio call dispatching an officer was broadcast over the department's frequency, and ten minutes later, a patrolman arrived at the Masters' home and took the initial missing persons report.

The news also had reached all of Alan's friends on the force. Sgt. Clarke Buckendahl, who had operated a detective agency out of Masters' law office, and another deputy, a detective named Mark Baldwin, were on their way to a late lunch but instead rushed to Alan's side.

"When I went into the house, he was sitting in the kitchen area," says Baldwin. "He was shaking. Very drawn and haggard looking, bags under his eyes like a person who hadn't slept."

Lt. Howard Vanick, the supervisor of the Sheriff's Police South Investigations Unit, whom Alan had once represented in a divorce proceeding, also heard the radio call. He drove to the house to take charge of the investigation.

Within forty-five minutes after his arrival, Baldwin obtained Alan's permission to search the premises. First he checked Dianne's bedroom. "I looked in her personal wardrobe closet to see if there were any gaps in the clothing, hangers; to see where maybe she had taken some clothing with her," Baldwin says. He found no indication that anything was missing.

Then he scrutinized the rest of the house. "I went through each room and I looked around on the floor, looked in closets," Baldwin says. "I looked at the furniture to see if I could find any broken furniture or anything out of place. . . . I looked all over the house to see if there was something unusual about it."

The detective also searched the yard and driveway. He found nothing amiss in the house or around the grounds. No signs of a struggle. No blood stains. No clues.

Before long, Lt. Keating arrived on the scene. Technically, Vanick was in charge of the case, but in the department pecking order, Keating, the commander of the intelligence unit, was his superior. Keating demanded that the investigators concentrate the probe on the premise that Dianne had run away.

During his interview with the police, Alan admitted that he and his wife had been having marital problems. He suspected that Dianne had been having an affair with a teacher at Moraine Valley Community College, Jim Koscielniak. When Baldwin asked where she might be, Alan replied that he thought she probably would be with her lover.

Alan told the police that he expected Dianne to file for divorce soon, but he was still hopeful that they would reconcile. He had brought travel brochures home for them to peruse and they were planning a trip. Next week was their anniversary, and to celebrate, he already had made dinner reservations at one of Chicago's fashionable restaurants.

He also mentioned that his wife recently had removed all of her expensive jewelry from the house—as much as $200,000 worth of necklaces, earrings, rings, and bracelets, including her distinctive wedding ring, a fabulous diamond and sapphire setting that spelled "LOVE."

To determine whether Dianne had taken any large sums of money, he gave the police a written letter granting permission to examine their account. A sheriff's investigator was sent to the Masters' bank, which was about two miles from the couple's home. There had been two withdrawals that week and a deposit. However, bank officials would not divulge the balances to authorities without Alan being present.

Investigators learned that Dianne did have sixteen credit cards with her. And both she and her husband were notorious for carrying large amounts of cash. It would not be unusual for her to have several hundred dollars in her wallet, Alan said.

But he was insisting that Dianne would never run away. "She would never leave Anndra," Alan told the police. He urged them to conduct a thorough investigation.

Vanick and Keating, who were extremely savvy in dealing with the media and had ties to some of the city's top reporters, understood that if the newspapers and television stations heard about the case, it would be a headline grabber. They knew that the press would relish a story about the mysterious disappearance of a beautiful blond woman employed by a political candidate for statewide office and married to a well-known suburban attorney.

Typically in this type of case, the police welcome publicity. It frequently leads to tips and sightings of the missing person. Alan, though, balked at releasing any information to the media. The two veteran cops realized, too, that if they didn't crack the case quickly, the image of the Cook County Sheriff's Department might be sullied.

So, for the moment, it was decided that Dianne's disappearance would remain a secret.

Chapter Four

March 20, 1982

CHICAGO's glimpse of spring vanished the day Dianne disappeared. A light layer of snow soon blanketed the ground and arctic winds were blowing in from the north.

Three hundred miles south, in St. Louis, Dianne's brother, Randy Turner, a regional manager for MacGregor Sporting Goods, was working. At five ten and 160 pounds, his youthful boy-next-door looks, brown hair, brown eyes, and gold-rimmed aviator glasses belied the fact that he was a shrewd businessman. He also possessed the ideal personality for sales: he was outgoing, enthusiastic, and exuded a charm that could disarm any recalcitrant client.

Randy had flown in Thursday afternoon, visited a few customers, and then dined with the buyer from Venture, one of his largest accounts, and the buyer's wife. He spent most of Friday wooing a lumber company and several department store chains.

Meteorologists call the cold front that swoops down from Canada into Chicago an arctic clipper. As this one traveled south from Chicago, it met the moisture-laden southern Gulf air in St. Louis, and by afternoon, cloud coverage was so thick that the city's famous Gateway Arch was almost obscured.

By the time Randy drove his rental car to Lambert's Field, the downtown airport, a miasma engulfed the city. He hoped the ground fog would clear so that his 4:30 P.M. flight eventually would take off, but within the hour, all flights were canceled. He called home to report that he was stuck overnight in St. Louis.

As soon as he heard the tone of Kathy's voice, Randy recognized that something was wrong. She quickly explained that Alan had called that afternoon to tell her that Dianne was missing. She told Randy that Alan had called the police and that they were already at the Masters' house. But she had not heard from him since.

Now Randy, incredulous, was desperate to get home. He and Dianne had had a special relationship since childhood, and she was more than an older sister to him. Because their mother had been blind, Dianne had assumed many responsibilities for her sibling. She had watched over and cared for Randy, who was four years younger, like a doting parent. She had taught him all of the niceties a young man needed to know.

"Dianne was my big sister, but she was more half-sister, half-mom," Randy says. "I'll never forget walking down the street one day and she said, 'Don't you know any better, damn it? Men are supposed to be on the outside of the street.' "

"I said, 'What the hell are you talking about?' "

"Well, if a car comes and runs up the curb, the man gets hit," Dianne explained. "That's proper etiquette!"

"She was always on me for etiquette, the way I dressed and the things I did."

When they were both in their teens, Randy's grooming habits inspired Dianne to bestow a pet name on him. "She was US and I was UB—ugly brother, ugly sister," Randy explained. "It started as a tease when I was in high school because of the way I dressed. I was not Mr. Meticulous. She started calling me her ugly duckling brother. I was the shaggy dog. It started off that way and we carried it on forever. Every note we sent back and forth was UB and US. It was our secret joke. It's kind of ironic because she was so beautiful and I called her that."

Randy suggested to Kathy that he could rent a car and drive the three hundred miles back to Chicago, but she convinced him that little could be done that day. It would be better to stay in St. Louis and catch an early flight out the next morning.

When he hung up, he called the nearby Ramada Hotel, where he had stayed the previous night, and got a room. He then went to the airport bar and grabbed a beer and a sandwich.

Initially, Randy's thoughts turned to Dianne and her lover, whom he had never met. He wondered if they had run away together. As he mulled over the possibility, he began to realize that it didn't make any sense. Dianne would have told him her plans. Something was terribly wrong. Randy knew that Dianne never would have left Anndra. Never.

He took the shuttle bus to the hotel and checked back in. After dropping off his suitcase in his room, he headed for the lounge.

It was 9 P.M. and the place was jammed. The Friday night crowd was in a party mood and many couples were dancing to the music of a live band, which was blasting rock tunes.

Randy chose a stool at the very far end of the L-shaped bar. He wanted to be able to think, so his seat was as far away from the band as possible, right next to the doorway.

He ordered a drink and began listing the facts. Dianne had planned to come to their house for Sunday dinner. She was filing for divorce on Monday. And she was definitely not the type to run away.

Dianne had been expressing some fears about her pending divorce to Randy and Kathy, but the couple thought at the time that she was being melodramatic—a woman caught in the throes of a nasty divorce. They tried to be supportive and sympathetic to her plight after she had revealed her plans to them right after Christmas.

A despondent Dianne had called Randy from the Masters' Florida condominium, where she was spending the holidays, and told him that she was going to get a divorce. She and Alan had argued continuously during their stay before he left her and Anndra to rush back to work.

After Dianne had returned home, her Sunday dinners with the Turners assumed an urgency, and suddenly Randy's and her roles were reversed. Dianne valued his common sense approach to problems, and she now sought the counsel of the man she referred to as "the kid"—in devising a monthly budget, on whether she could afford to remain in the Palos Heights house, on how to deal with her husband.

During one of her visits, Alan had called and wanted to speak with Randy. The men's conversation had erupted into a heated argument and Alan had started to belittle Dianne, saying she was nothing when she met him and would be nothing if she left him.

"She wouldn't be anything if it wasn't for me and the things I gave her."

"She's not your slave," Randy retorted, "she's a human being."

He knew Dianne needed companionship and they had discussed the question of her dating. But Randy had warned her early on not to get involved with anyone, because it could hinder her custody battle.

"Yes," Dianne had replied, "my lawyer emphasized that, too. Alan is going to be looking for anything he can."

Weeks later, she had admitted to Randy that she was having an affair with Jim, conceding that it was foolish for her to be seeing him while in the midst of divorce proceedings.

As the time approached for her attorney to file the papers, Dianne's apprehension grew, and she expressed her concerns to the Turners. She was scared that Alan would take Anndra and she would never see her daughter again.

She also began to worry about her own safety. She suspected that she was being followed. On several occasions, Dianne expounded on Alan's close association with the Cook County Sheriff's Police, because she had a terrible fear that one day she would be out driving, a cop would pull her over, and later she would be found in a ditch with a bullet in her head. She would never stop for the police unless she was in a heavily populated area, like at a shopping center.

"Alan has the power to make me disappear and never be seen again," she told her brother and sister-in-law. The Turners thought Dianne was becoming paranoid.

"It really didn't hit me until I had time to sit down and have a few beers and contemplate it," says Randy. Had Dianne met with foul play? "We grew up in the suburbs and we were immune to violence." People just didn't disappear, he thought to himself. "It may happen frequently in the city, but not in the affluent area where she was living."

Randy's anxiety about his sister's well-being grew. He pondered the possibility that Dianne might be dead. That night, the idea that she had been murdered haunted him, and he continually tossed and turned in his bed.

Early Saturday morning, he vowed that no matter what, he would find out what happened to Dianne.

The hour flight to Chicago's O'Hare Airport seemed interminable. When they finally landed, Randy grabbed a cab home. It was about 1 P.M. when he called Alan to pump him for information. But the exchange was brief and cold.

"What happened, Alan? I just got back from St. Louis. What's going on?"

"Well, she didn't show up after going out Thursday night. I called the police and they were here until late last night," Alan said.

Suddenly he turned on Randy, telling him that he suspected that Dianne was again staying with the Turners, as she had in the past when she and Alan had quarreled. "Don't hide her. If she's there, I want to know," Alan demanded.

"She's not here," Randy retorted angrily.

Trying to remain calm, he asked Alan to keep him informed of any developments and to let the police know that he was willing to talk to them.

"Calling Alan was one of the hardest things I had ever done in my life," recalls Randy. "After calling Alan and being shaken off, my determination to find Dianne was even stronger. I resolved myself to push on and not allow myself to be intimidated by anyone or any law enforcement agency."

Emotionally and physically exhausted, Randy went upstairs to take a nap.

Late that afternoon, a man identifying himself as Sgt. Mark Baldwin of the Cook County Sheriff's Police called the Turners to interview Randy about his sister.

Remembering how Alan had entertained members of the sheriff's department at his home and how Dianne had discussed their close relationship to her husband, Randy was reluctant to talk to the police now investigating Dianne's disappearance.

He told the officer he would have to return his call. Randy wanted to make sure the person was, in fact, calling from police headquarters, because he didn't trust them.

He hung up and then dialed the number left by the sergeant, who proceeded to ask very few questions. Baldwin wanted to know if Randy knew Dianne's whereabouts, if she had run off, and whether she had credit cards. It was clear to Randy that the police were treating his sister's disappearance simply as a runaway.

An hour or so later, another officer called, this time he said the police wanted to come to the house and conduct a personal interview. The lieutenant in charge of the investigation, Howard Vanick, had ordered the officer to take Randy's statement.

At 9 P.M., two detectives sat in the Turners' living room and began their interrogation. They wanted to know if Dianne was staying with one of her friends. "There were no questions, it seemed, about how was her relationship with her husband," Randy says. "Were they having marital problems? Nothing at all like that."

Randy and Kathy tried to change the direction of the interview. Dianne would never run away, they said emphatically. She never would leave Anndra. And she had promised them that she was coming for dinner the following day.

The Turners disclosed to the detectives that Dianne had become afraid of Alan and they told the police about how Dianne had said that Alan was capable of getting rid of her without a trace. Most important, Dianne's attorney was planning to file for divorce from Alan on Monday. The Turners were surprised when the officers then told them that Alan had said that the couple had reconciled.

The Turners also expressed doubts about how the sheriff's police would handle the investigation. "Mr. Turner voiced concern in talking to reporting officers as he had been told by Mrs. Masters that police worked for her husband and that he also had many friends within the sheriff's department," one of the detectives wrote in his report of the interview.

"Everytime we would say something that I thought would be a revelation to them, it would go right through them,"

Randy observed. "Then they would go back to their same basic premise—that Dianne had run away."

And the two cops kept implying during the forty-minute interview that Randy and Kathy were not telling the truth, that Dianne's brother and his wife really did know where Dianne was.

"They were accusing me of hiding something," says Randy. "They treated me not like a grieving relative, but like a suspect."

Randy surmised that Alan must have told the police about the time Dianne fled to the Turners' home after she and Alan had had an argument over money. Dianne's father, George, had cashed in a $7,000 life insurance policy and turned the proceeds over to Dianne for safekeeping. Dianne gave the money to a friend after Alan insisted that they should borrow the sum because they were in the midst of a cash crunch. Subsequently, the friend's home was burglarized, and the only thing missing was George's nest egg.

Dianne was furious at Alan and accused him of arranging the burglary. Their fight escalated, and Dianne took Anndra to the Turners. When two of Dianne's friends spotted Alan driving around their houses looking for Dianne, they called Randy and Kathy and told them to hide Dianne's car.

At that point, she became determined to leave Alan. "If I don't go through with this, I'll never get out of it," she told Randy at the time. Eventually, the couple reconciled.

When the detectives left and Randy reviewed his statements, he realized that he had just intimated that Alan might have had something to do with Dianne's disappearance to the very agency that he knew was in the lawyer's back pocket. Would Alan hear about it?

That night, he began keeping a journal. He wrote: "I felt all the police were owned by Alan and thought another means had to be found to answer the question of what happened to Dianne."

On Sunday, the Turners' telephone rang constantly. Even though the sheriff's police continued to suppress Dianne's disappearance from the media, Dianne's fellow board members knew she was missing. One by one, they began calling Randy to see whether Dianne had gone there and to exchange information with the Turners. Everyone wanted to offer their support and share their suspicions with him.

Randy wrote in his journal that he "began to realize how many friends Dianne really had. The friendships were not artificial." He also began to feel a deep sense of guilt. "I started to question my own availability and devotion to my sister during the troubled weeks before her disappearance. Did I miss a signal from her?"

As the long day ended, Randy, who had clung to the tenuous hope that his sister had run away, started to face reality. "He kept hoping that she had run away for the weekend," Kathy says. "But by the end of the weekend, she would have pulled it together and come back."

"If I haven't heard from her by now," Randy told his wife, "something has happened. She just didn't run away. This is the beginning of some horrible nightmare."

Chapter Five

March 24, 1982

RANDY was frustrated by Alan's refusal to publicize Dianne's disappearance. Randy wanted the story leaked to the press, so he turned for help to Lee Harris, a seasoned political consultant who had sources throughout the media.

"If you want to get it out, I can do it for you," said Lee. He, too, was convinced that Dianne had not run away. She had shared many secrets with him during their forty-five-minute commute downtown, three days a week, to their jobs. On the Wednesday before her disappearance, Dianne had handed Lee a piece of paper bearing a license plate number.

"Would you do me a favor and check this license plate out?" Dianne had asked.

"Why?" queried Lee.

"He's been following me for a couple of days and I think he's following us now."

"So who do you think it is?"

"An off-duty cop," she replied.

When Dianne disappeared on Friday, Lee, an administrative assistant to one of Illinois's top officials, decided to hide the piece of paper with the license plate number. For safekeeping, he placed it in the desk of his boss, then state comptroller Roland Burris.

That same day, Lee also called the sheriff's police several times, urging that they meet with him. Harris told the police that he might have some insight into the case and that he wanted to talk to them.

"We're treating this as a missing person and we'll get to you," a deputy told Harris.

"But it's not a missing person," Lee insisted.

"We're very busy. This isn't the only case we handle," the deputy said.

Lee, however, persisted. He called the sheriff's police twice on Saturday and finally arranged to meet two investigators at a south suburban restaurant. The department sent Sgt. Clarke Buckendahl, a close friend of Alan's, and another detective.

Lee told the police that Dianne never would have run away and that she believed she was being followed, and then he gave them the license plate number of the car that had followed them downtown. He was convinced that Dianne was a victim of foul play and tried to convince the authorities of this. To no avail.

"We think she's a missing person," Buckendahl told him. "Her husband does. We're treating this as a domestic problem. That's all."

When Lee suggested that perhaps Alan should be viewed as a suspect, Buckendahl had a ready answer. "Lee, if Alan Masters did it, we'll never know. Because Alan Masters is a criminal lawyer and if he wanted to commit a murder, he knows the right people, and he knows the law and the way around it to get it done. You'll never know."

Lee was anxious for the story of Dianne's disappearance to unfold in public, so he had anonymously tipped all of the area newspapers and television stations to the fact that Dianne had been missing for five days. His call to the hotline of Chicago's all-news radio station, a CBS affiliate that bills itself as News Radio 78, earned him the station's $78 prize for the best news tip of the week.

The station had begun broadcasting the story that morning, which triggered an avalanche of publicity. Alan's law office was soon barraged with phone calls from reporters, and when he learned that the story was breaking, even he helped hype it that first day, by offering a $10,000 reward for information leading to Dianne's return. Yet he declined to make any comment, a fact noted in all of the newspaper accounts and broadcasts.

Randy, on the other hand, was talking. To everyone.

Throughout the day, he granted at least ten interviews to city and suburban journalists. He and Kathy spent hours with the reporters sharing what they knew about the case. The Turners' tranquil tri-level house was transformed into a press conference locale.

An NBC minicam van was parked in the driveway outside the brown frame house and the vehicle's microwave antenna was hoisted thirty feet in the air, so that it could transmit live shots back to the television station, which was forty miles away in downtown Chicago.

Along the normally quiet street, neighbors gathered in small groups and gawked at the crew hauling its equipment inside the home. Inside, there was a kind of organized chaos.

The television interview was being done in the Turners' living room, where cables ran along the plush brown carpeting. The cameraman and his assistant plugged in their bright lights and conducted a sound check while Channel Five's Russ Ewing prepped Randy, who sat on the couch. Kathy watched the goings-on from the doorway of their family room.

The Turners were fortunate that the interviewer was Ewing. A veteran broadcaster who had interviewed hundreds of grieving relatives, he didn't jam a microphone in front of their faces and ask tear-jerk questions, as some of his colleagues did. He used his own low-key approach, which always earned the respect of his subjects.

As the crew set up, Randy came to the sudden realization that he wasn't just going to be asked background questions about Dianne. They wanted him to do an actual on-air, television interview. Ewing saw Randy tense up and tried to soothe him. "He put me completely at ease before the cameras started, so much so, that I barely realized it when the interview began," Randy recalls.

Step-by-step, Randy reconstructed the events. Dianne had gone out for drinks after the board meeting, and the return trip home was only a four-mile drive from the restaurant. Yet the car had not been found and the police had no clues. The Turners reiterated that she never, never would have run away and left her daughter. And Dianne's attorney was filing for divorce on Monday.

During the interview, Randy never mentioned Alan or his own theories about the case, but he already had reached the conclusion that Alan was responsible for Dianne's disappearance. He had spent hours replaying in his mind his conversations with his sister concerning Alan and her divorce, conversations he hadn't taken seriously until she vanished.

Now her ominous warning that Alan was capable of getting rid of her without a trace assumed new import. Randy believed that Dianne was the victim of foul play. But how to convince the authorities was another matter.

He was relieved when the TV crew left and he had a few minutes to himself. The couple's phone had started ringing at 9 A.M. when the news media in Chicago finally had learned of Dianne's disappearance, and on their private line, the Turners were receiving a continuous stream of calls from reporters and Dianne's friends.

In the downstairs bedroom, where he had his office, Randy tried to conduct business as usual. There were complaints and inquiries from clients and his salesmen to handle, but all he could think about was his missing sister.

"I finally felt I was accomplishing something," Randy says. "I continuously thought about the biblical story of David and Goliath and felt the little people would win this one."

In Chicago-style journalism, most stories have a one-day life cycle; almost everything becomes old news overnight. But Dianne's disappearance was different. It was a running story for three days on television and in the newspapers that offered numerous intriguing facets: college trustee vanishes with $200,000 in jewelry after board meeting. Beautiful blond disappears just days before she was to file for divorce. The fact she was married to a renowned, controversial attorney further enhanced the mystery.

Dianne's political connections were newsworthy, too. As the office manager in State Treasurer Jerome Cosentino's bid for secretary of state, her disappearance, reporters pointed out, was the second bizarre incident to jolt his campaign. One of Cosentino's chief staffers, who had been in town attending a meeting, had been found slain two months earlier in his hotel room.

The television crews returned to the Turners' home the next day. Deborah Norville, who was then with the local NBC affiliate, did the interview and CBS sent a crew as well. Both reporters confided to Randy that the evidence in the case pointed to Alan. "These confessions brightened my hopes even though no innuendoes were mentioned on the newscasts," Randy wrote in his journal.

At 1:30 A.M., hours after the Turners had gone to bed, they were awakened by a phone call. It was Alan, and his voice was quivering. It was the first time the men had spoken since Randy returned from St. Louis.

"You asked me to keep you informed if there were any developments. That's why I'm calling you. There was an extortion attempt tonight."

He explained that late that afternoon, he had received a call at his law office from a man who claimed that he had Dianne. For $25,000, he would return her. Alan immediately contacted Lt. James Keating and told him what had occurred. He then took $25,000 from an office safe and met Keating at a hotel in Waukegan, a town about eighty miles north of the Masters' home.

The plan was for Alan to go to the Waukegan train station and wait at a public telephone for further instructions. Keating had informed the Waukegan police and requested backup. He then drove with Alan to the train station.

Just after 10 P.M., the phone rang. Alan was instructed to go to a local restaurant about two miles away, order a cup of coffee, and await further instructions. He begged to talk to Dianne, but the caller told him that she was sedated and unable to speak.

He waited at the restaurant for the next communication. Within minutes, the manager summoned him to the telephone. The caller told Alan that he had been followed by the police and the deal was off. The extortionist warned Alan that he would receive Dianne's hand in the mail in the next few days.

Alan told the Turners that the police had traced the call to the Lake County College campus in Grayslake, about a ten-minute drive from their home.

When Randy hung up the phone, he and Kathy began discussing the likelihood of whether Dianne had really been abducted; if the kidnapper would carry out his brutal threat to cut off her hand. They quickly concluded that either it was a hoax or Alan had arranged it.

Still, the fact that the police, led by Lt. Keating, were chasing imaginary kidnappers in such close proximity to their home frightened them. Randy and Kathy immediately contacted their local police department, an agency that wasn't involved in the search for Dianne, and explained what had happened. They asked the authorities to watch their house.

"After Alan's call, Kathy was petrified," says Randy. "Kathy just trembled for one solid hour. No way could we get back to sleep that night. Only when daylight arrived did we feel any better."

The morning after the alleged extortion attempt, Randy phoned the sheriff's police to see what he could learn about the incident. A detective told him that the police could have caught the caller had it not been for a communications error. They believed that he was a nut who just wanted a fast buck.

Randy realized that the incident could be the impetus needed to get the FBI to investigate Dianne's disappearance. He already had talked to one agent and begged him to get involved, citing several reasons why the agency might be interested in the case. He noted her work in the campaign office of a candidate for a statewide post and his belief that Alan controlled the police. None of the reasons were enough to bring the agency into the case, but the FBI did say that a file would be started in the event that any new developments surfaced.

Now that the alleged extortion attempt had occurred, an agent from the FBI's Mt. Prospect office made an appointment to come to the Turners' house at 4:30 P.M. to interview them. But at 5 P.M. the agent called and told them that her superior felt that the matter should be handled through the downtown office and it would have to be Alan who requested the assistance of the agency.

Randy felt demoralized and powerless. He desperately wanted to take some action. But what? That single phone call from Alan had exacerbated all of the fears that he and Kathy had struggled to suppress. Were they and their children truly safe?

"Driving alone, I was so phenomenally careful. I'd write down license plate numbers all the time," Randy says. "One of my biggest fears was turning on the car in the morning."

He even considered buying a gun for protection, and he sought advice from an acquaintance about obtaining a weapon. But Randy, who had never fired a gun, quickly concluded that he wouldn't know what to do with a gun even if he got one. "It is not going to solve anything," he decided. "If they want to kill me, they're going to kill me."

Randy realized that he could not rely on the professionalism of the Cook County Sheriff's Department to solve the case. Burt Odelson, the college board president and a politically powerful suburban attorney, had contacts in every sector and suggested that Randy might want to explore another avenue.

"Maybe you should look into getting a private investigator," Burt said. "It doesn't look like Alan is doing much of anything. I've got this guy who's willing to come over and tell you a little bit about the agency."

It was called Special Operations Associates, and it was headed by James O'Grady, a former Chicago police superintendent. Burt arranged for one of the agency's detectives to meet with the Turners at his home on a Saturday. Included at the gathering was Dianne's lover, Jim Koscielniak. It was the first time he and Randy had met.

"My God, Dianne, this is not exactly the guy I imagined," Randy said to himself. For some inexplicable reason, he had expected Jim to be the type who left women breathless—not someone so ordinary.

But when Jim started talking about his fondness for Dianne and their secret life together during the past three months, Randy understood his sister's attraction to him. "He was obviously a very sensitive person," Randy concluded. "He seemed like a sincere person, very concerned and very nice."

During the meeting, everyone recalled how Dianne continually had voiced her apprehension shortly before she disappeared. Like Randy, Jim and Burt felt they had ignored her fears. While no one had any solid evidence, they all concurred that she had not disappeared of her own free will.

Then the private investigator spoke. Special Operations could ferret out facts that the police could not, and the detective agency's resources exceeded those of the police department's.

Randy was impressed. "They had methods and contacts to find information which could not be used by the Cook County Sheriff's Police. After their presentation, I knew I had to hire them." But he wanted to mull over the idea and discuss any possible ramifications with Kathy. Within days of the meeting though, SOA received its $4,000 fee.

The Turners also turned to the supernatural for help, in the form of a psychic, Patrick O'Brien. Randy's belief in this world was strong. When he and Dianne were children, their mother entertained them with the tarot cards and the Ouija board and often had tried communicating with them through telepathy.

For Randy, working with the psychic was reminiscent of the happy times he and Dianne had shared with their mother. The Turners, along with some of their relatives and friends, formed a three-car caravan to try and trace Dianne's last movements.

Starting near the restaurant where she and her colleagues had met after the board meeting, the group followed the psychic around the rolling hills, lakes, and streams that surrounded Dianne's home in Palos Park.

They stopped at one of the lakes and walked around the shore. Near the water's edge, there was a poster of a man, dressed in a top hat, pointing toward the lake. It looked almost like a tarot card. "It was just very strange, and it was pointing towards the water," Randy says.

The procession also drove down a road in Willow Springs near an old canal that served as a shipping lane. "I got a tingling feeling," Randy said. "We must have walked around the area for hours with the eerie feeling continuing."

A more difficult task awaited Randy. The private detective agency had told him that it was imperative that he telephone Alan regularly because they wanted to see what Randy could learn from him about the status of the sheriff's investigation. He hadn't spoken with Alan since the extortion episode, and now the detectives wanted him to call Alan again but Randy resisted. "I am supposed to be calling the man I think killed my sister. That's not an easy thing to do."

After fortifying himself with a glass of wine, Randy phoned Alan and asked if it would be possible to meet and discuss Dianne's disappearance. Alan refused.

He bluntly told Randy that he was angry with the insinuations the media was making and that he blamed Randy, in part, for the tone of the stories. "How dare you come out with those statements to the press," he rebuked.

It was an odd conversation, partly because there had been no blatant antagonism a few days earlier, when the two men had last talked. And all Randy had said in the broadcasts was that Dianne had been fearful and that she had suspected that she was being followed.

Alan seized on those words and stated that Dianne had had nothing to fear. He said that if Dianne had only told him she was afraid, he would have hired a bodyguard to protect her. He also said that he knew that Randy had talked to Jim. The comment baffled Randy, because he had never mentioned meeting Jim or talking with him in any previous conversation with Alan. However, Randy had told the sheriff's police.

SOA had wanted Randy to coax the attorney to reveal his views on what had happened to his wife. Alan continued to claim that he had no idea. His only theory was that Anndra was continually mentioning Acapulco, so perhaps Dianne had gone to Mexico for a holiday.

"How?" Randy retorted. "She had no money. No credit cards had been used. Didn't the police check for her car at the airport? Didn't the police check the airlines?"

Randy pointedly asked Alan if he had made someone angry enough to kidnap his wife. Alan said that he doubted it, but that he had given the police the name of an old nemesis who had beaten him after he successfully represented the man's wife in a divorce.

Randy then inquired whether Alan had ties to organized crime, as newscasts had indicated. Alan maintained that it had been at least five years since he had represented anyone with syndicate connections and that he had been nothing more than a bookie.

"What's the clicking noise on the telephone?" Alan asked suddenly.

"My phone was probably bugged by the police," Randy replied jokingly, suspecting that either the police had tapped the line or Alan was recording their conversation.

Because it was necessary to maintain communication with him, Randy tried to convince Alan that Anndra should at least visit with her cousins. "I'll think about it," his brother-in-law snapped.

It was evident that Alan was severing all ties with the Turners, that he never wanted to see any of Dianne's family again.

The telephone call to Alan was just another element of the emotional roller coast ride that had engulfed the Turners since Dianne's disappearance. One day, developments looked promising, and the next, the situation appeared hopeless. They spent hours worrying about the eventual outcome and whether there would ever be any resolution.

The nights were the worst. Kathy went to a doctor and obtained sleeping pills, while Randy resorted to quaffing beers or wine before bedtime.

"I was starting to use alcohol to help me forget and also to help me sleep. I would wake up at four o'clock in the morning and feel horrible. That's when I started jogging. That is the thing that kept me alive. Every morning that cleared my head and it would be my time for thinking."

Randy could not obliterate the guilt feelings that also emerged. He continually replayed the conversations in which Dianne had confided her fears. "We thought Dianne was exaggerating. I look back and think maybe I was selfish during that period of time. Maybe I should have been more aware of her. Maybe I should have had her move in with us for that last month or so. Maybe we should have tried to force her to do that."

Now, even the weekends, which once were cherished, had become intolerable. There was never any news, and this void depressed him. One Sunday he and Kathy drove to the cemetery where his parents were buried. Randy was overcome with emotion.

"I was ashamed, embarrassed, and frustrated that we had

trouble finding the graves," he wrote in his journal. "When we finally did find the graves, in the old section, I had nothing to say. All I wanted to do was leave and once we left, all I wanted to do was chide myself for not praying over the grave."

Sitting inside his car, Randy's eyes filled with tears that were impossible to stop. For the first time since Dianne's disappearance, he cried for his lost sister. Overcome with grief, he confronted the terrible possibility that Dianne might be gone forever from his life. "I kept thinking that my sister might never have a grave I could visit."

Chapter Six

April 5, 1982

Randy Turner was trying to relax in the straight-back wooden armchair, but finding a comfortable position was difficult. Electrodes were connected to his fingertips and chest, and strapped around his right arm was a sensor measuring his pulse.

First came the standard control questions that are part of every polygraph test. These measure the person's response to known, veritable answers and are then compared with the responses to the three or four key questions detectives want resolved. Randy watched the machine's needles jump and register each time he replied.

"Is your name Randall Turner?"

"Yes."

"Are you the brother of Dianne G. Masters?"

"Yes."

"Are you thirty-two-years old?"

"Yes."

"Do you know the whereabout of your sister Dianne?"

"No."

"Have you heard from your sister since she disappeared on March 19, 1982?"

"No."

"Are you withholding information from the police about the disappearance of your sister?"

"No."

Randy and Kathy's lives had changed inexorably since

Dianne's disappearance. Every day it seemed like the, trapped in a never-ending nightmare.

The sheriff's police still suspected that they were lying. And despite their pleas for a homicide investigation, the detectives were continuing to adhere to the theory that Dianne had run away.

Lt. Howard Vanick had called Randy requesting that he and Kathy take a lie detector test. While Vanick claimed to believe the couple, many of his colleagues thought they were hiding information. "He again tried to prepare me for the possibility that they might never find Dianne. He was sympathetic. He said a break could occur in six months or six years," Randy wrote in his journal.

So the couple drove to the Cook County Sheriff's Police headquarters in west suburban Maywood to prove, once and for all, that they were telling the truth. When they reported for the polygraph, they were met by two detectives who treated Randy and Kathy with total disdain, almost as if they were criminals.

The investigators barked orders for the Turners to follow them down the hallway and waited outside the testing room while Randy and Kathy were questioned individually. Randy could barely control his anger at his interrogators. "I just kept a calm voice and answered the questions. I just remember thinking this is ridiculous."

His thoughts turned to his wife. "I was concerned about Kathy's temper and how she would react to some of the hard questions. . . . I wondered whether she would overreact."

During the test, Randy tried without success to keep his mind from wandering. Three days after Alan reported Dianne missing, police had asked Alan to submit to a polygraph. Alan had refused, explaining that he didn't believe that such tests were accurate and that he was going to follow the same advice he had given his clients over the years: don't take one. The irony wasn't lost on Randy.

Nor was it lost on Jim Koscielniak. When he was asked by the police to take a polygraph, he, too, declined, saying he wouldn't take one until Alan did. He later relented and passed the test. It was Alan who had urged the authorities to question

Dianne's lover extensively. And until Jim passed the lie detector test, investigators had believed he knew far more about Dianne's disappearance than he let on.

To Randy, it seemed as if he would be grilled forever. "They asked the question 'Do you know where your sister is' three different times. Then they would ask, 'Do you have any knowledge of the whereabouts or the possible whereabouts of your sister?' I never thought they would be so extensive. It seemed a lot of the questions were to find out how much we knew. We had to prove to the police that we had nothing to do with this." By submitting to the test, he hoped that the police would realize that he and Kathy were telling the truth: Dianne had met with foul play.

The Turners, though, were not shy about voicing their opinions on the case. Randy bluntly told the detectives that he thought that Alan was responsible for Dianne's disappearance and that the sheriff's police—the very ones administering the test and conducting the investigation—were Alan's partners in crime. "Even after I told them that I suspected the county police, they continued to claim that they were complete professionals," Randy says.

When the hour-long test ended, the detectives told the couple they had passed. Their results were never entered into the department's official case file.

After the Turners' ordeal, they wanted nothing more than to go home and spend the remainder of the afternoon relaxing. Instead they received an unexpected shock from the private detective agency. "We don't trust the phones," an SOA secretary told Randy. "We think they may be tapped. From now on, make sure you use a pay phone when you call us."

So contacting the private detectives changed Randy's daily routine into a cloak-and-dagger existence. He would get into his car and make a five-minute drive to the nearest pay phone, which was located on a busy thoroughfare outside a drugstore. Here he placed his calls to the agency, and only then did he receive any information or instructions.

Meanwhile, Bénédicte Kagy, an intimate of Dianne's for more than a decade, had learned of Dianne's disappearance while visiting relatives in France. Her boyfriend, an associate of Alan's, had called her.

"Is Anndra home?" Bénédicte asked after hearing the news.

Her boyfriend assured her that Anndra was home and doing well.

"Then Dianne's dead and Alan has killed her," she told him.

Bénédicte was enraged at what had befallen Dianne, and she had spent several days trying to track down Randy's telephone number. Despite Randy's warning that his phone lines might be tapped, during a phone conversation with him, she immediately accused Alan of murdering Dianne. She then related a series of conversations that had occurred between Alan and her after Dianne had informed him that she intended to file for divorce.

The first call to Bénédicte had come on January 14, her birthday, she told Randy. Alan telephoned her at the office while she was preparing for a party given by her coworkers. He was sobbing. Alan's not the kind of guy who is going to cry, she thought at the time. He begged her to talk to Dianne and persuade his young wife to change her mind about the divorce. He couldn't live without Dianne, he told her. Then, amid the tears, he blurted out, "I'm going to blow my brains out if she leaves me. I have a gun. I can't accept this."

For the next six weeks, Alan phoned Bénédicte almost daily, pleading with her to convince Dianne to reconcile. The calls came late at night or at five o'clock in the morning. But after his initial call as the despondent husband, his conversations became more ominous, and they never varied.

"You're her best friend. You're her confidante. If you don't make her change her mind, I'm going to destroy her," Alan told Bénédicte. "As much as I love her, I'm going to hate her if she leaves me. And you know what that means with me. You know what I do to the people I hate," Alan said.

In the past, he had told Bénédicte that he had done terrible things to people, but she had concluded that the man was bragging. But as Alan's Jekyll and Hyde personality unfolded during that six-week period, she had an epiphany: "I was convinced that Dianne was in danger of being killed."

And Dianne herself was terrified. "If he decides to kill me," she told Bénédicte, "you'll never find my body."

Bénédicte consulted a psychiatrist about Alan's behavior to see what action she could take to thwart his plans. "Most people who brag about these things don't do it," the psychiatrist reassured her. Then she talked to a friend who was a policeman. "There's nothing you can do," he said simply.

So Bénédicte begged Dianne to go with her to France, where she would be safe. But she refused, saying she couldn't leave Anndra.

An hour before Bénédicte was to depart for the airport, Dianne called to say good-bye, and the conversation had an eerie tone. "We may never see each other again," Dianne told her friend ruefully, and she thanked Bénédicte for her years of friendship. "You are one of the only people who believed in me and supported me."

Yet all Bénédicte could do was give Dianne her address in France in the hope that she would change her mind and join her there.

Randy was amazed by Bénédicte's revelations. He asked her to meet with the private detectives, and she agreed. She was overcome by remorse that she had been unable to help Dianne, and she wanted to do everything she could to make amends.

Bénédicte, however, wasn't the only person who had been receiving phone calls from Alan. He also had contacted Dianne's divorce attorney, Gretchen Connell, threatening a "bloodbath" if the divorce was not dropped. "You keep this up, and you'll be sorry," he told the attorney.

Gretchen was also approached by judges who were friends of Alan's. It seemed that every time she appeared in court, the judge would call a short recess and ask to see her in his chambers.

Inside their sanctum, the judges would ask whether she could get Alan and Dianne back together. Even Gretchen's father-in-law, a Cook County judge, had intervened on Alan's behalf. Her answer was always the same: Dianne never would reconcile with her estranged husband.

Although Gretchen's statement, along with those of the Turners, contradicted Alan's claim that he and Dianne were reconciling, it did not change the direction of the investigatı From the onset, Lt. Howard Vanick, who was heading the case, had been trying to turn it into a homicide probe focusing on Alan. But Lt. Keating, Vanick's superior, was quashing all of his attempts.

Unbeknownst to the Turners, Keating had been heavily involved in the investigation, but his role was shrouded in secrecy. The day Dianne was reported missing, he and Vanick had quarreled on the driveway of the Masters' home about the direction the case should take.

"Dianne Masters did not voluntarily disappear," Vanick had told Keating. Vanick said he was convinced that Alan was somehow responsible for her disappearance and he suggested that the investigation should be looking at Alan as a suspect.

An angry Keating reprimanded his subordinate. He warned the lieutenant that he was not being objective and implied that Vanick easily could be removed from the case.

Keating, the commander of the intelligence unit, was a powerful figure in the sheriff's department and a man to be reckoned with, the private investigators told Randy. An informant who was on the force had tipped them to the fact that they should not dig too deeply within the department for answers relating to the disappearance of Dianne Masters.

Dan Davis, the president of SOA, warned Randy that he never should discuss Lt. Keating's relationship with Alan. "Never mention the name Keating. If you are over at your inlaws, don't even bring it up there. We just don't want that name to get out."

Randy recalled meeting Keating frequently at Alan and Dianne's parties. On one occasion, he and Keating had discussed the law enforcement profession, a job Randy was considering at the time. Keating tried to deter him from pursuing a career by describing what a cop encountered at Chicago's worst housing project, which had a nationwide reputation for its rampant crime and where police are often the targets of snipers. "One little look at Cabrini-Green and you'll never want to be a cop again," Keating assured Randy.

Despite the fact that Keating had Vanick walking a tightrope, Vanick was sympathetic to the Turners. He had hinted to Randy during a telephone conversation that they had some new clues, but he warned him not to become excited, because they might not pan out.

Vanick also asked if Dianne might have gone to Acapulco. Randy immediately recognized that Alan had repeated to the police his comment that Anndra had been mentioning the Mexican resort town and that it might indicate that she had overheard something about her mother's plans.

Kathy Turner, however, recalled that "Sesame Street" recently had completed a special on Acapulco. "Anndra loves that show, so that must be where she heard it," Vanick concluded.

The detective's response took Randy by surprise. "Odd that he knew what television show Anndra preferred," Randy noted in his journal.

Chapter Seven

April 8, 1982

THE Turners struggled to maintain a semblance of normalcy. Kathy had asked her mother to come over and babysit for her two sons while she went grocery shopping and ran errands. Randy was working in his office in the basement when the phone rang. It was Jim Koscielniak.

Something odd had happened at the college campus that day, he said to Randy. He'd run into Genevieve Capstaff, a humanities teacher and the faculty association's grievance committee chairperson, who had attended the college board meeting on March 18 and then gone with the group to the Courtyard for drinks.

Genevieve had left the restaurant at about 12:30 A.M. But after saying good-night, she moved her maroon station wagon from its space in the west lot to a spot along a wall of the restaurant, where she could sit unobserved and scrutinize the departure of her colleagues. The inquisitive Genevieve wanted to see if anyone was having an affair. Dianne, who emerged forty minutes later, was the last to leave the parking lot. Genevieve followed her as both women headed toward their homes on that chilly, overcast night.

At that hour, there was virtually no traffic. Genevieve easily could see the taillights of Dianne's car, which was about a block ahead of her, as they traveled west on 123d Street, a hilly thoroughfare that had streetlights at irregular intervals. The women drove about a mile and a half before encountering their first traffic signal at 123d and LaGrange Road. Though Genevieve had to stop, she never lost sight of Dianne's car.

Past LaGrange Road, the two-lane street became a dark, lonely stretch of pavement, and for about a mile, no homes would be visible. This route intersected forest preserves. Genevieve followed Dianne as she passed tranquil Papoose Lake, which was adjacent to the roadside, where the street leveled off. Many of the area's expensive homes, set far back from the street, then came into view.

When Dianne reached Wolf Road, which was just a hundred yards or so north of her house, Genevieve was still about a block behind her. But Dianne's car remained clearly in sight. Genevieve observed her at the intersection, where Dianne stopped for the stop sign and then turned south toward her own home. In less than thirty seconds, Dianne would reach her winding driveway. With the exception of Dianne's killers, Genevieve was the last person to see her alive.

Randy immediately recognized the importance of Jim's discovery. It was the first major clue that indicated that Dianne appeared to have reached her home that night and that Alan might be lying.

Genevieve had agreed to be interviewed by Randy's private detectives, Jim said. Afterward she would make an official statement to the sheriff's police.

Shortly after Dianne vanished, Cook County detectives had interrogated Genevieve, but they never asked her when she had last seen Dianne. Instead the investigators' questions centered on who was at the restaurant that night and what times they left. Genevieve did not volunteer the information about following Dianne because she did not want the embarrassment of being known as the nosy professor who lurked in the shadows to spy on the private lives of board members.

For Jim, the encounter with Genevieve was devastating. He had rationalized Dianne's disappearance from the moment he learned that she was missing. Dismissing any other possibilities about her fate, the day after she vanished, he went on a ski trip to Michigan. "I didn't want to believe she was dead," Jim would say later. "She said she was going to run away."

He and Dianne had discussed the ramifications. She told Jim her fear that if she took Anndra out of state, Alan would wield his clout and get a judge to issue a restraining order against her and then use it in a court battle, where she might lose custody of her daughter. If she ran away without Anndra, she worried that the court would view it as abandonment and Alan would use this in a custody battle. Again, she could lose Anndra.

When people told Jim that Dianne never would leave without her daughter, he had hoped that Dianne might have found a loophole in the law that skirted the abandonment issue. He had clung to any lifeline he could, to the extent of believing that Randy might be hiding his sister. "I thought she would go to her brother. I thought Randy wasn't telling me because she told him not to tell me."

When Randy turned to the private detectives for help, Jim expressed skepticism. "Randy, she must have run away. It's a lot of money. Are you sure you know what you're doing?"

For Jim, there were many unanswered questions and many lonely hours to fill. To keep busy, he decided to hone his skills at one of Dianne's favorite games, Pac-Man. "I would go and play Pac-Man to practice up for when she came back," he said.

Suddenly, after listening to Genevieve Capstaff's story, he knew there would be no tomorrow for Dianne and him. He thought back to the last time they had made love. Jim was holding her tightly in his arms when Dianne asked him, "How come you're not afraid? He's going to hurt us." Then she leaped out of bed and went to grab her purse. "I want to show you a picture of him, because I think you are going to be meeting him very soon. And you'd better watch out!" she warned.

Dianne returned to bed shaking. Jim recalled later that Dianne was more frightened that day than he had ever seen her, and he tried to soothe her frazzled nerves. Enveloped in his arms, Dianne then related a conversation that had occurred between Alan and her.

She had mentioned to Alan how much she missed her parents, who were both dead, she explained to Jim. "You're going to be seeing your mom and dad real soon,'' Alan had told Dianne, giving her a wink.

Jim was struck by the realization that Alan had made the insinuation sometime during the week prior to Dianne's disappearance. He was horrified that he had not taken her fears more seriously. ''I just didn't think that people murdered their wives in this day and age.'' Now Jim had to confront that likelihood.

The discovery of Genevieve Capstaff was significant for everyone involved. Randy and SOA's president, Dan Davis, were elated. He told Randy that the fact that she had seen Dianne turn south on Wolf Road should change the whole complexion of the investigation.

With a new development in the case, Randy again decided to contact the FBI. He told an agent that they had discovered a witness who had followed his sister virtually all the way home the night she disappeared. Randy was told again that the bureau could not officially become involved until proof of some interstate action occurred, though an agent would be assigned to watch developments.

When the media learned that an eyewitness had spotted Dianne practically turning into her driveway, there was another flurry of telephone calls to the Turners' home. But this time to avoid irritating Alan, the private investigators told Randy to decline any comment.

Armed with the knowledge that Dianne had arrived home, Randy's latest assignment from SOA became an even greater ordeal than before. They wanted him to try again to get Alan to discuss the case. The detectives wanted Alan's reaction to the news that Randy had hired them and they wanted to see whether Randy could engage him in a longer conversation.

''We thought the best way to do that was to invite him to Easter dinner. I thought that was proper. It was a good reason for the call and it gave me a good entrée,'' Randy concluded.

But Alan quickly declined the invitation, explaining that Anndra was leaving for Florida and he was going to visit his parents.

Following his gruff refusal, Randy immediately segued to the hiring of SOA. ''Alan, I know you are doing your part by offering the $10,000 reward. I didn't want to sit back and do nothing, so I hired a private investigative firm, Special Operations Associates."

"Good," Alan replied.

"I hope you'll cooperate with them and help them . . . in the investigation," Randy said.

"We'll see."

After their exchange, Randy dutifully reported to Dan Davis, telling him that Alan had refused his invitation. When Davis learned that Randy was calling from home, he quickly terminated the conversation. He insisted that Randy not say anything more on the phone and promised that they would discuss it fully at their next meeting.

While Alan spurned Randy, he did agree to meet with one family member: Dianne's aunt and godmother, Laurie Willcoxon. Outspoken and gregarious, she also was glib, and from the moment she and Alan were first introduced, they enjoyed casual banter.

"I'm the only one that would make cracks to him," Laurie explains. "I always talked back to him. He and I always had this kind of rapport." Yet Laurie was uncertain how Alan would respond when she telephoned him to see whether she could visit Anndra, and she was surprised by his invitation to Sunday brunch.

Alan opened the door and kissed Dianne's favorite aunt. Next he went into the kitchen and popped a Valium, telling Laurie that he was living on tranquilizers.

She was surprised to find that Alan's older son by an earlier marriage, was joining them. Alan had compartmentalized his two families, and it had always been a point of contention between him and Dianne. This was the first time Steven had met his four-and-a-half-year-old stepsister.

After brunch, they returned to the house, where Anndra took her Aunt Laurie and Steven into the backyard to show them all of her playthings. Later Laurie had the opportunity to talk to Alan alone. They sat at the dining room table.

"Alan, where's Dianne? What's happened to her?"

"I don't know," Alan replied.

Anndra then came into the kitchen. "Daddy, when's Mommy coming home?" she asked.

"I don't know. You better take your nap now."

After that encounter, Alan never again permitted Anndra to see any of her mother's relatives.

Meanwhile, Randy felt stymied in his efforts. The investigation was not moving quickly enough for him and his troubles at work were growing. It was evident to Randy that MacGregor was experiencing financial problems. The cash-strapped company had undercut their sales force by making deals with major retailers that left the salespeople trying to sell sporting goods at prices higher than those offered at the local discount chains. Randy discovered that he was losing part of his staff and that territories were being combined. He thought it might be an opportune time to start his own business. "I was finally beginning to believe in myself enough where this is what I wanted to do."

His decisive moment came in the last weeks of April. He flew to Ohio for a regional sales meeting that was supposed to last until Wednesday. He had to be back in Chicago on Thursday morning to leave for a family vacation to Florida.

But when the company announced that it was eliminating the regional sales manager's position—Randy's job—and demanded that he delay his trip to discuss his new role, he balked. He flew home and went on his holiday, vowing that he would leave the company in the coming months.

On April 23, 1982, he wrote his last item in his journal: "Vacation, job and lack of positive leads have not only drained all my emotions but also brought my writing to a halt.

"Vacation seemed to cleanse our minds to the situation but not remove our hatred. The knowledge that Alan killed my sister was *almost* becoming bearable, but anger, and perhaps pride, would not allow it. Knowing that Alan probably thought I would forget everything, keeps me hanging on."

An SOA employee, the late John Waters, gave Randy hope that his brother-in-law would be charged with Dianne's murder. Waters, a Chicago cop who was moonlighting for the private detective agency, was a consummate professional. Unlike some of his bosses, he wasn't a politician. He was a grunt, working for what soon would become one of the most politically connected detective agencies in the metropolitan area. One partner,

James O'Grady, would become the Cook County sheriff. Another, James Dvorak, would be named undersheriff and O'Grady would have him elected as the head of the Cook County Republican party.

Waters made sure that Alan knew he was not going to let Dianne's murderer escape prosecution. Some days, Waters suddenly would appear in the picture window of the Masters' home, so that Alan only saw a silhouette, then he would disappear.

Other days, he would position himself across the street outside Alan's law office in Summit, where Alan vaguely could see Waters' shadow watching him.

After paying Special Operations $4,000, Randy demanded that they give him a written report. Waters wrote a fourteen-page, single-spaced account outlining his findings. When the Turners received it, it had been edited into a four-page, triple-spaced rendition. Much of Waters' passion and painstaking detective work was missing. It offered little new insight. For instance, Dianne had been missing four months when the agency noted that a thorough investigation had revealed that Dianne Masters had disappeared without a trace. SOA also took credit for locating Genevieve Capstaff.

The version that Waters originally penned on May 25, 1982, which the Turners never saw, was far more telling. More important, his report raised the issue that the men who were investigating Dianne's disappearance—the Cook County Sheriff's Police—were covering it up.

Waters' superiors worried that this kind of shocking disclosure could hurt their agency's reputation if the report were leaked to the press and later was assailed by the sheriff's department. Moreover, O'Grady, who harbored political aspirations, was concerned about how the report would affect his candidacy for an office.

Waters noted that Masters had been the divorce attorney for Lt. Howard Vanick, the veteran cop in charge of the investigation, as well as for Sgt. Clarke Buckendahl, who was assigned to the case. And he pointed out Masters' close relationship with Lt. James Keating.

He found that Alan was a friend of a reputed member of the

crime syndicate, a top figure in Chicago's notorious First Ward, Democratic political machine. For years, Chicago's mob and the First Ward politicians had exchanged favors, and Alan's crony had long been a major player. Alan's associate was also a close friend of the judge who ran the Cook County Circuit Court, the nation's largest judicial system.

Waters quickly learned about Alan's sphere of influence, how he nurtured his friendship with judges and sent them from his home with gifts of pornographic movies and the refrain, "See you in court in the morning." Alan liked to brag about having several judges in his pocket and he had developed unusually strong relationships with judges in the suburban municipal districts in which he practiced.

The private investigator had uncovered a spate of new clues that the sheriff's police had seemed to overlook. "Alan had the phones bugged at home," Waters concluded. "He often repeated word-for-word conversations or made reference to things that he could not possibly know unless he overheard the conversations," he wrote.

Five days before Dianne disappeared, she had called Jim from her home phone, Waters learned. She told the college professor that she was definitely leaving Alan, whom she characterized as a crook in the taped phone conversation.

He traced the license plate number of the car that had followed Dianne to a thug who possessed a criminal record. He ascertained that Dianne had met with George Dunne, the clout-wielding Democratic president of the Cook County board, to talk about her divorce.

Waters speculated that Alan knew Dianne would never return. He noted that two days after she disappeared, Alan contacted a local florist saying they could stop the daily delivery of flowers to their home. That same day, Alan had taken one of Dianne's dogs to the vet. The dog had a mysterious cut over his eye and stitches were required to close it. Was it possible, Waters wondered that the dog had been struck as it came to Dianne's rescue while she was being attacked inside the house or outside in the driveway?

According to the report, in the fall of 1981, when Dianne and a friend had gone on vacation in Germany, Alan was having an affair with a woman from his office. Dianne, he said, had found the woman's underwear and other personal items in her car when she returned from her trip and demanded that Alan fire the woman.

During his investigation, Waters developed a certain disdain for Dianne, whom he described in his report as a rich housewife with little to do. But he also understood that she was a loving mother and an apparent murder victim and that Alan was the chief suspect in the case.

It was his theory that she had been attacked, probably in her driveway, by a known auto thief working for Alan. He believed that her body was dumped in her car and was either destroyed by a shredder in a nearby junkyard or taken to a mortuary belonging to a friend of Alan's and cremated.

None of these details were in the SOA report that Randy received. It did, however, agree with Waters' conclusion. "Dianne was the victim of foul play; not in the form of an accident, but as the result of a planned, deliberate action upon her life. Her body and her automobile were disposed of in such a way as to never be discovered," the report speculated.

CHAPTER EIGHT

December 11, 1982

FOR nearly three months, scuba diver Tom Skrobot had been exploring the murky depths of the Chicago Sanitary and Shipping Canal as a favor to local police. A cop from Willow Springs, a suburb known for its all-night taverns and laissez-faire government, had spotted tire tracks leading into the waterway, and initially authorities feared that someone had died in a car accident. So divers were dispatched.

When Skrobot and his partner searched the waters, they had trouble locating the auto—not because the visibility was so poor, but because there were so many vehicles buried in the canal. In the ensuing months, divers had recovered twenty cars. All had been deep-sixed to collect the insurance money.

The pitch-black canal was ideal for perpetuating a scam. It is a thirty-two-mile shipping channel that was hailed as a modern miracle at the turn of the century. Its opening meant that ships cruising the Great Lakes could travel from Chicago downstream to rivers connecting all the way to New Orleans. Tug boats still pushed cargoes of grain, coal, and sand up and down the channel, but with the onset of modern transportation, the canal had lost its former grandeur and its primary purpose had changed. It was now a dumping ground for millions of gallons of treated sewage and chemical waste that was collected from the industrial plants lining its banks on the southwest side of Chicago.

It was the kind of place where mothers warned their children not to play. The canal is 160 feet wide with a six-foot drop from the edge of its banks to the top of the water. Slip into the canal and it is virtually impossible to climb ashore.

Here the past coexisted with the present. More than a hundred yards overhead was a giant, modern overpass with steel-beam girders and concrete pillars. Graffiti covered the columns, evidencing the canal's use as a local teen hangout and lover's lane.

Expert stonemasons carefully had laid the giant slabs of limestone walls, which had been obtained from the nearby quarries that flourished in the early 1900s. Towering oaks and maples, now leafless in December, dominated the banks of the canal.

The tree-lined shores were easy to reach via the main thoroughfare of tiny Willow Springs, called Archer Avenue. Rumor had it that disgruntled car owners would simply turn down the road just off Archer, drive seventy-five yards across the dirt where the roadway ended, then plop their vehicles into the canal and report them stolen.

Diving in the vile waters, littered with the rusty ruins of cars, required special preparation. To protect his rubber wet suit from cuts and tears, Skrobot donned denim coveralls. He wore mittens over his wet suit gloves to feel his way through the muck, which the current deposited around the cars and could be as thick as two feet in spots.

Forecasters' promises of bright sun, blue skies, and temperatures that would hover in the mid-teens were meaningless to Skrobot and his buddy Jerry Los, who would be spending most of their day submerged in twenty-five feet of water. The search began at 10:30 A.M. underneath the Willow Springs Bridge. The bridge spans not only the canal but also a local river that parallels the waterway for several miles. The overhead roadway also serves as Willow Springs' major link with the more fashionable suburbs of La Grange and Burr Ridge.

Because of the height of the canal's walls, the two men used a crane borrowed from a local junkyard to enter the thirty-two-degree waters. The crane was portable and its long arm could be extended mechanically far above the canal banks to retrieve the metal hulks from the bottom after they were discovered by the divers.

To enter the water, Skrobot and Los sat atop a four hundred–pound wrecking ball. The crane's arm gently lifted the men from the canal bank, swung them over the water, and then slowly lowered them into the abyss.

To avoid tasting the putrid water, the divers bit down as hard as they could on the rubber mouthpieces that fed air from the scuba tanks. They descended, feet first, by letting out air in their vests and allowing the weights around their waists to carry them down until their fins struck the bottom of the canal.

With the push of a button, air flowed back into their vests and gently raised them above the bottom sludge. The visibility was so poor that they could not see their hands in front of their faces. Using ropes tied to the crane's wrecking ball, they searched in ten-foot circles, with each man gliding through the darkness in hopes of finding the metal carcasses.

During the first hour, the men located a 1981 Plymouth Reliant and a 1975 Lincoln Town Car. With each discovery, the car quickly was lifted to the surface so that the hunt could begin anew.

Skrobot and Los took a short lunch break and resumed their task at 1:15 P.M. After nearly an hour, the divers were getting cold. Their body temperatures had dropped as water seeped into their wet suits. Just as the more experienced Skrobot was ready to call it quits until warmer weather returned the following year, he literally ran into a Cadillac. The car sat on its roof on the floor of the canal.

The men quickly rose to the surface and announced their latest find: the twenty-third car discovered in the deep water. Then they returned to the vehicle and tied ropes around its front and rear so it could be lifted by crane onto the shore. By the time the car was sitting on the south bank of the canal near the concrete pillars—still upside down—the sun was sinking in the west, casting an orange glow over the water.

Green algae covered the white chassis of the 1978 luxury car and the yellow vinyl roof was completely collapsed, the result of a smashup between the submerged vehicle and heavily loaded barges. A thin layer of slime covered the license plate, distorting its numbers. One of the tires was flat. A key ring containing the car and trunk keys was in the ignition and the switch remained in the on position. The gearshift was in drive. And the dashboard clock had stopped at 1:50.

As had been the procedure over the past few weeks, the divers alerted the police whenever they located a vehicle. Willow Springs police chief James Ross was at home when he received the news, and he came to the scene to see the car lifted from the murky depths. By the time he arrived, the Cadillac's doors were open and water was pouring out of the interior.

Skrobot and Los were warming themselves by a log fire that was being stoked on the canal's banks. The divers were ready to pack up their gear and head home when Ross ordered them to remain there.

The police chief did not immediately recognize the license plate, because the letters were inverted. But he did recall that the distinctive yellow-and-white Cadillac fit the description of the missing car belonging to Dianne Masters. For months, every local law enforcement agency had been on the lookout for it.

Ross wanted to make sure he was right about the ownership of the car, so he drove to the nearby police station, about a minute away, and called Burt Odelson. It was Odelson's birthday.

"Burt, I just pulled a car out of the canal. I think its Masters'. It's a DGM 19, yellow Cadillac."

"That's it," Burt replied.

Ross returned to the canal to inspect the vehicle. The trunk was locked, so workers used the crane hook to pop it open about three or four inches, enabling them to peek inside. They saw a badly decomposed body. The men were overwhelmed by the smell of rotted flesh. "It just smelled to high heaven," says Skrobot, who stood watching the drama unfold, "My God, what a smell."

"We popped the trunk open because that is routine procedure and we realized something was wrong," Ross recalls. "I saw the legs of the victim and said, 'Oh my God' . . . and we immediately called the county police and the coroner."

The police chief ordered one of his men to guard the car while he went to the office to call the Cook County Sheriff's

Police. Lt. Vanick and Sgt. Buckendahl were among the nearly dozen officers who came to the canal.

With dusk approaching, Ross gave orders that the car be loaded onto a flatbed tow truck and moved to the fire station, where it was placed in an empty ambulance bay alongside the department's refrigerator and cold drinks machine. Evidence technicians could not search the car until the arrival of Dr. Robert Stein, the Cook County medical examiner. Then the trunk was opened and the body removed.

The corpse, obviously that of a woman, was nude from the waist down. Her panties and pantyhose were missing and her skirt and white lace slip were pushed above her navel over her chest. Her brown blouse was almost completely unbuttoned and her classic brown suit was badly deteriorated. Her shoes and purse were gone. The victim was wearing a blue raincoat, and a shell casing from a .22-caliber bullet was found in the cuff of the coat.

Her jewelry was still intact. On her right hand she wore a gold ring with a cobalt blue stone surrounded by diamonds and a chunky yellow-gold bracelet distinguished by two interwoven swirls; a Baume and Mercier watch and a gold linked bracelet adorned her left hand. Around her neck was a religious medal.

It was around 7 P.M. by the time Stein finished his tentative exam. He couldn't positively identify the body until dental charts were obtained, but he and the police believed the woman to be Dianne Masters. Authorities had determined that the car was definitely hers, and the clothing and jewelry found on the corpse appeared to match what she was reported to have been wearing the night she disappeared. And the body was about the same size and weight as Dianne.

Because the Cadillac was wet and muddy, evidence technicians could not complete their investigation until it dried out. As a result, the car would remain in the fire station for several days. Ross took security measures. He posted an officer on the premises for the entire night and installed a security camera so that a dispatcher could monitor it from the radio room.

The police chief went to notify the next of kin, Alan Masters. Ross later told investigators that the husband had taken the news with aplomb.

"When Chief Ross went to Alan Masters' home to advise him that the body had been positively identified as Dianne Masters, Alan displayed no visible signs of loss or sorrow, just a troubled look," investigators would write later. Ross characterized the expression as, "Jim, why did you find her?"

It was Saturday, December 11, 1982. Dianne's body had been at the bottom of the underwater graveyard for nine months. It was a fluke that she was ever found.

"They could have dumped this car anywhere. Why here, I don't know, but obviously they didn't think anyone was going to search there at all. They had to be pretty confident no one was going to look," Ross says.

The police chief had started the dredging operation weeks before at another location about a mile south after police had spotted some evidence indicating that a car had been pushed into the canal. After a few cars were pulled from the waterway, Ross received a tip. "Word had gotten around about the discoveries. I got this call one night telling me that if we looked under the bridge, about a mile north of where we found the first ten cars, we would find more."

The Turners were expecting college friends for dinner when they received a telephone call from Vanick informing them about the discovery of the car.

"We couldn't believe that this finally actually happened," Randy recalls. "We always suspected she was dead, so it didn't bring out horrible grief." Instead the news produced a feeling of cautious optimism that Dianne's murder might now be solved. "We had been through so many ups and downs by this time that one of the things we were very frightened of was getting our hopes up too much."

But Randy thought that maybe now the case would go forward. Perhaps the FBI would become involved.

"Obviously this was the most important thing that had happened in the whole case. No longer would I get that bullshit from Cook County. No longer could I be pushed around." Randy could not be told now that Dianne had run away or that she was in Acapulco. "No longer could they give me any of that crap, because they found her in the trunk of her car."

Nonetheless, the Turners' elation was short-lived. It was just two weeks before Christmas, and the joys of sharing the upcoming holiday with their young sons, Sean, three, and Austin, fourteen months, had ended abruptly with the realization that Dianne had, indeed, been brutally murdered. "It was a very trying time for us," Randy said. "A very sad time."

In some ways, Laurie Willcoxon was relieved that her niece's body finally had been found. "This is just what we wanted and what we didn't want. I used to sit here and the doorbell would ring and I'd push the buzzer and hope that she would say: 'Auntie, it's me.' It will eat at us the rest of our lives that someone walking the earth could say you are no longer fit to live."

She also hoped that now Anndra might learn the truth about her mother's disappearance. "Maybe now Anndra can be told her mother died and did not leave her. Out of this tragedy at least one little life can get back on an even keel."

For the Turners, there were tasks to complete. They immediately called the coroner's office to see whether he had determined the exact cause of death.

Stein, who normally starts working at 5 A.M. each day, had gone home to bed, an aide told Randy. But, the aide related, before leaving the county morgue, Stein took an unusual precaution, one that he rarely had done in all of his years as medical examiner: he took home the key to the drawer containing Dianne's remains. He was concerned about someone tampering with the evidence.

Using dental charts, Stein made a positive identification of the body. The formal autopsy was performed the next day. He concluded that Dianne had died of two gunshot wounds to the head.

But Stein also contacted an old friend from Oklahoma about the murder, forensic pathologist Dr. Clyde Snow, an expert at skull reconstruction and a consultant to the Cook County Medical Examiner's Office. Snow quietly flew into Chicago to confirm Stein's findings. Snow's work showed that Dianne had been beaten before the killer had fired the two fatal shots. Someone had struck her twice on the head with a blunt instrument, possibly a police-type sap, that had crushed her skull.

With the grisly discovery of the body, Alan was again the focus of the media. They hounded him at work and at home, but he ignored them.

Randy forced himself to call Alan to discuss his sister's funeral.

"What are the arrangements and where is the wake going to be?" Randy asked.

"Well, she requested in her will she wanted to be cremated. And I am going to follow her wishes and she is going to be cremated," Alan replied.

"What?" Randy was incredulous. "I didn't know that. She was a Catholic. She would never want to be cremated."

Dianne recently had returned to the church, and cremation was not part of the dogma. Though the Turners had witnessed the will that Dianne had executed on June 22, 1980, they had no recollection of such a provision.

"It's in her will. That was what her request was and I am going to do what she wanted," said Alan.

Randy argued with him. "I can't believe my sister would ever say that. That's not right."

After the conversation, he contemplated what Alan planned to do. "Then of course I saw a red light right away. It would be another way to hide evidence."

The Turners called Stein on Monday to try to stop the cremation.

"Did you realize that the husband is going to cremate the body?" Randy asked.

"You can't do that," Stein replied. "It's a homicide and the body can't be cremated."

Stein told the *Chicago Tribune* on Monday night that he had blocked the cremation.

"I turned Masters down," Stein said. "Possibly we might have to exhume the body sometime for further examination."

Alan turned to someone he trusted for help in handling the funeral arrangements, Alan Schiefelbein. The men were long-time friends and the couples had taken vacations together.

Schiefelbein had combined two disparate careers: he was an undertaker and at one time, had been the police chief of Lyons, a small town known for its topless dancing spots, its prostitutes, and the mob and motorcycle gang members who controlled many of them. He served an eight-year stint as top cop and was on the force for nearly three decades before retiring to devote full time to his mortuary.

According to police interviews, Schiefelbein was in Florida just days before Dianne vanished. Then, suddenly, he was summoned back home to see Alan.

On Tuesday, Randy called Alan again to say he would like to be involved in Dianne's funeral.

"What are you going to do? Bring the press and everything and make this a spectacle?" Alan snapped.

"No," Randy replied. "I would just like her to have a nice funeral and ceremony."

"There will be a memorial service. If I find out that you talked to any press at all, I will not tell you anything about her funeral," Alan stated flatly.

The Turners felt that Alan was blackmailing them. But they had no recourse but to comply with his wishes. "He used the press thing so much against us," Randy says. "We were very careful about that because we certainly wanted to go to my sister's funeral."

As Dianne's godmother, Laurie called the priest at St. Michael's Catholic Church in Orland Park, where Dianne had been a parishioner. Anndra had been baptized there. She told the priest that she wanted to arrange for a Catholic mass for her niece. The priest, however, said Alan was coming in later to make the plans.

Despite the fact that Alan did not place any obituary notice in the newspapers, a throng of more than two hundred mourners attended the memorial service. Among them was John Waters, who stood in the back of the church observing Alan. The private detective would not let Alan forget that he was being pursued.

"I remember Alan looking back there at Waters," Randy says. "Waters wanted him to know that he was there."

The Turners and their immediate family sat in the front right pew; Alan sat in the left pew with Anndra, his brother Leonard, sister-in-law Carol, and their daughter Allison.

It was evident that Alan had made the funeral arrangements,

for all Catholic rituals had been shunned. No requiem mass was said, nor was there a casket present. Only a large single wreath stood in the middle of the floor. There is no written record, either, that Dianne had received the last rites.

Monsignor John Gorman, who was also a psychologist and had counseled Dianne on numerous occasions, eulogized her as a woman who had been involved in the community and who had worked with battered women. He also discussed how her religious beliefs had been tested and how she had found her way back to the church. No one else spoke. Within a half hour, the memorial service was over.

Jim Koscielniak wanted to bid a proper good-bye to Dianne. He had intended to go to the church but was advised against it by the president of the college. Instead Jim drove around the St. Michael's parking lot copying down some of the license plate numbers belonging to those inside. When he was done, he went to a neighborhood bar to lament the loss of the woman he loved.

Somehow the media had learned of the service and had gathered outside St. Michael's to await the departure of the mourners. As the family exited, photographers snapped pictures. Alan became enraged, and he confronted Randy afterward.

"He blamed me for it. We didn't tell anybody. That's the last conversation I ever had with him," Randy said.

The following day, December 17, 1982, Alan secretly buried Dianne in St. Adalbert Cemetery in Niles, near the graves of her parents, without notifying the Turners. Besides Alan, the only ones present were his lawyer, Alan Schiefelbein, and a priest.

A reporter, Ray Hanania, was tipped off about the burial and called the Turners to inform them.

"It bothers us immensely," Kathy told him, "because I know that Dianne would not have wanted it this way."

The Crisis Center for South Suburbia decided to hold its own prayer service in Dianne's memory. Reverend William Smith, a local Methodist minister and former crisis center board member, celebrated Dianne's life. He asked her friends to share their own stories or remembrances of her.

Smith started by recalling his first encounter with Dianne in 1979. She had dropped by his church asking to borrow a "room or two" for the fledgling center that would aid victims of domestic violence. Dianne was so persuasive that the minister offered his church as its first headquarters.

Randy told the gathering that his sister had been the happiest during the last years of her life, when she was helping others.

There were tears, laughter, affectionate tributes. But none from Dianne's husband, Alan, who was conspicuously absent.

A few weeks later, Randy went to the cemetery to find his sister's grave. But because of the cold weather, a headstone would not be in place for some time, so Randy had to ask a maintenance worker where Dianne was buried. It was as though Alan had committed his final affront.

CHAPTER NINE

July 4, 1941

DIANNE and Randy's parents' courtship was like a storybook romance. Boy meets girl on a double date and they fall in love.

Anne Strzalka was a striking twenty-year-old. She had gorgeous blond hair and a captivating smile that stole the heart of George Turner. It did not bother him that she was blind. He treated her as an equal, and within months, they were engaged.

George, a quiet, good-looking, and talented musician, had formed a ten-piece swing band called the Rhythm Kings, while attending Leyden Township High School, with his older brother, Nathan. The group played the party circuit at night and on weekends. By day, George attended a music college on Chicago's south side.

Within a year, he became disenchanted with school and landed a job teaching music in Arkansas. He would drive home nearly every weekend to see Anne. But he couldn't tolerate being so far away from her, so he returned to Chicago and took a higher-paying job at a factory so that they could marry. The couple wed on July 4, 1941.

George and Anne bought a two-bedroom home in the western suburb of Franklin Park in 1951. The couple's apartment on Chicago's near north side, where they had lived since they were newlyweds, had become overcrowded with the addition of Dianne, now four and a half, and Randy, who was six months old.

For George, it was like a homecoming. In 1926, when he

was six, his parents, brother, and sister had migrated from Storm Lake, Iowa, where he was born, to Franklin Park. The family rented an apartment in the downtown section and his father, John, obtained a job as an auto mechanic. George and his siblings had grown up there.

Serendipity had brought Franklin Park's founder, Minnesota real estate magnate Lesser Franklin, to the area in 1890, where all he saw for miles were cornfields and prairie. But he was a man with vision. He purchased four farms, land that once had belonged to the Chippewa, Ottawa, and Potawatome Indians, laid out homesites, and built a depot. Then he bestowed his name upon the tiny town, which he called "the home of the Goddess Opportunity."

Initially Franklin lured urbanites to his rural locale with much fanfare. Parades and brass bands marched down Chicago's LaSalle Street and he ran free excursion trips for prospective buyers on the two railroad lines that traversed the countryside. Many were visitors to the Columbian Exposition, who relished the idea of free beer, free food, and free entertainment that ran the gamut from balloon ascensions to dancing.

The savvy developer knew that not everyone possessed the imagination to envisage Franklin Park's future. So he planted catalpa trees and built some imposing buildings, including a hotel, a business block, and a pavilion, where real estate lectures were held, to captivate potential denizens upon their arrival.

Franklin also opened his own stately home, which had a wide portico, high-ceilinged rooms, a sweeping staircase, and stained glass windows, to the public. His elegant third-floor ballroom provided the perfect spot to view his would-be village.

And his strategy worked. Lot sales exceeded $1 million, and in a special election held in 1892, the residents voted sixty-three to nine to incorporate.

But two years later, a depression gripped the country. Investors everywhere refused to pay taxes and abandoned their property. Franklin Park, which had become a boom town almost overnight, now lay dormant, struggling for survival.

Few visitors now paid a call at the home of the Goddess

Opportunity. But in 1929, the city fathers declared that "Franklin Park has been rediscovered." Civic leaders proudly cited accomplishments pointing to its revival: several industries, attracted by the railroad facilities, had relocated to the town, a new grade school had been built at a cost of $40,000, twelve streets had been paved, and a local businessman had been investing heavily in Franklin Park property.

Yet the village did not really flourish until World War II, when factories producing combat goods sprang up. Soon developers were scurrying to transform fields into subdivisions offering affordable housing for returning GI's. The basic models included two bedrooms, unfinished basements, and large yards. Franklin Park was an up-and-coming suburb once again.

Just a few miles away, a former military base was now a major commercial airport. It was called O'Hare, in honor of an air force hero, and every few minutes the silence of the countryside was shattered as propellor-driven planes dropped from the sky to land on the runways. And within blocks of the Turners' new home stood one of the nation's largest railroad yards.

Franklin Park had become industrialized. Land was so inexpensive that owners of machine shops, manufacturing facilities, and warehouses had moved there from the city. Many of George and Anne's neighbors were blue-collar workers who had followed their jobs.

The Turners' home on Reeves Court, named for Mayor Barney Reeves, was built in the mid-1940s by Steven Lonnquist. He had purchased the former Mills Farm at a foreclosure sale and had converted it into a small subdivision.

Anne learned every nook and cranny in the new house. Her blindness was the result of a terrible accident. When she was fifteen, she was in the coal cellar of the family's Chicago apartment near Milwaukee Avenue and Division Street when a neighborhood youth who was standing outside the building and playing with a gun pointed the weapon at the basement window, pulled the trigger, and then fled. The errant bullet struck Anne in the head.

She was rushed to the county hospital, but doctors said there was little they could do. They suggested that a priest be called to administer the last rites. But the priest refused, saying the young girl would recover. He further prophesied that eventually she would have two children, one of whom would become famous.

While doctors fought to save Anne's life, they removed her eyes and replaced them with glass ones. The shooting was a terrible blow for her. She had been a gifted child who already had demonstrated her ability as an artist by winning a scholarship to the prestigious Art Institute of Chicago.

Her talents, however, were varied. Before the accident, a family of circus performers living in the same six-flat had taken the lithe Anne under their wing. They had given her private lessons on the building's rooftop and had turned her into an accomplished acrobat and dancer. A theatrical troupe had wanted to hire her before discovering that she was a minor.

Anne's tragedy was further compounded when her father, thinking she was asleep, said the teenager would have been better off dead than blind.

A second calamity soon followed. Anne's father, John, died of a heart attack on Christmas Eve. After putting up the tree, he told his wife he wasn't feeling well and went into the bedroom to nap. He never awoke, and hours later, his family discovered him dead.

Anne's mother, Rose, always had worked. She was employed at night as a cleaning lady in the executive offices of a Chicago railroad company. The job allowed her to care for Anne and her three siblings during the day and provided enough cash to support her family.

At an early age, she taught her children the rudiments of running a household, which she had learned at her mother's knee. She gave them daily chores to perform, including a designated room to clean, and no one shirked his or her duties.

Their mother demanded that the apartment sparkle. The youngsters often could be found down on their hands and knees scrubbing the floor with a brush, soap, and water, until it shined. The three girls learned to cook all of the traditional Polish dishes. By the age of ten, they knew how to pluck and clean a chicken as well as iron a white shirt.

Anne was forced to continue her formal education at a school for the blind in Jacksonville, Illinois, a small rural town in the central region of the state, hundreds of miles away from family and friends. She hated the school, but she hated her fate even more. She learned braille and how to cope with her handicap, yet she never forgot how much she had lost and how cruel life could be. It was a lesson she later would instill in her children.

Anne was thrilled to have a home of her own. Like most young couples, the place was simply furnished with hand-me-downs from her family. But it was cozy. The living room held two stuffed chairs and a matching couch in earth tones. Gold carpeting and gold drapes, which covered the venetian blinds, completed the room.

In the master bedroom was an art deco–style bedroom set. For the first few years of their childhood, Dianne and Randy shared the second bedroom. The basement boasted a knotty pine rec room that had a bar and a slot machine. Before long, construction began downstairs so that Dianne could have a small room of her own.

The previous homeowners had planted a plethora of peonies and lillies of the valley and Anne loved gardening in the yard. The fingertips that had helped her discern the braille letters soon distinguished between weed and flower. Workmen added a rose trellis around the porch, but it was Anne who planted and tended the garden that transformed their plain-looking house into a neighborhood showplace.

Dianne was George's little princess. He doted on her. He adored seeing his young daughter dressed up. Her frilly outfits often were complemented by a straw hat, and there was always a bow in her long blond hair. A tomboy she was not.

George showered Dianne with gifts. At an early age, he bought her a clarinet, and there were ballet lessons, too. For her seventh birthday, she received her first Schwinn bicycle, which had a light and training wheels. He wanted his little princess to have everything.

And for the first few years, the family lived the suburban dream. They were one of the first on the block to own a television with a six-inch screen and there were new Oldsmobiles in the driveway annually.

George's business was booming. In 1945, while working as

a production foreman at a coil manufacturing plant, he and two coworkers had decided to start their own company. Industrial Coil Manufacturers, which produced audio transformers, was born in a little storefront on Irving Park Road in Chicago, and it grew rapidly.

George soon bought out his partners and asked his brother Nathan to join him in the firm after he returned from the war. George ran the front office; Nathan oversaw the factory. The plant had contracts with all of the biggest electronic manufacturers of the day, Motorola, Zenith, and Sonora. At its peak, three thousand to five thousand transformers were being manufactured daily.

But prosperity became a fading memory. In 1953, George's company collapsed, partly because of his excessive drinking. He drank especially when things weren't going as planned, and alcohol was a panacea for him, an escape from any problem that arose.

Nathan, who had a degree in music, fled the company and returned to teaching when he could no longer tolerate George's inattentiveness. "The minute things started to go bad, he wouldn't show up," Nathan says. "He wouldn't face it. He lost interest . . . but [the] drinking was responsible." With the demise of the company, the good life ended for the Turners.

George found work as a milk truck driver. Though home delivery was not yet passé, his route included only retail outlets. It was a union job, paying union scale, and the money was enough to support his family. There was always food on the table, but life was now a financial struggle. Still, it was a happy household filled with love, occasional laughter, lots of music, and pets galore.

The family always had a menagerie—cats, birds, and, at one time, a monkey. George had picked up the animal at one of his regular haunts and had taken it home as a joke. Both Anne and Dianne were enthralled with the little creature.

"It had the run of the house," Randy says. "I was a little kid and I just remember how much I use to hate it because he would always jump on my shoulder and bite my ear. It would get mad at my mom and it would go and take her coffee cup and pour it on the bed. Or take a sugar bowl and pour it on the bed."

Parakeets were another family favorite. There was always a bird-in-residence, named Pretty Boy, who would perch on Anne's shoulder and drink out of the faucet.

George urged everyone in the family to take up an instrument. He had played the trombone well and won numerous awards in high school and competed in the National Solo Contest. Anne played the piano and also taught herself the accordion. Dianne's instrument was the clarinet, while Randy followed in his father's footsteps. He not only inherited and played his father's slide trombone, he also started a band when he was in the seventh grade.

Whenever Randy or Dianne practiced, George would sit in the kitchen and listen to their drills. "He always got a kick out of that. He would sit in the other room as we practiced, and every five minutes, when you hit a wrong note or you hit it flat, he'd come in there," Randy recalls.

Both children became proficient musicians. Dressed in their high school band uniforms, they looked like decorated war heros, their chests hung with medal upon medal. Dianne and Randy regularly competed in state championships and won dozens of top honors. And it was a big disappointment if they finished second.

The less George Turner accomplished, the more Dianne seemed to achieve. Not only was she a talented musician, but she continuously was making the honor roll. His princess was everything he had hoped she would become.

When the Turners lived in Chicago, Anne's mother, Rose, who resided across the hall, helped her daughter care for her two children. After they moved to Franklin Park, Anne managed on her own, feeding, washing, and diapering Randy. When he got older, Anne relied entirely on Dianne to supervise her younger brother. With this awesome responsibility, she matured more quickly than her peers and, as a result, missed much of her own childhood.

Randy remembers her as a "mini-mom." "She wasn't just like a sister. She was the one who had to watch me. If I wanted to go in the yard, she was the one who had to watch me to make sure I didn't leave the yard. If I was going to be playing outside, she had to be the eyes. She was just from the beginning always a part of that."

Randy was a mischievous lad. Sometimes, as a trick, he would conceal himself under a bed. Dianne would tell their mother, who would then chase him out of his hiding place with a broomstick.

On one occasion, to outsmart his mother and sister, Randy snuck into the family's car, thinking that the broomstick would never find him there. A few minutes later, Dianne came outside and knocked on the car window. She told him that the neighbors had called and that they were contacting the police. Randy was so scared that he ran back inside the house.

The children's friends never realized that Anne was blind. Anne had developed her other senses to such an extent that it was difficult to discern her handicap. For example, she could pour a beverage into a glass without spilling a drop, and when someone addressed her, she would turn her head in the direction of the speaker, so it appeared that she was looking at him or her. "Most of our friends never knew, because you just couldn't tell," says Randy. "Every step in that house was counted. She knew exactly where everything was. It was amazing. I can remember having my friend over to my house four times before he asked if my mother had a problem with her sight."

In junior high, Dianne became clothes conscious, but there was no money for extravagances. Aunt Laurie, a seamstress, provided her with fashionable hand-me-downs gleaned from some of the most affluent women in the Chicago area. Unaware of how Dianne obtained her wardrobe, friends often asked what her father did for a living.

The family made do with what they had. And Randy, Dianne, and George all turned to Anne for strength.

The Turners never had been regular churchgoers. Anne's accident and an insensitive encounter with a priest in the old neighborhood had ensured that. Home from Jacksonville, she had gone to confession and accidentally walked into a church pew. The priest, not knowing she was sightless, yelled at her, saying she was a stupid little girl and asking sarcastically if she was blind.

It was the last time that Anne had entered the church, with the exception of her children's christenings and a few funerals. George, a Lutheran, had accompanied Dianne to her first communion and confirmation. Anne stayed home.

Yet she had an abiding belief in God. At night she would read the Bible in braille. Dianne would say later that her mother never lost her faith.

Like her mother, initially she was drawn to the church. Alone, Dianne would walk two miles to St. Gertrude's for Sunday services, and she attended catechism classes regularly. But the more she read and learned, the more her interest in Catholicism waned.

Anne's wisdom was valued by her children. "My mom was always trying to teach us to be very tough and resilient, because she always was of the feeling that life can deal bad things to you and you ought to be prepared for them," says Randy.

"My sister couldn't quite cope or learn that. She had a very difficult time, because she was an emotional, poetic person. She was very emotional and had big swings of emotion. She could get tearful over reading a poem. Dianne could probably recite two hundred poems for you verbatim, but when it came to common sense, the simplest of things, that wasn't her strong suit."

Anne was the kind of mother who delighted in hearing about her children's day. She always was ready to listen.

"Randy adored his mother," notes Laurie. "They had a relationship that's rare. He would come home from a date and he would go in her room and talk to her. He was such a talker. He would kneel on a kitchen chair and he could sit there for hours like this and talk to you. He would talk and talk and talk."

Dianne, on the other hand, was less communicative and would disappear into her room. "She was really Ms. Academia. She loved school. She was the one who'd come home and go to her room and study for two hours," says Randy.

Her room, though, was also her sanctuary. The soul-searching adolescent spent hours reading, exploring myriad topics, from Zen and existentialism to Freud.

Dianne was cognizant of what her life lacked. She wanted hugs and kisses from her parents, but they were not demonstrative. And she desired things that her family could not afford. So she spent hours dreaming. Dreaming of the future. Dreaming of riches and a better life.

She confided many of those dreams in Bengt Naslund, who lived directly behind the Turners' home. Dianne and Bengt had known each other since kindergarten, and they were kindred spirits. They grew up together going to the beach and playing clarinet in the Lincoln Grade School and East Leyden High School bands. For nearly thirty years, they shared each other's secrets.

Dianne was a typical adolescent, a head taller than the boys in her class. Her blond hair was cut short and she was skinny and gangly.

But in high school, she blossomed. The boys whom Dianne had chased in grade school now were chasing her. She fell head over heels for a fellow band member who played the French horn and was a year older than she. Until he graduated, they went steady and frequently double-dated with her friend Bengt.

She was just as popular with girls as she was with the boys. "Everybody knew her," recalls Randy. "She was in so many things. When I came, it was 'Oh, another Turner!' "

Dianne and Bengt, who were both brilliant students, also shared a penchant for literature and art, although they had diverse tastes. Dianne liked modern art, "what I would term the bizarre," says Bengt.

"Even in English, her favorite subject, she was attracted to the unusual," he says. Poetry, though, was Dianne's raison d'être. When she wasn't reading it, she was writing it. She particularly was fascinated by verse that had melancholy themes.

"I remember her favorite poem because I had to recite one in sixth or seventh grade," says Randy. She recommended that he learn "Little Boy Blue." "And that's a sad, sad poem. I can still recite it to this day."

LITTLE BOY BLUE

The little toy dog is covered with dust,
But sturdy and stanch he stands;
And the little toy soldier is red with rust,
And his musket moulds in his hands.
Time was when the little toy dog was new,
And the soldier was passing fair;
And that was the time when our Little Boy Blue
Kissed them and put them there.

"Now don't you go till I come," he said.
"And don't you make any noise!"
So, toddling off to his trundle-bed,
He dreamt of the pretty toys;
And, as he was dreaming, an angel song
Awakened our Little Boy Blue—
Oh! the years are many, the years are long,
But the little toy friends are true!

Ay, faithful to Little Boy Blue they stand,
Each in the same old place—
Awaiting the touch of a little hand,
The smile of a little face;
And they wonder, as waiting the long years through
In the dust of that little chair,
What has become of our Little Boy Blue,
Since he kissed them and put them there.

Dianne and Bengt collaborated on short stories, which always had a bizarre twist to them; they read like takeoffs of the then-popular television show "The Twilight Zone." They also worked together on the high school creative writing magazine, the *Eagle's Feather*. But their writing styles were vastly different.

Bengt's poem "Trepassey," penned during his and Dianne's

sophomore year, was an ode in iambic parameter. It was among those published in the 1962 *Eagle's Feather*.

Dianne's "Endless Payment," which was in the same edition, was far more sombre and introspective. Written in first person, the poet explores the themes of killing, the control that someone has had over her in the past, the lack of meaning in her life, and the examination of her black soul.

Dianne was an energetic, free-spirited girl, notes Bengt. "She was creative, and creative people tend to have a mind of their own."

Nonetheless, she was the kind of girl all parents hope their child will be. Well schooled in the social graces. Polite. She possessed a keen sense of humor and a quick, acerbic wit. Dianne would verbally joust with anyone and had rarely met her match.

As she approached adulthood, she turned her sharp tongue on her father. George and Dianne shared at least one personality trait—both were stubborn and strong willed, and they clashed frequently. "It was pretty much a love-hate relationship," Randy says. "He was never close to us."

Dianne had become extremely critical of him. She was angry particularly about her father's drinking, and she hated his nightly stops at his favorite watering holes.

George often came home after the family had eaten dinner. He'd ask for his meal, take several bites before complaining that the food was unacceptable, and leave the table. He'd then slam the door and go to bed.

Dianne also resented her father's disregard of her mother. She insisted that he take Anne, who rarely left the house, out on weekends, even if it was to a bar. She often screamed at her father to make her point, and he would capitulate.

During Dianne's senior year, her boyfriend went off to college and she began seeing someone her parents frowned upon. "Even I, who was four years younger than she, looked at the situation and thought she was nuts," Randy says. "She had this great guy. I couldn't understand what she was doing with this jerk who nobody in high school liked."

So Dianne dated him on the sly. Late one night, George caught the teenager tapping on the Turners' window. The scene erupted into a tremendous shouting match between Dianne and her father.

There was something almost sinister about the relationship, Randy recalls. Dianne had done more than pick a fellow who was not socially acceptable at school. The young man treated her badly, and she still was attracted to him. "Looking back, she always had problems with men," Randy said. "The meaner they were, the more she fell for them." Yet after the fight with her father, the relationship ended.

When Dianne argued with her parents, she sought solace from Aunt Laurie. "If she was unhappy at home about something . . . she'd call me and cry. I'd go pick her up."

Dianne and her father were now increasingly at loggerheads. The biggest blowup occurred over college. Dianne desperately wanted to go away to school, but George refused.

He maintained that girls didn't need to leave home to continue their education. And the family did not have the money for such an expenditure.

She would have to finance college herself. While Dianne had saved some of her earnings from her job as a cub reporter covering night meetings for the community newspaper, she knew she couldn't afford the type of school she yearned to attend.

She opted for Wright Junior College in Chicago. It was a two-year program that provided a way station for students hoping to improve their grades so they eventually would be accepted at a larger institution.

After the first semester, a college dean wrote George and Anne informing them that Dianne didn't belong there. She needed a four-year school that could challenge her intelligence, and he implored them to find funding for her education.

In high school, Dianne had heard a lecture given by poet Gwendolyn Brooks, who also taught at a local university, Elmurst College. She was so inspired by the woman, who later would be designated the poet laureate of Illinois, that she wanted to attend her classes.

Aunt Laurie took Dianne to enroll at the nearby campus. They spent the day touring the facilities and meeting some of the faculty. Dianne almost balked when she learned that she had to take a religion class to meet the small, conservative school's graduation requirements.

Meanwhile, George had decided that for his princess, he would do anything to help send her to college. Even if it meant taking a part-time bartending job on weekends to scrape her tuition together.

Although Elmhurst had dormitories, Dianne could not afford such a luxury. She lived at home and commuted to school. George had saved to buy her a baby blue Mercury, which she shared with Randy when he turned sixteen.

Dianne's sophomore year was a reunion of sorts. Bengt Naslund transferred to Elmhurst after he ran out of money attending Northwestern University, and Sally Meador, a friend from high school, was an incoming freshman.

On most college campuses during the 1960s, radicalism prevailed, but Elmhurst remained a bastion of conservatism. Dianne and Bengt were backers of the ill-fated Barry Goldwater campaign in 1964, and they, along with Sally and her future husband, were members of the school's chapter of the Young Republicans.

While Dianne met many young men, she dated only sporadically. "She was very much her own person," says Sally. "She had almost a women's libber mentality. Once she opened her mouth and men heard how she could think, that turned away a lot of them. Blondes with a brain are not in popular demand with a lot of men."

Dianne, however, was attracted to the junior chamber of commerce types, Bengt says. Ronald Mueller, an impoverished transfer student from the University of Wisconsin at Whitewater, was of that ilk.

He had spotted Dianne in one of his classes. He liked the young woman's quick wit and sense of humor. "She was kind of like a wiseacre," Ron recalls. "Smart-alecky. She was like I was. We'd make flip remarks . . . and be so sarcastic that people didn't know how to take it. We'd exchange barbs back and forth in classes. It was just a game."

And their ongoing battle of the sexes resulted in their first date. "We just wanted to see who was going to drink who under the table," says Ron. "We went to a drive-in and we had a bottle of something. We both got half-snockered. We started dating. . . . Doing the inexpensive things we could afford.''

Dianne and Ron would play cards for hours at the student union. ''We started cutting classes to play Hearts because we didn't want to leave the hand,'' he says. And they'd go on outings to the lake or to the arboretum. Sometimes they'd wage their war on the tennis court or the golf course.

Finally, just before Christmas in 1966, he approached Aunt Laurie about getting Dianne an engagement ring.

''Dianne's Uncle Joe had some jewelry connections. I think he had jewelry stashed all throughout his Chicago house. I contacted Laurie and said that I wanted to surprise Dianne with an engagement ring. . . . Laurie took me to the house and he'd go back there and bring some diamonds out. I remember I wrapped it around a stuffed animal on a ribbon.''

During the next few months, Dianne vacillated about whether she should marry. She wasn't sure that a life with Ron was what she wanted, and she expressed her uncertainty to him. ''Oh, yeah, we talked about it,'' he says. ''Any engagement, it's a shock to a person when you have to make the commitment.''

Theirs was an off again, on again relationship. Dianne returned the diamond ring at least once to Ron. But she was eager to leave home and longed for a change of any kind. And marriage certainly would be a change.

Chapter Ten

August 19, 1967

RONALD Mueller was everything Dianne wanted in a husband. He had a wonderful physique, blond hair, blue eyes, a solid, square jaw, and he had played split end on the college football team. And he adored her.

It rained the day they got married—August 19, 1967—at the St. Paul Lutheran Church in Melrose Park. Where to hold the ceremony had caused consternation. Ron's parents, who were strict Lutherans, would not consider a Catholic wedding.

Dianne's grandmother, Rose, could not understand why she wasn't getting married in the church. Laurie told her mother, "That's all right, Ma. If they get a divorce, she's still Catholic."

Dianne was a glowing bride. Her beautiful white lace and satin gown, which had short scalloped sleeves and a long train, came from one of Chicago's most exclusive stores, Bonwit Teller. Aunt Laurie, who had gotten the dress from one of her customers, had added matching fabric to the hem to lengthen it for her niece.

Dianne's bridesmaids were her two closest friends, Sally Meador and Daviene Hanson, and her cousin Sharon. Ron's groomsmen included his brother, Phil Bowdenstab, and Bengt Naslund. A beaming George, sporting a new, dapper gray suit and red-print tie, gave his princess away. Anne wore a baby blue print dress and her mink stole, a momento from her husband's more prosperous days.

Dianne had planned every detail of the wedding. "She loved

doing things like that," Randy says. "My dad just provided the money."

Afterward, there was a large reception at the local VFW hall, where a panoply of Polish and German food was served. Sixteen-year-old Randy sneaked beers from the bar. Couples danced to a live band. The group's first song, "Strangers in the Night," drew a chuckle from Sally, who knew that Dianne and Ron would not be strangers on their wedding night.

The rift over the church selection had strained relations between the Turners and Muellers and it was evident at the festivities. Guests recall that the families never seemed to talk to one another. "The whole thing started off wrong. His family all sat here on this side of the hall and we sat here and no one spoke to each other the whole evening from either side," says Laurie.

Perhaps that was an omen. At least two of the members of the wedding party did not believe the marriage would last. They were right. "They were totally unsuited for each other as far as I could see," says Sally. "Kind of like she liked jazz and he liked rock music. She liked to read and he liked baseball. He was cute. And I think he made her feel special. And at least initially, he looked up to her because of her vocabulary and her drive. You know opposites attract. And she liked him because he was very cute and he was sexy. He was athletic and he had a nice body and all of that. It was not enough to make it last."

Bengt, too, had warned Dianne that she and Ron did not seem compatible. "He was strong-willed," Bengt recalls. "I think that was one of the attractions. She never liked anyone who was Milquetoast."

Yet Dianne did not stop to analyze the basis for their relationship or think about the future. She was more concerned with the present. Both Dianne and Ron viewed the marriage as a means of escaping their home life, a one-way ticket to independence.

"She rushed into marriage, which is always bad," notes Sally. "The object was to get out of the house. She had only been married a few months [when] she realized it was a real big mistake."

After honeymooning in Canada, they returned to campus. Dianne was in her senior year and Ron had to complete twelve hours before he would graduate in January.

They already had rented a cute one-bedroom apartment at 125 West Virginia in Elmhurst, within walking distance of the college. Ron had been working mornings as a circulation assistant at one of the local weekly newspapers and his bosses knew the owners of the building. With their help, he and Dianne leaped in front of others on the waiting list for the inexpensive flat.

The newspaper job, though, did not pay enough to support two people. Ron also was employed full time in an administrative position at the nearby Automatic Electric plant, which manufactured telephones.

Dianne enjoyed decorating the apartment, but their budget was so tight that the couple could afford to buy only a new couch. Like other newlyweds, they had little furniture and had to improvise. With Randy's help, they built bookcases, which also housed their television, from bricks and shelving.

Dianne and Ron's life-style was a frugal one. They dined frequently on macaroni and cheese, and at night they watched television or went to an occasional movie. Sometimes there was a more exciting type of entertainment—strip poker.

Ron watched the pennies carefully. He was making only $125 a week at Automatic Electric and their rent was one week's salary. There was food to buy, never-ending school expenses, and student loans to repay.

Then the couple was offered a deal enabling them to purchase a new Plymouth for $3,000. Ron had gotten it at cost through his secretary's husband, a car salesman. The car came sooner than they expected and they furiously had to scrape together the down payment. "Finances were really difficult," says Ron. "It was a struggle."

In some ways, Dianne was realizing that marriage had not changed her life. She was just as poor as she had been before.

And there were more problems on the horizon for the newlyweds. In 1967, the nation was at war and Uncle Sam was drafting scores of men for the action in Southeast Asia. Ron had the misfortune to live in the suburbs, where the number of eligible draftees were few, because most had obtained student deferments. As soon as his expired, he knew he would be drafted.

He pulled even tighter on the purse strings. He wanted to accumulate a nest egg for Dianne before he went away, so he quit his accounting job at the factory and went to work for his uncle in the construction business, which paid nearly twice what he had been making, sitting behind a desk.

As soon as he received his draft notice, their relationship changed. "The tension was there," Ron says. They fought like cats and dogs. They constantly were sniping at each other.

Their game of one-upmanship had escalated into angry, acerbic arguments. Occasionally, Bengt and Sally witnessed their vituperative confrontations.

"Dianne would tell you exactly what she was thinking and she didn't pull any punches," Sally says. "Tact was not her forte. Dianne also baited Ron. Well, anyone who is intelligent and knows they are more intelligent than their mate can use that against them."

It was clear that Ron was leaving a frightened woman behind. Dianne wanted a career in journalism but knew those jobs were nearly impossible to find. And she really had no marketable skills. "I think the fear of her not having a job and me leaving put an awful strain on her," concludes Ron.

Despite the uncertain future, she never would move back home. "She wanted to be independent," remembers Ron. "She had a lot of pride. It was easier to rough it than go back to her parents."

When she received her degrees in English and psychology in June 1968, she took a job as a life insurance salesperson for the Independent Order of Foresters. Three months later, Ron was ordered to go to Ft. Leonard Wood, in Missouri, to begin basic training in the U.S. Army, and he knew that ultimately he would be sent to Vietnam. Dianne saw him off at the train station and kissed him good-bye.

They had been married for one year.

Weeks later, Ron received a letter from a lawyer, whose name he does not remember, advising him that Dianne wanted a separation. "I wrote a nasty letter back to whoever the lawyer was and told him to let us mind our own business and let us settle our own problems,'' he says.

For Dianne, her marriage ended on September 1, 1968, the day Ron went off to the army. Intellectually it did not matter that they were not divorced. That would happen eventually.

''She must have felt, even though I got drafted, that I had deserted her,'' says Ron.

What happened during the next 18 months was one of the more bizarre times in Dianne's life and the most difficult to understand. It was as if she had a split personality. On one side was the conservative little girl from Franklin Park who loved the arts and music and enjoyed reading at night. On the other was a Dianne who led a clandestine existence unbeknownst to her family and friends—a young woman who lusted after the good life and wanted to savor every possible experience that came her way.

It started with an affair with an older, married coworker at the Independent Order of Foresters. During the holidays, Ron made a surprise trip home for a three-day weekend. He and three of his army buddies had rented a tiny four-seater plane and flew into Chicago's Midway Airport.

When he arrived that night at their Elmhurst apartment, he remembered he had left his keys in the barracks. He went to the back door and knocked. The lights were out in the flat, so Ron went to the front entrance and rang the intercom. He waited and waited.

Just as Dianne was buzzing him in, he heard the back door slam. He went into the bedroom and it was filled with smoke, and there was a package of cigarettes in the kitchen. Dianne didn't smoke. Months later, Ron learned that he had caught his wife and her coworker, who was at least twenty years her senior, in the midst of a tryst.

''Knowing what I know now, I couldn't fault her,'' Ron said nearly twenty-two years after the incident. ''I had nothing. I might not ever come back. He wined and dined her. The maturity of an older man overwhelms younger gals. It's like a stacked deck.''

On January 20, 1969, Dianne's attorney filed a lawsuit in Cook County Circuit Court on her behalf seeking a divorce from Ron, but she never informed him of her intention, nor did she tell her family. It stated that they had been separated since September 1, 1968, the day Ron left for basic training.

There were several oddities about the lawsuit. At the time of the filing, Dianne was living outside Cook County, and technically, she would have had to reside in that county for at least a year before a judge could even consider her suit.

The divorce file indicates that Ron was served notice of the pending divorce case on February 6, 1969. According to Ron, he never received any such document. Federal law also prohibits judges from granting divorces to military personnel assigned to combat duty.

Ron left for Vietnam on February 20 from O'Hare International Airport. Dianne accompanied him, but their farewell was not what he had anticipated. "She just lost it," Ron says. "She tore out of there like a bat out of hell, as if something really had to be troubling her."

When Dianne's lease expired in 1969, she moved from Elmhurst to a dingy six-flat building in Harwood Heights, a suburb bordering Chicago's northwest side. The only redeeming quality about her basement apartment was that it was cheap.

She started dating immediately. She frequented a bar just a few blocks from her new home, where she met the owner, whose nickname was Bull. He, too, was married and about twenty years older than Dianne. Sally recalls that Dianne referred to him as though he were a Texas oilman, not the owner of a neighborhood tavern. "She kept a lot of her private life private. She would like drop little tidbits and never give you the full story. So it was virtually impossible to link things together."

On December 12, 1969, despite the fact that Dianne had filed for divorce eleven months before, she flew to Hawaii to visit Ron, who was on his first R and R. It was a much-needed respite for him.

As a photographer, he crawled into enemy tunnels after they were cleared by friendly troops and took pictures of the North Vietnamese underground military camps. He was also an engineer—one of the most dangerous assignments in the army. He piloted troops along the Vietnamese rivers in small motorboats that were easy targets for enemy soldiers. Later he managed the clubs that catered to the officers and the enlisted men.

Initially, Dianne had no intention of joining Ron in Hawaii. Until she received a tongue-lashing from Aunt Laurie. "She wasn't going to see him, and I am the one who made her," says Laurie. "I talked and talked and told her you have to because he is going back to the war and this is something you'll have to live with. You know he might not come back and you have to go see him."

From the onset, their reunion was a disaster. Ron was devastated by the change in his wife. She feigned no affection, no happiness at being together. All love between them appeared to be lost. And she still had not revealed to Ron that she had filed for divorce.

When Dianne returned home, she and Aunt Laurie discussed the trip. Dianne explained that she was particularly repelled by Ron's punctilious attention to expenses. His habit was to write down every expenditure. "Auntie, we weren't together an hour or two and out came that damn little pencil," Dianne told Laurie. "I knew right then and there, we'll never make it."

Within weeks of returning to Vietnam, Ron began to receive a series of eight letters. The first, dated February 13, 1970, began:

> I wouldn't be writing this, but I know that you're on the verge of divorce anyway, so this shouldn't hurt you. I guess we both realize she's pretending to get along with you so that you would continue sending her money.
>
> Did you notice that her letters to you have been nicer since about December 1st?
>
> I think you've suspected all along she's been going to bed with several different guys since you went into service (I can give you names and addresses of 4 guys—3 are married).
>
> But right now she's going mostly with a guy named "Bull." She stopped working in November, so she'd have more time with him. He owns the Heights Restaurant next door to your apartment.

The letter was signed by a woman named Jane Jerrold, who gave her address as 2238 North Kimball Avenue in Chicago.

In her next letter to Ron, she said she knew that Dianne had left for Hawaii on December 12 to see him and she provided detailed descriptions of Dianne's previous assignations. "The first time she met Bull was in May, June, or July of 1969," she wrote. "This was on a Friday Night. This very first night she spent the *entire* night with him in bed." The writer provided his license plate number and a description of his car. The letter continued:

> Since Bull is rich, he probably has influential friends. He owns a bar. . . . Don't blow this Ronald. I involved about 12 persons, and also spent considerable time and money to give you all this information. But the main reason would be *your own welfare*.
>
> Even though you knew or suspected that she ran around, I know that this hurts you at least a little bit. *BUT*,—keep your head, keep it cool . . . I know that you don't want to pay alimony *the rest of your life*!

The third note enclosed diagrams and suggestions of ways that Ron could trick Dianne, so he could find her with another man. "If all this fails, then you can just holler, 'Diane [sic], this is Ronald. I know you're in there. Let me in.' "

When the letters arrived, Ron was shell-shocked. "I didn't believe the letters. I really didn't," he recalls.

He desperately wanted to talk to Dianne and he waited in line for hours to try and get a call through to the States. His efforts were fruitless, however, because even though it was the middle of the night, there was nobody home.

Ron wondered if perhaps Dianne had written the epistles. He consulted a chaplain, a surgeon, and finally the division psychiatrist. "We talked it over and we didn't know if she wanted to get me killed . . . to get me out of the way or to force me to come home." Although Ron was to be discharged within a month, he was concerned about Dianne's well-being. He and the psychiatrist thought it prudent to inform the Turners' family physician about Dianne's recent behavior. A letter was sent in care of George Turner.

"He describes a history of his wife having episodes in which she felt frightened of her neighbors and would act on her feelings by moving to a new apartment without informing her husband," the army psychiatrist wrote. "Specialist Mueller said his wife seemed distant and indifferent during their R & R in Hawaii in December. He said his wife accused him of being unfaithful." Ron would later deny the allegation.

Ron also sent a letter to Jane Jerrold. On February 25, 1970, she responded:

> Either you are a complete fool or *very clever*. I received your letter yesterday. I was shocked: I believe one of three things:
>
> 1. You want to close your mind, and don't want to believe the truth.
>
> 2. You really think Diane sent these letters, and you're showing how smart you can be by using psychology etc. You're trying to show her that you're one step ahead of her.
>
> 3. You believe the letter, hired a detective, and are trying to throw me off. You probably have a duplicate of the letter.
>
> As a matter of fact, I know that *someone* other than me is *checking* Diane. Is it you? I just found out yesterday.
>
> When I received your letter, my first thoughts were to tell you, *O.K. sucker*, you're *the fool, I* tried *to help you. Good Bye*. . . . And you'd never hear from me again. But I invested too much time and money to stop now. This isn't a game I'm playing.

Ron then sent a certified letter to Jane Jerrold's address, trying to see who would sign for it. She informed him that she had not picked it up.

> I phoned the post office, they won't say who the mail is from, and they'll return it if I don't pick it up in 5 days. I know it's probably not from you, but on the slight chance it may be, I'm letting you know, so that whatever you sent me, you can send the regular way.

The last missive was dated March 17, 1970. The writer was trying to determine whether Dianne had renewed her Harwood Heights apartment lease.

All of the letters were typed; only one bears any handwriting. The date had been written in, and it clearly was not Dianne's handwriting. The letters also included three pages of maps detailing Dianne and Bull's apartment complexes. None of the printing appeared to match Dianne's. Throughout the series of letters, Dianne's name is misspelled. For Dianne, it was common practice to underline words for emphasis. But the letters lack her writing style and vocabulary. They are filled with grammatically incorrect sentences, unlikely mistakes from an English major.

But the missives detail so much of Dianne's life at that time that it is evident that the writer was someone very close to her. Perhaps a confidante who was out to hurt her? A girlfriend of one of the men she was seeing? Or someone who was writing the letters on Dianne's behalf without even telling her? At one point, the writer indicates that she knew Dianne during her precollege days.

Concerning the motive behind the letters, the author raised that question in her first communication:

> Are you wondering why I'm doing this? Maybe she stole him from me. Maybe she stole some other guy from me. Maybe I'm her ex-boy friend. Maybe I'm your friend. Maybe she crossed me when we used to double date. Maybe I'm Bull's wife—or ex-wife. Maybe I hate Bull. Maybe he owes me money that he won't pay. Maybe I didn't state the real reason.

When Ron returned from Vietnam, he took a cab from O'Hare Airport to the Harwood Heights apartment where Dianne supposedly was living. When he knocked on the door, an eighty-year-old woman answered.

He called Dianne's parents at their house in Franklin Park and asked what was happening. Anne dispatched George to break the news to her son-in-law that Dianne was filing for divorce. Over a beer at a local tavern, George told him that Dianne never wanted to see him again. And she never did.

Dianne later contended in her divorce case that Ron had forced her to have sex with him during the Hawaii interlude. Ron, who did not appear in court, refuted the charge. At the time, Illinois was one of the few states without no-fault divorce. It wasn't unusual for lawyers and their clients to make outrageous claims of mental or physical cruelty, because such conduct had to be established by law before a judge could grant a divorce.

"Since September of 1968 have there been sexual relations between you and your husband?" her attorney asked at an April 28, 1970, divorce hearing.

"No, not since September, just one time in December," Dianne replied.

"And that was a unilateral act where he forced himself?"

"Yes," she said.

As part of the agreed divorce settlement, Ron asked that Dianne pay him $300 and return all of the couple's credit cards. She complied through her lawyer.

His name was Alan Masters.

Chapter Eleven

January 20, 1969

Cook County's divorce court is located in the heart of Chicago's Loop in an office building that was known as the Civic Center. The courtrooms were on the sixteenth floor, and here, Alan Masters almost always could perform his kind of magic.

His downtown office was within walking distance, just four blocks south on LaSalle Street. Dianne's first appointment with Alan occurred several weeks before he filed the divorce case against Ron on January 20, 1969. It was a typical bone-chilling winter day, but Dianne wore only a lined raincoat and her head was uncovered. Details duly noted by Alan.

"I can remember he took her for lunch that day. The first day he met her," says Aunt Laurie. "And he asked her if she had something to wear on her head. They walked into Saks and he bought her a $25 scarf for her hair and who knows what he paid for the lunch. And then of course, he chased her."

There were phone calls and flowers almost daily. And later, expensive gifts from toney stores on Chicago's Michigan Avenue. Months went by before Dianne, astonished by Alan's perseverance, capitulated and started dating him.

"He bought her," Aunt Laurie explains. "I know she was impressed. There's no question she never knew anybody like that who could spend so freely. He bought her the best of clothes and jewelry and furs. It was like show and tell. You know, look what I got! Well, that's how he used her."

Dianne was anxious for her friends and family to meet her

sophisticated new beau. Not everyone understood the attraction, though.

"I didn't like him from the onset," Sally Meador admits. "He was a user. . . . I can remember asking Dianne what she saw in him."

"Well, he's got his good points," Dianne said. "You just don't know them."

Sally spoke bluntly. "I don't see it, Dianne. I think you're fooling yourself."

When Dianne's family was introduced to Alan, they, too, were surprised by her choice. "None of us liked him," Aunt Laurie admits. "But for her sake, we were as nice to him as if he were the greatest guy in the world."

They were concerned about the age difference between them—Alan was eleven years older—and they tried to discuss the issue with Dianne. "You didn't sway her," Aunt Laurie says. "The mind was made up and it stayed that way. She'd listen, but she'd do it her way."

Dianne did not want her relationship with Alan scrutinized. So she concealed from everyone the fact that he was married and living with his wife and two sons. "All along, she would tell me that he was separated from his wife," says Aunt Laurie.

Sally heard a similar story. "The impression I had gotten was that they had been separated awhile and he was still seeing the kids, of course."

For years, few knew that Dianne was his mistress.

Alan and Dianne came from two disparate worlds. Alan was raised in an ethnic neighborhood, Lawndale, which was the heart of Chicago's Jewish community during the 1920s through the 1940s. Located on the west side just three miles from the Loop, Russian and Polish Jewish immigrants flocked to the tiny enclave. Lawndale was the city's most densely populated neighborhood. Gorgeous three-story apartment buildings and spacious homes had sprung up along the tree-lined streets.

The hub of the neighborhood was Douglas Boulevard, a wide, verdant parkway that linked the neighborhood to the gigantic Douglas Park. During Chicago's steamy nights, denizens congregated there for a stroll through the acres of woodlands or rented boats for a quiet ride on the lagoon.

Alan's parents, Sam and Esther Masters, lived at 1811 South Central Park. The address was convenient to everything. Alan, who was born on March 9, 1935, could walk to Penn Elementary School, and just two blocks north was Douglas Boulevard, where dozens of Orthodox synagogues and other religious and cultural institutions were located. The main shopping district along Roosevelt Road was nearby, too.

Sam Masters typified the area's inhabitants. He was hardworking, industrious, and he sought a better life for his family. At one point, he sold insurance. Later he owned a hardware store and opened a currency exchange in the suburbs. Early on, Sam impressed upon Alan and his brother Leonard, who was two years younger, the value of the dollar. It was a concept that Alan took seriously.

He was a smart youngster. One of those who could successfully juggle his studies with extracurricular activities. His day began at 5:30 in the morning, toiling as a janitor in an apartment building and hauling garbage. At Farragut High School, where his nickname was Rock, he played on the football team and was a movie operator, which earned him letters. With his excellent grades, he joined the honor society. After classes, he worked in his father's hardware store. The perspicacious Alan, whose ambition in those days was to be a doctor, realized that high school had taught him an important lesson in life: how to get along with people.

Upon graduation, his parents moved to West Rogers Park, another Jewish area on the city's far-north side. Rather than go away to college, Alan opted to live at home and attend the University of Illinois at Chicago and, later, De Paul and Roosevelt universities. He received a bachelor's degree in commerce from Roosevelt, a private institution that trained many of Chicago's prominent leaders, including the late mayor Harold Washington. Alan made his parents proud—he was the first in his family to obtain a college degree.

He then enrolled at De Paul University's law school, where, like most of the students, he worked while earning his degree.

Alan opted for day courses. There was contract law with Arthur Anderson and Lawrence Daly's corporations class.

During his first year, the school was situated in downtown Chicago and consisted solely of rented space in a high rise near Michigan Avenue and Lake Street. Public transportation was just a block away, so the rumbling of the els overhead often could be heard in the classrooms.

The only semblance of a hangout was a twenty-four-hour eatery located on the first floor of the building. Over a cup of coffee that was as black as midnight, students crammed for exams or socialized. Alan, who was a member of a Jewish legal fraternity, spent little time with his classmates, though. His life revolved around his fiancée, Benita, and they married during his waning days of law school on March 22, 1958.

That same year, De Paul moved to its current campus on Chicago's near-north side. Alan Masters was among the best and brightest of his graduating class, having finished law school in two years. The dropout and attrition rate had been tremendous. The conviction rate of the class of 1958 was equally impressive. Later in their careers, 5 of the 109 graduates eventually were found guilty in the federal courts on charges ranging from bribing judges to embezzling more than $1 million.

Initially, Alan chose the traditional path for a fledgling attorney. He went to work for a major law firm in Chicago. But within six months, he was disenchanted. He decided to form his own practice with Norman Sands, and a De Paul classmate, Arthur Zimmerman, joined them later.

At the end of his day, Alan was eager to go home. Benita was the perfect wife and a meticulous housekeeper. In 1959, the couple had their first child, Steven David. Four years later, Benita gave birth to another boy, Douglas Neil.

But by the late 1960s, the marriage had begun to disintegrate. Alan gradually was distancing himself from his family. There were meetings to attend, court cases to prepare. He abandoned the couple's friends, preferring to socialize with the judges, politicians, and police officers he was meeting through the practice he had started in Summit.

Alan began having nightmares and sought counseling, Benita would say years later. His behavior changed and he talked less and less to her about his problems. Their marriage basically ended in September 1975, when Alan moved out of their near-north suburban house into what the family thought was a dingy apartment. Unbeknownst to them, he was going to be living with Dianne, and he managed to conceal their clandestine relationship from Benita and his sons until 1982—two years after he had wed Dianne.

But throughout his marriage to Benita, he had been a gentle husband and loving father. He had never raised his voice or demonstrated any violent tendencies, though the family knew he kept a number of guns at his law office and occasionally there was a firearm in the glove compartment of his car.

Alan was a master at secrecy. Benita knew little about her husband's financial dealings and law practice. She knew even less about his personal life.

Alan moored his boat at one of the harbors along Chicago's scenic lakefront and he frequently entertained on it during the summer. On one occasion, Dianne invited her friend Sally Meador and her fiancé aboard.

But the couples did not socialize often. Alan's personality irritated Sally. He was "very condescending," she explains. "He was always talking about the big shots that he knew. And all the cases he won. And how much he paid for this and how much he paid for that. We were not the type of person he liked to be with. We had nothing to offer him."

Sometime in 1970, Dianne moved into an apartment complex in the far-western suburbs. Four Lakes Village was very different and far more expensive than her Harwood Heights flat. Alan paid the rent and gave her the money to purchase the furniture.

There were dozens of the twelve-unit buildings offering myriad amenities designed to appeal to young professionals. In Dianne's one-bedroom unit, the living room featured a working fireplace. Sliding glass doors led to a balcony that provided views of a ski slope during the winter and immaculately tended gardens during the summer. The kitchen was small, but in the dining area that was adjacent to the living room, there was ample room for entertaining guests.

At the community center, a throng gathered at the bar and the outdoor swimming pool. It was the ultimate single's scene in suburbia and men and women alike were filling it as soon as there was a vacancy. Alan was now introducing Dianne to some of his acquaintances. One of the few women she met was Bénédicte Kagy, a native of France who was dating a friend of Alan's. Like Alan, he, too, was married and a lawyer. Because of the similarities in their situation, Alan tried to bring the women together.

"I was surprised," says Bénédicte of her first meeting with Dianne. "For some reason, she wasn't Alan's style like the other girlfriends he had. At this point, Dianne was shy and very overwhelmed by his friends. By the life-styles of his friends."

So the women did not chat long. The next time they encountered each other was when Alan brought Dianne to Bénédicte's apartment. "After we talked a long time, we found we had things in common. She touched me very much and I guess I touched her very much."

Over the years, Bénédicte had watched Alan's modus operandi with women. And it was always successful. Dianne had succumbed to his charms just like those before her. "Money and power were Alan's way of doing everything. Alan bought everybody everything. And his power. He needed that all the time. Even back then, I always remember that. That was the way he was through the years. He always overwhelmed people. And he always chose his women that way. He'd pick ones who needed him. He wanted them to look at him as the god. One day the woman was poor; the next day she had everything. He did that all his life."

Dianne's existence had changed drastically since meeting Alan. There was no need to work. He provided an opulent world that surpassed all her dreams, filled with caviar and fine wines, a world thousands of miles away from the little four-room house in Franklin Park. And she was duly impressed by what Alan had helped her attain.

During the first stages of courtship, Dianne seemed happy. And the family noticed that Alan treated her kindly. At least in the beginning.

The couple frequently entertained at her apartment. There was always a horde, most of them Alan's friends—judges, cops, business associates. Half of the people attending, however, weren't there with their spouses, which shocked Dianne's relatives.

Finding a married couple at these gatherings was such a rarity that Alan teased Aunt Laurie about it. On one occasion when she was a guest, he offered to arrange a date for the matronly housewife.

"Auntie, I've got a guy for you! He's a judge. He'd go for you."

"Get out of here. What would I do with the Irishman I've got?' " she replied, referring to her adoring husband Russell.

Not surprisingly, Alan prioritized his life, and when something more important than seeing Dianne arose, he cancelled his plans with her, which would spark a quarrel and often made her physically ill. One of those battles occurred just hours before she was to be in Sally's wedding party on December 12, 1970.

Dianne, who was prone to colitis at the time, had had several attacks before she arrived at Sally's home, where the women were changing into their bridesmaid dresses. "She was in a flurry; she was running late," recalls Sally. She didn't even have a slip. Mother and I cut up a bed sheet. . . ."

Alan had agreed to escort Dianne, but at the last minute, he had broken their date. Dianne was furious. "Alan isn't coming. There was some sort of stupid appointment he couldn't get out of," she told Sally.

"She figured it was something he should have gotten out of," says Sally. "You could tell they argued about it by the look on her face."

Dianne had to be content with the few stolen moments that Alan gave her. So she and Bénédicte saw each other frequently. They went to the theater, concerts, the opera, all of the cultural events that Dianne had craved as a girl.

"We tried all the new places," Bénédicte says. "She loved to come downtown."

One of the women's favorite pastimes was shopping. "There was always a place we could shop," says Bénédicte. "Dianne liked to buy everything.'' Her style was classic elegance with a little touch of extravagance here and there. In jewelry she liked the unusual.

Bénédicte explains their shopping routine: ''That's pretty,'' one of them would say. ''Don't you think that's a little too much?'' ''No. Buy it!''

''Dianne was really perfect. She became that way. Everything had to be coordinated. At one point, she was very into tailored suits. She was a very elegant lady and she could carry it. She really had extremely good taste.''

But it took some time before Dianne was comfortable with the idea that she now had money. She wasn't the type of person to abuse what she had and she frequently waffled before making a purchase.

Besides the furs, jewels, and trips, Alan had given Dianne something else: a gun. Laurie's son found it in Dianne's bedroom when they were visiting. Alan said he had given it to her for protection.

He also employed other methods to protect Dianne, depending on the situation. When he learned that one of her old flames was harassing her, intimidation sufficed.

''This guy kept bugging her,'' Randy recalls. ''He was constantly calling her, constantly giving her a hard time. So she mentioned it to Alan and Alan said he would take care of it. He told Dianne he was going to break the guy's kneecaps. He sent a policeman to talk to this guy.''

Bénédicte spent weekends with Dianne, because Alan would be at home with his family. ''We'd go to the pool and it was all a singles scene. So he would walk in on us all the time in the middle of Saturdays and Sundays. He would walk in on us to see if we had the entire navy fleet and everybody around us. But he was always, even then, very jealous.'' It wasn't long before Alan came to the realization that perhaps Four Lakes wasn't a suitable place for Dianne.

Within a year, the couple started fighting. ''The problems started because he was married,'' Bénédicte explains. ''He didn't want to give up Dianne at this point. Only a woman can understand. It's okay at the beginning. For the first year, she accepted it; maybe.

"When you're apart, there are all these things in the back of your mind. Where is he? He's with his wife. He's in bed with his wife. . . . And I'm here. It was all these things. They had fights, but they weren't that serious at the time."

Their arguments escalated, however. Alan continuously accused Dianne of having an affair. On several occasions, he literally exploded in a jealous rage that culminated in physical abuse.

Dianne confided in her friend Teri Swanson that Alan had swung a roundhouse at her, missed, and instead smashed a hole in the hallway wall near the front door of the apartment. She escaped from him by leaping off the balcony and sprained her ankle.

Later, at one of the couple's parties, the hole in the wall became a conversation piece. Alan explained to Teri, who was among the guests, "that he was trying to punch Dianne and she moved her head and he went in the wall instead." Throughout the evening, everyone congregated around the hole and commented over its origin. "It was a big joke," Teri says.

Alan eventually solved the problem of where Dianne should live. He bought a house in the far-western suburb of Naperville. Land records show that he purchased the home on February 18, 1972.

He wanted to keep his ownership of the property a secret, so he used what is called a land trust to buy the home. Illinois is one of the few states in the nation that allow individuals to conceal ownership in this manner, and land trusts have become a favorite among politicians. As a result, every attempt to change the state law to eliminate this type of landholding has been defeated.

Land records show that the owner of the property was a bank trust called the American National Bank Trust 76421, but Alan was listed as the beneficiary in bank records. The home cost just $48,500. The CPC Corporation, the makers of Argo Corn Starch, located in Summit, had sold the house on behalf of an employee who was transferred to Ohio.

Like the apartment, the home at 116 Tupelo was the setting for many galas. The gregarious and fun-loving Alan desired that the occasions be a standout, so he usually hired performers.

"Whenever they had a big party, they always had some entertainment," says Randy. "I remember at the Naperville house, he always had a hypnotist. Hypnotists were his favorite."

For one of the parties, Alan engaged the famous psychic Irene Hughes. "It really upset my sister and my mother because she saw something," Randy says. "Irene Hughes told my sister and me to be very nice to my mother because she didn't have long to live. And she said she saw some dark things. Irene Hughes knew. She saw it all. And everything she said and told my sister, happened. She didn't tell Dianne to be aware, but she said you are going to have some hard times. There are going to be some dark things in your future."

Dianne's life-style was taking a tremendous toll on her. "It was pretty much of a known fact that she was never really happy with him," says Kathy. "It seemed like they were always fighting. She'd always complain about something. . . . He's got to visit his kids or he's never here. She'd complain and you'd kind of look at her like she's being bitchy. But you have to realize that we didn't know that he was living with his wife. . . . There were things she wanted from him that he wasn't doing."

After an argument, there was always a conciliatory gesture by Alan—a new fur coat, a piece of expensive jewelry, or a trip to some exciting destination. "There was always something exchanged there," Kathy says.

Just months after moving into the house, Dianne sought psychiatric help. Police records show that Dianne began treatment on October 23, 1972, and continued therapy through 1975. The psychiatrist next saw Dianne for an eight-month period in 1980. However, she did not seek treatment again until January 8, 1982. Her last appointment was on March 11, just a week before her murder.

At the sessions, Dianne, who suffered from lack of self-esteem and depression, discussed the inner demons that haunted her. She felt painfully empty inside and had no enthusiasm for anything. "The only thing worthwhile was life in the fast lane, because it made her feel alive," explains her psychiatrist.

"She knew it was a crazy thing to be involved with Masters.

She was the main doll in a dollhouse. She couldn't get loose from him. She skated on the edge of death all the time. More than once he had a gun pointed at her. . . . She had somewhat of a fascination with violence but rode on the edge of risk all the time. It's the same thing that gets people to skydive and drive Formula race cars. It looks logical, but it's a bet against death. With some people, there's a certain tension that gets played off inside by riding off this danger."

Having affairs provided Dianne with the same kind of excitement. They revitalized her and, for a short time, made her feel alive.

Ironically, her therapist blames Dianne's problems on her bonding with her mother, not the stormy relationship she had with her father. "Her mother was not emotionally available or tuned in to her, not physically demonstrative," he says.

Dianne didn't hide the fact that she was seeing a psychiatrist from her family. "She right away went back to her mom and told her the doctor said the way you brought me up is the problem. Annie was real upset about that," Kathy notes.

Dianne required hugs and kisses from her mother and everyone else close to her. Being held was just as important to her as making love.

She was selective, though, in what she told her family. And sometimes what she told them were lies. For instance, Dianne once announced to her family that she and Alan had gone to Las Vegas and gotten married. So Anne and Laurie held a small wedding party at the Naperville house for the couple. "We all behaved like Dianne had just gotten married," says Laurie. They did not actually wed, though, until years later, in 1980.

But there was no reason for anyone to doubt Dianne. Alan had obtained a driver's license for her in the name of Masters as well as credit cards. Naperville police records indicate that Dianne was using Alan's last name shortly after moving into the house in 1972, when she reported a possible prowler. Then in 1975, she reported that someone was harassing her by ringing the doorbell and running away. Later that year, she called in to report a stray dog.

"She'd do anything for an animal," recalls Kathy. "She

would spend more money on the cats than she did on herself. It always troubled her that she liked mink coats and she was never quite able to resolve the conflict about the origins of the garment.''

Dianne recognized that she had to change her life. She needed fulfillment, so she began looking for a job. ''She really wanted to be an independent woman and do something,'' Bénédicte says.

She became a realtor with a large west suburban real estate firm. While she was working, she met Patricia and Robert Casey.

''They'd hold weekly meetings of all the offices and we seemed to hit it off personality-wise,'' notes Pat. ''Our friendship sort of grew very naturally and gradually. She was very honest . . . and we could talk about any subject. We tended to think the same way. We were both avid readers and had the same sense of humor. We would see the same humor in a situation, really inane things, and start giggling.''

Pat recalls a trip the two took to Acapulco years after they first met. During a shopping excursion, Dianne purchased a bathing suit for Anndra while Pat bought a two-foot, stuffed armadillo to add to her collection. Afterward the women were sitting by the pool when Dianne said she wanted to take a nap and suggested that her friend stay out awhile.

Pat shortly went inside to use the bathroom. ''I let out a yell when I flicked the light on. She had taken the armadillo and put Anndra's new bikini on it with a Mexican hat and had sat it on the john.''

Pat first met Alan at one of the numerous gatherings featuring a hypnotist. ''At the party were all of Alan's friends and associates. He had *strange* friends. My husband and I use to say we were probably the only normal couple they knew.''

When the foursome first went out for dinner, Alan played the big shot. He extracted a huge roll of cash from his pants pocket. ''We set a precedent right from the start that we wouldn't let him treat us,'' says Pat.

If there was one thing that Alan truly enjoyed, it was food. ''Alan's whole life was eating. By the time we took our first bite of food, Alan was finished.''

The couples often vacationed together. Yet Alan would travel to an exotic locale and then not want to do anything.

"We'd all be at the pool laughing at Alan, who would be sitting under the umbrella wiping his brow. Bob and Dianne went parasailing and Alan would sit in the shade and wait. He never did anything physical. Alan was always twenty paces behind us. We always had fun," Pat concluded.

By 1974, the happy times were becoming increasingly rare. There were more and more violent arguments. And Alan didn't care whether someone witnessed his tirades.

Bénédicte was spending the weekend with Dianne when she observed one of their scenes. "I was in the kitchen and I heard Dianne and Alan fighting. There were loud voices. They were yelling at each other. I ran around to the living room and I saw them on the top of the stairs. Alan was hitting Dianne with his fists."

Alan once again had accused Dianne of being unfaithful. Bénédicte ran upstairs to try to stop Alan. "Alan pushed me aside and he was holding Dianne by her hair," she says. Alan then pushed both of the women down the steps. When Bénédicte landed, she looked up at Alan and saw him holding a clump of blonde tresses in his hand.

Another time, Bénédicte saw Dianne's face and body covered with bruises and asked what had happened. "He beat me up," Dianne told her.

Dianne did not conceal Alan's brutality from her friend. During one of their conversations, she told Bénédicte that Alan had grabbed her and pounded her head against a tree.

"He was so totally overweight and you don't picture people like that having much strength and muscle. His arms were incredibly strong. He would love to show off his strength. One time he took a car and moved it just by the strength in his arms. It was amazing for a man of his obesity to be that strong. When he grabbed her, his strength was incredible. She was very slim, very tiny. She had all kinds of bruises. After Alan hurt Dianne, he would apologize and tell her he didn't realize his own strength."

Dianne stayed with Alan despite the beatings. He provided security, a commodity that she feared she would never attain without him. "She was afraid to lose what she had," Bénédicte explains. "She was terrified to go back to Franklin Park and be poor. She knew that there was no way. No way she was going back there."

That same year, Dianne was growing desperate to change the status quo. She stopped taking birth control pills and became pregnant, hoping to force Alan to marry her.

Instead he accused her of cheating on him, says Bénédicte. "He believed it was his, but he accused her of having stopped taking the pills. At the time, he didn't want a child." Dianne opted for an abortion, though she desperately wanted to have the baby. At the time, abortions were illegal in Illinois, so Dianne, accompanied by a friend, went to New York to have the procedure.

Her scheme had backfired. "He totally turned away from her," Bénédicte says. "He was very mad. He left." Yet Dianne expected a peaceful separation. Instead she was threatened, beaten, forced to sign the house over to him, and cut off from credit cards and money, she told a friend.

Dianne turned to her Aunt Laurie for help. "All I know is I spent days with her looking for an apartment because she had to go somewhere and he gave her so much time to get out of there. That's when I found out he wasn't living there and was still at home," she says.

Laurie felt that Alan was being unjust. She called him at his home in Lincolnwood, where he resided with Benita. When Alan answered the phone, she made sure he recognized her voice. Then she posed as Dianne's attorney so that Alan could engage in a charade in front of his wife.

"I'm calling for my client," she told him. "I understand she has so many days to leave and she's not allowed to take anything."

"That's right."

"Well, I don't think that's fair," Laurie said. "I think she should be able to furnish up a home with what is in there."

Alan agreed. Dianne received some money and relocated to a condominium in Woodridge.

He immediately found another girlfriend, who looked remarkably like Dianne, and he brought her to Bénédicte's apartment. "When I opened the door I thought it was Dianne," Bénédicte remembers. "I threw them out."

As the weeks passed, Alan suddenly decided that he did indeed love Dianne. One morning, he appeared on her doorstep clutching a black plastic garbage bag filled with his possessions. He finally had left his family and now he would marry her, he said.

Dianne later told Bénédicte that she had agreed to the rapprochement only if Alan met certain conditions. One was that she would get pregnant. She also had negotiated a new house. Alan promised Dianne that it would be even better than the one in Naperville, which he had sold to a good friend, Lt. James Keating of the Cook County Sheriff's Department.

More important, he swore that *this time*, he was going to get divorced.

It was all part of their deal.

Chapter Twelve

March 25, 1980

Dianne had finally gotten the man she loved. Or so she thought.

In some ways, Alan was attempting to adhere to their reconciliation agreement. She had insisted that he put the new house in Palos Park in her name as an act of good faith, and he had acquiesced. And she was pregnant.

But he had yet to seek a divorce. He worried about how it would affect his sons and did not want to divulge to them that he was involved with another woman. And there were monetary reasons that made it prudent to wait. So Alan continued to lead a double life, while assuring Dianne that he would legitimatize the situation when it was propitious.

Dianne viewed herself as a twentieth-century woman. A marriage license was unimportant to her. What she wanted was a commitment from Alan, and that eluded her. Meanwhile, she spent countless hours alone, evenings, weekends, and holidays, endlessly waiting for Alan to share her life. He had vowed, though, that he would marry Dianne before their child was born.

Alan's sexual problems had made it difficult for her to conceive. The couple slept in separate bedrooms and Alan frequently was impotent. He also had Dianne observe certain rituals as a prelude to lovemaking. According to Bénédicte, "Whenever she wanted to have sex, she had to perform The Dance of the Seven Veils. She had to parade in front of him. Then he wasn't interested anyway."

Dianne complained to her friends about Alan's impotence and said that most nights, when they were attempting to have sex, he fell asleep before she got into bed. She joked about how difficult it had been to become pregnant, calling it the "immaculate conception."

Despite their mutual decision to start a family, Alan was unhappy at the prospect. Dianne discussed the problem with Bénédicte. "But she was so thrilled," recalls Bénédicte. "She did not have the child to trap Alan. They had discussed it. He agreed to it just to keep her around, I guess."

He and Dianne continued to argue vehemently over his failure to file for divorce and inform his children that he was remarrying. Dianne told Bénédicte that Alan had become so angry at her during one of their fights that he punched her in the stomach. She was bitter after that happened.

Dianne also was angry because Alan was seeing other women, yet she resigned herself to it. She confided to Kathy that there were nights when Alan wouldn't come home. He would tell Dianne that he had been out late at some meeting and had grown so tired that he'd just pulled the car over and fallen asleep. Alan underestimated her intelligence.

Nevertheless, Dianne was truly happy when she became pregnant. "She was at peace," Bénédicte notes. "So serene. Glorious. It was something she wanted all her life. She had it."

When Dianne was five months pregnant, her mother died. It was a strange tragedy and it affected Dianne dramatically. This marked the beginning of her rebirth—a transformation that ultimately would lead her to embrace the values that she had forsaken nearly a decade before.

It was Easter weekend and Anne had come to visit. She used Dianne's home as a refuge when George drank too much. He was coming to see his wife and daughter for dinner but was returning to Franklin Park because he had to work the next day. Anne was staying overnight.

Anne had familiarized herself completely with the layout of the Palos Park home as soon as Dianne and Alan had moved in. For nearly a year, she had been carefully counting the steps from room to room, just as she did in her own house.

Dianne had invited Aunt Laurie, Uncle Russell, her grandmother, Rose, and a friend for the holiday meal. She set the table with the cloth that Aunt Laurie had made for her and prepared a large ham. At about 11 P.M., the guests departed, leaving Dianne, Alan, and Anne in the house, along with the menagerie of dogs and cats.

The Masters' ranch-style home was L-shaped. On one end of the L was a large sunroom that looked out over the couple's swimming pool and Dianne's garden. A small hallway connected the sunroom to the kitchen and living room. Walking straight ahead down the hall, you walked passed Alan's bedroom and then you would make a right turn into the kitchen. If you didn't turn, you ran directly into the stairs leading to the basement.

Dianne was in her bedroom at the other end of the house when Anne decided to go to the kitchen to make herself a ham sandwich. Alan was in the sunroom when Anne plummeted head-first down the basement steps.

One theory, according to Randy, was that she had tripped over Baron, Dianne's aging Irish Setter. The other was that she had been pushed down the stairs.

Anne was on a respirator for nine days before she died, but she never regained consciousness. George, who never had liked Alan, was outraged.

Alan always had doted on Anne and she had enjoyed the attention. It was a practice that irritated George and caused antagonism between the two men. Also, Alan had written nasty letters to George, belittling him. George collected them over the years, intending to show them to Dianne eventually, Laurie says.

"Alan interfered so much in their marriage. He was Mr. Big Shot and Annie liked him. I never paid attention to it until we were having a whole bunch of people over and Anne walked in. She had a spring coat on. She walked in with George and I mentioned that her new coat was pretty. She told me Alan got it for her. I could see George's face drop."

Later, Alan and Dianne took Anne's wedding band and added little diamonds to it. No one had bothered to ask George how he might feel about this, and Anne somehow had lost the ring in the Franklin Park house.

Anne's death produced another clash between the men. Alan had assumed control of her funeral arrangements and he refused to listen to the wishes of other family members. He scheduled the wake for the same day that she died at a mortuary on the south side. "Half the people we know couldn't come. Everything was *his* way," says Laurie.

Dianne was grief stricken over her mother's death. Anne had told people that she was not going to live to see her daughter's baby born and the premonition had come true. Dianne was inconsolable and consumed by guilt over her mother's having died in her house.

With Anne's death and the impending birth of her child, Dianne returned to the church that she had abandoned. She began attending mass and confession at St. Michael's. Earlier Alan had tried to convince her to convert to Judaism and she even had taken the required instruction. But at the last minute, she had opted to forego the conversion. Now the church sustained her.

Anndra Lori Masters was born on July 20, 1977, at 8:59 A.M. The birth, attended by Dr. A. William Schafer at Hinsdale Hospital, was routine.

Alan adored his baby girl and willingly shared the parenting responsibilities with Dianne. He couldn't do enough for his daughter. "Alan went totally crazy about that girl," says Bénédicte. "I think that was the end of Dianne. Alan was like a different person. He probably fell in love for the first time in his life."

Anndra's birthday parties were extravaganzas. A tent was erected in the backyard and there were pony rides, clowns, and magicians to entertain the children and lavish, catered buffets for the adults. "You knew he was obsessed with her," Kathy says. "I remember birthday parties where this child would have so many gifts from him, he'd bring them in big boxes." Anndra was so overwhelmed that she once asked, "Mommy, can I stop opening these for awhile?"

Every day was like Christmas for his daughter. Alan's gift

giving never ceased. There were fur coats and designer clothes, and even a diamond ring.

For Dianne, Anndra's birth provided the roots she had been seeking. But although there was a family, there was still a chasm between her and Alan—a void she attempted to fill with numerous activities. She joined the local tennis club and became active in the South Suburban Chapter of the American Association of University Women, and she founded the Crisis Center. She made recordings for the blind and ran for the Moraine Valley Community College board.

Dianne had acquired all the trappings of upper-middle-class respectability, and this changed her stature with her relatives. Cousins now sought her advice on topics from etiquette to locating a reputable jeweler.

She took pride in her home and decorating it became almost a full-time occupation. Dianne's decorator would join her for dinner and they would sit in the living room and decide to change everything. Wallpaper was replaced, furniture was re-upholstered, and later, a pool was installed in the backyard. Oftentimes the workmen were off-duty police officers who were part of Alan's cadre and were doing the job as a favor.

Alan rarely drank, and one of the reasons he abstained was that when he consumed alcohol, he talked too much. That's when the family would hear about payoffs and his more unusual cases.

In a social setting, Alan turned on the charm. He was glib and liked to tell jokes, although his sense of humor sometimes bordered on the bizarre. He enjoyed shocking people.

During a visit to the Turners, he placed a contractor's business card on the table for all to see. It belonged to John Wayne Gacy, one of the nation's most infamous serial killers. While authorities were digging up the bodies of young boys Gacy had murdered, a policeman friend of Alan's had searched Gacy's house, snatched the card, and later given it to the attorney.

Often Alan related anecdotes about his clients. Among his favorites was a domestic quarrel that had escalated to violence. After a shouting match, the husband ran out of the house and took his wife's new car. She followed him, and when he rolled the window down, she pulled out a gun and killed her spouse.

When Alan came to bail her out of jail, she immediately complained that her husband had bled all over her new car.

Because of Alan's unorthodox methods of practicing law, he frequently carried a gun. He found it a necessity, especially after a disgruntled husband on the opposite side in a divorce case had beaten him up after the conclusion of the proceedings.

But Alan's intimates were not typical citizens. Dianne often told her friends about his involvement with organized crime figures.

Always a blowhard, even Alan referred to some of his friends as his "bad boys," Bénédicte says. "And they're *bad* boys," he would emphasize. One day Alan took Bénédicte to a house to show her where a policeman lived. "He told me he was a killer," she says. The cop was among those who frequented Alan and Dianne's parties.

Laurie recalls that at one of the parties, Dianne pointed out a man in the room and said, "Auntie, that guy over there is a hit man."

"How could you have him in your house?" Laurie inquired.

"Auntie, I didn't invite him. That's Alan's friend."

At one of the gatherings at the Palos Park home, Dianne chatted about the guests. "Alan has all these people in his pocket," she told a confidante. "You're sitting next to a sheriff. . . . All he does is pay them off." On another occasion, Alan introduced her childhood friend, Bengt Naslund, to a judge. Dianne told him afterward that the judge was one of the individuals Alan paid off.

But Dianne had known about Alan's corruption from the beginning of her relationship with him, because it had made front-page news in 1971. One of Chicago's long-established watchdog groups is the Better Government Association. The BGA usually teams up with one of the media to uncover governmental corruption. On June 9, 1971, the BGA and the now-defunct *Chicago Today* broke the first story linking Alan to a court referral ring. The investigation started when an eighteen-year-old youth named Leo Mens of Palos Hills had called the BGA complaining about the police and Alan. Mens had been arrested in the south suburbs for drag racing, a serious charge that could result in the loss of his license, as well as for the minor charge of failing to report a change in address to state licensing authorities.

That same day, Mens got a telephone call from a Bridgeview policeman who had witnessed the arrest. The cop suggested that he get a good lawyer and that he had just the attorney who could help: Alan Masters. Alan called the youth later and they made an appointment.

But Mens contacted the BGA and reported the referral, so when the youth met Alan, he was accompanied by a BGA undercover investigator and an undercover reporter from the *Chicago Today*. Alan told the trio that for $500, he would get the drag racing charge thrown out, but he would have to plead guilty to the minor charge. "We've got to give them something," he said. "It's tit for tat. Be happy to settle for a fine," Alan told the group.

Three days before the court case, Mens and the two undercover investigators returned to Alan's law office to pay part of Alan's fee. The two investigators noted that Alan had just fed a tankful of piranhas a lunch of goldfish when they asked how he could assure them that the charges would be dismissed. "Just let me handle it. You didn't ask Blackstone how he did his magic tricks while he was on stage, did you?" Alan parried.

The day the case came up in court, the investigators talked with the man who had been arrested along with Mens. He, too, had received a referral call from police and had Alan representing him. Alan had charged the second driver $700 but had given the man a money-back guarantee. Alan told the driver the reason for the high fee: "Some money will go to the judge and some to the cops to keep everybody happy." Both drivers had the charges dismissed in pleas negotiated with the prosecutors.

When confronted about the referral system Alan had established with the police, he denied everything. "That would be unethical," he told *Chicago Today*.

Today's June 10, 1971, report revealed how Alan also used clerks to make similar referrals. The story noted that when a man who had been arrested for drunk driving and had spent the night in jail went to pay his $100 bond so that he could be released the next day, a clerk suggested that he was going to need a good attorney. "She winked at me and smiled and said that she was not allowed to suggest any attorney's name and then slipped me a card bearing the name of Alan Masters, a lawyer."

When the driver contacted Alan, Alan asked for a $1,000 fee to handle the case. "I balked a little at the price, and Masters said, 'I wish I was going to be able to keep all of the $1,000 myself; however, I'm afraid I'm going to have to spread some of it around, if you know what I mean,' " the driver told *Today*.

Alan had met one of his most trusted associates, Ted Nykaza, a private detective, in much the same way in 1963. Nykaza was just sixteen at the time and he had been out drinking and rammed his car into a parked auto. He then left the scene but later was caught. Nykaza was referred to Alan, and that started a relationship between the men that would last more than two decades. Later Nykaza would figure prominently in Dianne's murder case.

Alan did nothing to deter those who thought of him as a court fixer. Rather, he often bragged about it. "If they got the money, I can get them off," he boasted to Kathy.

Although the news accounts prompted the state attorney's office to conduct a criminal investigation of Alan, he never was charged. But being in the public eye had made him reluctant to handle high-visibility cases.

Sometimes Alan's fees were outrageous. Kathy recalls one case where he represented a murderer. The client's mother was footing the bill and she had balked about giving the attorney her condominium in lieu of payment.

"Well, can you get him off?" Kathy asked him.

"Yes, as soon as she comes through with the condominium," he replied.

From the onset, the corruption bothered Dianne, but at the time, paying off judges and cops was more or less a common occurrence in Chicago. It was part of the city's mystique. Motorists once carried a folded-up $20 bill with their license, which they would hand to the police officer when pulled over for speeding or going through a stop sign.

"I think it was something that she accepted," says Bénédicte. "First of all, you have to remember more than twenty years ago, there was no Greylord [a federal investigation of corruption in Chicago's courts]. Most lawyers did it. It was a fact. It was a common thing to do. Payoffs. Everybody laughed about it more or less, but it was OK. I think she ignored it. We knew he owned the judges. We always knew if you were caught with a revolver in your hand with a warm body in front of you, you would call Alan Masters. Because if you had money, he would get you out of it."

However, the more Dianne learned about Alan's illegal activities, the more outraged and repulsed she became. Nothing disgusted her more than Alan's ownership of a brothel. He had purchased it in 1978 and his partners were the best kind to have in the operation of an illegitimate business—cops, veterans of the Cook County Sheriff's Department, Clarke Buckendahl and Jack Bachman. Land records show that they concealed their ownership in a land trust.

The whorehouse, which operated over the years as the Astrology Club, the Gigilo Club, and the Western Health Spa, was the ultimate sleazy strip joint. Proud of his holdings, Alan frequently led expeditions of friends to the poor black suburb of Dixmoor where the club was located.

Just after Thanksgiving in 1978, he took a caravan of partygoers there following a dinner sales meeting held by Domes America. Alan was the corporate attorney of the firm owned by his friend Robert Casey, and he had been one of the speakers that night. When the group entered the Astrology Club, the room was still. Its only inhabitants were the bartender and a lone customer. An angry Alan went to the telephone, and fifteen minutes later, dancers appeared and began their striptease acts, recalls Pat Casey. One of the three black dancers sported a hairdo that spread out like an open fan, which elicited catcalls from one of Bob's salesmen. The Folies-Bergére it was not.

As the genial host, Alan took Pat on a tour of the premises. In the center stood a circular bar, and booths flanked the walls. She noticed cubicles in the room and asked Alan what they were for. "They look like phone booths," Pat commented.

"That's silly. That's where the girls take the guys," Alan explained.

Alan promoted the club whenever he could. One night he wanted to take Bénédicte and some of her friends, who were visiting from France, to the whorehouse. She was shocked. "Alan, don't you think you're going to be in trouble? How can you do that?" she asked him.

"Don't worry about it," he replied laughingly. "I have the judges. I have everything covered. I've never had any trouble."

Yet the Astrology Club proved to be a losing venture for Alan and his two partners. Its profits were nil.

A chop shop owner later bought the club from Alan, Bachman, and Buckendahl. The price was cheap, a mere $40,000, but it only included the sale of the business. Alan and the cops continued to own the property.

The buyer had known the police officers even before the sale. He testified in federal court that prior to purchasing the club, he had referred customers from his chop shop operation to the brothel.

The new owner renamed the club the Western Health Spa, but shortly after he took over, the mob muscled in, demanding 50 percent of the profits. Instead the auto thief handed them the keys to the club and walked out the door.

By 1979, Dianne was totally disenchanted with Alan. She kept telling him that their relationship had to change, but Alan ignored her. Finally she left him, taking Anndra with her. For days, they secretly stayed with the Turners, and it was during this period that Dianne revealed to her brother and sister-in-law that Alan had abused her physically.

Kathy previously had noticed Dianne wearing a bandage around her arm while they were sitting at her pool. When she asked what had happened, Dianne said the dog had bitten her. Now she told them the truth—that Alan had grabbed her and twisted and bruised her arm. But she didn't want it to show, so she put a bandage over it and concocted a story.

Dianne was so worried about how Alan would react if he found her at the Turners that she called the police, Kathy says. "She reported that she had left him, that he could become violent, that he owned a certain kind of gun." Dianne had made up her mind to leave Alan for good, Kathy says. "Dianne said that if she didn't get out then, she never would."

Several days after their arrival, Anndra injured herself. She was playing on the uncarpeted stairs and slipped and hit her head. It was a hard blow and Dianne and her brother and sister-in-law were scared that she might have suffered a concussion. They drove to a local hospital and Anndra was examined for two hours by a specialist, who reported that the little girl was fine.

When Dianne was completing the paperwork, she mistakenly gave her home telephone number rather than Randy's. Later, when the hospital had to obtain some additional insurance information, they contacted Alan. He went crazy upon learning that Anndra had been hurt. He suspected that a friend of Dianne's knew her whereabouts, so he called her and demanded that she tell Dianne that he must see his child.

Alan arrived at the Turners' and convinced Dianne to return to him, promising a trip together to the exclusive La Costa Spa in Carlsbad, California. It was the typical tactic that he had used throughout their relationship, and once again it worked. Dianne returned home.

Nearly three years after Anndra was born, Alan finally took the necessary step toward legitimatizing his daughter. He filed for divorce from Benita.

And one day after the divorce became final, he and Dianne were married. They wed extemporaneously on March 25, 1980, and of course, a judge performed the ceremony.

The nuptials at City Hall were not what she had envisaged. "Yeah, I went down to get married in my blue jeans," she told Kathy jokingly. "The way I live and the way I dress and I get married in a pair of blue jeans!" she exclaimed. It was a fact that never ceased to amaze her.

Days after the marriage, Alan changed the ownership on the Palos Park house, so that instead of the title being held solely by Dianne, it would be in both of their names as part of a land trust.

Dianne told everyone that they honeymooned on the *Queen Elizabeth II*. This was not the romantic interlude Dianne had been expecting. Nothing seemed to go right, and to make matters worse, Alan had asked another couple along. It was a voyage that friends said marked the beginning of the end of the couple's relationship.

That spring, Dianne and a friend took a trip to Germany. When she returned, she found a woman's panties in her Corvette and a credit card slip bearing the name of a young, good-looking secretary in Alan's office. He concocted a story about giving the woman Dianne's car to use while hers was being repaired. Based on past experience, however, she knew that her husband had been unfaithful.

"He cheated all along," says Bénédicte. "I met him downtown with other women. I never told her, because she knew."

For Anndra's sake, Dianne attempted to keep peace within their home. She was afraid of Alan's violent outbursts and was concerned that he might vent his anger in front of their daughter.

Dianne's psychiatrist describes her relationship with Alan as either ecstasy or rage. When he lost control of his temper, it was an incredible experience to behold. And the psychiatrist had first-hand knowledge: he had witnessed one of Alan's explosions.

Arguments between them were inevitable. Alan continued to accuse Dianne of having an affair, and her therapist noticed that she was bandaged and bruised when she came to one of their sessions. Dianne bluntly stated that Alan had beaten her a week earlier.

His fists were not his only weapons. During another one of their fights, Dianne took Anndra and left the house. Alan followed them out, brandishing a gun. "If you leave, I'll blow your head off," he told Dianne. According to the psychiatrist, she believed he would have used the gun if she actually had gone.

By 1981, Dianne realized that her marriage never would be the true union she desired, and she often cried herself to sleep out of frustration and loneliness. She finally had accepted the fact that despite her continuous pleas, Alan was not going to change. She was tired of his promises. Agreeing to see a marriage counselor with her was a ruse on his part, a way of maintaining the status quo. She felt she had given selflessly to their relationship but had gotten nothing in return. She had had enough.

Now it was time to seriously think about herself. She wanted to be truly independent, to have a rewarding career and the chance to make her own decisions. What she yearned for was freedom. It was at this turning point in her life that Dianne Masters fell in love with Jim Koscielniak.

On December 20, 1981, Dianne, Alan, and Anndra left for their condominium on Long Boat Key near Sarasota, Florida. She had used the small inheritance from her father to buy the apartment.

She viewed the trip as Alan's last chance to keep their marriage together. She had been warning him in letter after letter about his inability to relate to her, his failure to diet, his lack of physical activity, and his disinterest in sex. If he failed to demonstrate in some way that he was going to change, she would leave him.

The vacation proved to be disastrous. He returned home early, claiming that there was pressing business at the office. Dianne assumed that he was lying, because from Christmas through New Year's, the county courts virtually shut down.

Dianne was miserable. She missed Randy and his family and phoned her brother several times seeking consolation. She promised that she would never again go away for the holidays.

Alone with Anndra, Dianne spent many hours contemplating her impending decision. She called Bengt Naslund in Washington, D.C., and told him she finally had made up her mind. She was divorcing Alan.

Dianne flew home on January 4. In the ensuing weeks, she began her torrid affair with Jim. It would be the primary reason for her brutal murder.

Chapter Thirteen

April 28, 1983

Alan Masters fortuneless? Attorney Gretchen Connell could not believe it. His reputation depicted him as a multimillionaire, a man of wealth and property. He had luxury cars, a summer home on the shores of Lake Michigan, a Florida condominium. In short, he had all the trappings of success.

Before her murder, Dianne had given her attorney a list of what she presumed were the couple's marital assets. Gretchen believed that Alan had virtually no cash and his real estate holding didn't seem extensive. She told authorities investigating Dianne's murder that she believed that one of the reasons Alan had contested the divorce so strongly was that it would disclose that he was not the prosperous man his friends thought him to be.

After all, Alan's settlement with his ex-wife Benita had been costly. He had support payments of $2,000 a month. And to discharge his ex-wife's claim to their property, he had agreed to pay her a sum of $300,000 in increments of $1,000 a month. The settlement also called for him to defray the cost of his two sons' college education as well as maintain some hefty life insurance policies.

What Gretchen did not know was that Alan was still a man of means, but he had hidden many of his assets from both Dianne and his ex-wife.

Alan had invested heavily in real estate over the years. He owned the building in Summit, where his office was located. He and his friend Bob Casey had been partners in the purchase of two suburban buildings and also owned a property in the western Illinois resort town of Galena. Alan and a Cook County judge were partners, along with five other investors, in thirty-five acres of land in the southern suburbs and within several months, he and the same judge bought 120 acres in Florida.

On April 28, 1983, Alan Masters became even richer. On that date, an attorney who was a longtime friend of Alan's filed the necessary papers in the probate division of Cook County Circuit Court to settle Dianne's estate. The will that she had executed two years earlier, shortly after her marriage, named Alan as the sole heir. If he had died before Dianne, everything would have gone to Anndra in the form of a trust.

As a result, after Dianne's death, Alan took possession of the thirty-four pieces of jewelry worth as much as $250,000 that she had locked in the safe deposit box. Because the title of the Palos Park home was now in joint tenancy, he assumed sole ownership of the house. He also became the owner of the Florida condominium that she had purchased with proceeds from her father's estate. When the car insurance company paid off the claim on Dianne's Cadillac after it was dredged from the canal, Alan received that $6,525. He took the $4,929 that was in her checking and savings accounts and got a small-denomination Israel bond.

The month after Dianne's body was found in the canal, Alan learned that in 1979, she had named him as the beneficiary of a $100,000 life insurance policy that covered college board trustees while traveling to and from their meetings.

The Hartford had conducted an investigation into the claim and had resisted paying it because they believed that Alan had killed Dianne to collect the insurance money. But the Cook County Sheriff's Police had refused to indicate to the company that Alan was even a suspect in Dianne's murder. As a result, they had no choice but to pay the claim.

The sheriff's police no longer had responsibility for the case. The murder now was being investigated by detectives in Willow Springs, the suburb where the body had been found. It was an agency that had been rocked by turmoil in recent years. The town's mayor, Frank Militello, had ousted police chief Michael J. Corbitt, who had headed the department for ten years, as well as fifteen other full- and part-time police officers. Then he hired James Ross as the new chief to clean up the tiny department and its soiled reputation.

Ross formed a special task force to investigate the Dianne Masters murder. He brought in the Illinois State Police and asked the FBI for assistance. Strangely, Ross, a former sheriff's deputy, refused to involve the Cook County Sheriff's Police in the new probe.

But Lt. Howard Vanick, the sheriff's policeman who headed the investigation into Dianne's disappearance, seemed reluctant to relinquish the case. He told Ray Hanania, a reporter who had covered Dianne's disappearance extensively, that Ross was a backward hillbilly. And Vanick, who had not unearthed one solid clue during the nine months he headed the investigation, told Hanania that he doubted that Ross ever would solve the crime.

Authorities had found little in the way of physical evidence from the car. The main clues from the body had been the discovery of two .22-caliber bullet wounds to the head and the shell casing from the suspected murder weapon, an automatic, that was found in the sleeve of Dianne's coat.

That was enough, though, for police to speculate to the press about the identity of Dianne's killers. Most of Chicago's newspapers and television stations were reporting Dianne's murder as a possible mob hit. They called it a "mob-style" killing and an "execution-style" murder—buzz words for hits carried out by Chicago's infamous organized crime figures. Hanania quoted FBI agent Robert Scigalski as noting that, in the bureau's experience, "gangland murders are done with .22-caliber guns, with shots to the head area."

In fact, the gun had become the weapon of choice for underworld assassinations and it had gained in stature after the head of Chicago's outfit, Sam "Momo" Giancana, was gunned down in his Oak Park home with such a silencer-equipped weapon. Thereafter, every slaying that occurred in the area, where a .22 was used and the victim's last name ended in a vowel, was labeled a mob hit. It wasn't exact police science, but the pronouncements by authorities always made good headlines.

The new theories also shifted suspicion away from Alan Masters, the husband whom the sheriff's police said had waited patiently for his wife to return home that evening. As far as the authorities were concerned, he had no ties to the crime syndicate.

Although Vanick had said that Hanania would find Ross a bumbler, he found the man to be honest and forthright. And in the ensuing days, the police chief and the reporter developed an unusual bond. Hanania became Ross's trusted confidante. Ross allowed the reporter to go through every police document on the case and introduced him to FBI and state police agents who were assisting the department in the murder investigation.

There were deep background sessions between the police, the agents, and Hanania, and he wrote a column based on one of those sessions that angered the sheriff's department. The headline read WHO MURDERED DIANNE MASTERS?

"Was a police officer involved in the mob-style murder of Moraine Valley Community Board Vice Chairman Dianne Masters?" Hanania wrote. "That is one of several theories being explored by the FBI and the Willow Springs Police Department." Hanania reported for the first time several startling details of the investigation that somehow had been kept under wraps by the sheriff's police. He disclosed that Dianne had been dating a Moraine Valley College professor and that Alan had been aware of the relationship. He also reported that Dianne had told friends that she was being followed and that she and her paramour had been spotted by two off-duty suburban police officers whom she had recognized.

The day after the column ran, Hanania and his editors were inundated with phone calls. The reaction was not what the reporter had expected after breaking a major story. The callers, particularly politicians, were complaining. "Vanick was the man who really fought it the hardest," says Hanania. "He called me the next day yelling and screaming." Hanania said that more than one prominent south suburban politician also called his editors to complain about the column, including one county official who had sat on the crisis center board with Dianne.

The response from Hanania's editors was unusual, too. They didn't back their reporter.

The man who was then Cook County sheriff, Richard J. Elrod, also wanted to meet with Hanania to discuss the allegations that members of his department were involved in the murder. Elrod's father, who for years had been a powerful Democratic ward committeeman on the city's west side, had helped his son obtain a job at City Hall following Elrod's 1958 graduation from Northwestern Law School. Over the years, he rose through the ranks to become the city's chief prosecutor.

But it was an incident during a 1960s demonstration against the Vietnam War that catapulted the lawyer into the spotlight and into the hearts of voters. During one particularly violent demonstration, Elrod tackled a protester and the blow partially paralyzed Elrod from the waist down. Police had claimed that the demonstrator had struck Elrod.

The Chicago media declared Elrod a hero of the Days of Rage, the name of the protest in which he was injured. Only later was it disclosed that Elrod's injury had resulted from his hitting a wall while tackling the unarmed demonstrator.

He was an easy victor in almost every election since he first won the sheriff's post in 1970 following the publicity that hailed him as a hero. He was reelected handily to the job in 1974, 1978, and again in November 1982.

Elrod was running one of the most patronage-rich offices in Cook County: five thousand employees were under his jurisdiction and most owed their allegiance to the Democratic ward boss who had recommended them for their jobs. Yet the actual number of sworn police officers who patrol the unincorporated sections of the county and investigate homicides and vice, is a small percentage of the total jobs. There are only about 500 such officers and 120 civilians assigned to that division. Most of the positions are those of bailiffs and court personnel in the Cook County Circuit Court, the nation's largest court system, or guards at the county's mammoth detention facility.

In addition, Elrod controlled what was called his private patronage army, a group of twelve hundred deputies. Often they were political contributors or thugs whom he hired for part-time work on the weekends. The job had its privileges. The men were entitled to carry a gun and a badge.

Hanania was not looking forward to his session with the sheriff. Elrod had a reputation as a whiner, one who always complained about the media coverage. And that is exactly what occurred. What Hanania did not anticipate while he was being dressed down for his column was the presence of Lt. James Keating—Elrod's trusted aide and the commander of the department's vice unit—standing behind the sheriff during the meeting.

During the ensuing months of the murder investigation, police tried to find a link between the cars in the canal and Dianne's murderers.

As the Willow Springs dredging operation continued to raise cars from the canal, it did not take long for authorities to surmise that it had been used by a ring of individuals trying to cheat insurance companies. The canal had become a well-known dumping ground, the perfect hiding place for someone who owned a lemon and was interested in submitting a large claim to an insurance company.

Whoever had dumped Dianne's car into the canal either had been part of the ring or had heard about it in one of Willow Springs' many bars. The only mistake was that no one ever had expected the police to conduct a dredging operation for the vehicles.

Part of the probe focused on the Willow Springs Police Department itself. It did not take a genius to figure out that the cops in the suburb probably had heard about the dumping in the canal long before any cars were discovered and well before Ross ordered divers into the water. Many of the cars being pulled from the canal were linked either directly to police officers who had been dismissed from the department or to their relatives and friends.

One of the more than seventy cars and trucks that eventually was pulled from the underwater graveyard was of particular interest to the authorities. It was a 1979 Chevrolet truck owned by a former part-time Willow Springs policeman named Anthony Barone. He had reported the car stolen in 1981. At the time of the discovery of Dianne's body, Barone was a Chicago

Police Department patrolman. He was also the brother-in-law of the former Willow Springs chief of police, Michael Corbitt.

For four months, the investigators continued to try and crack the case. Facts were rechecked. Every lead was pursued. They talked to Randy and all of Dianne's friends. They interrogated Jim Koscielniak and reinterviewed Alan. While they uncovered some new clues, they found little tangible evidence that could bring about an indictment.

Despite the mammoth effort, Vanick had been correct. Ross and his task force had not solved the mystery of who killed Dianne Masters. It looked as though no one would be charged with her murder.

CHAPTER FOURTEEN

August 20, 1984

THE Willowbrook Ballroom was the jewel of Willow Springs during the 1950s and 1960s. Nestled between the canal and the roadway just off Archer Avenue, the nightclub attracted hundreds of patrons each night who were devotees of the big band era. All of the greats had played there once upon a time—Count Basie, Duke Ellington, Glenn Miller. But like most things in Willow Springs, it was not what it seemed to be. In a secret room above the piano bar was a small casino.

And down the road was Willow Springs' seedier side. Here, waitresses, called B-girls in the lingo of the day, hustled drinks. They would rub a customer's thigh and whisper in his ear as long as he kept buying them $2 soda waters.

At the nearby American Legion Hall, seventy slot machines lined the walls. It was such a popular spot that most nights, it was difficult to get a parking space. Gamblers then rushed inside to stuff nickels and quarters into the rigged one-armed bandits.

Throughout this era, Willow Springs was wide open. The mayor and the police chief adhered to the "anything goes" form of government—so long as they were taken care of. The rackets were all controlled by the syndicate, and the town's southwest location caused frequent infighting. The mobsters who ruled the west suburbs and the gangsters who ran the south suburbs would kill one another deciding which local boss would run Willow Springs' lucrative vice dens.

On several occasions, there were casualties of the war. One

was a collector of juice loans known as Action Jackson, a three hundred–pound gorilla whose job was to scare the Willow Springs gamblers when they welched on paying their debts. He was found stuffed in his car after the mob wrongly suspected him of being an informant for the FBI.

His death wasn't pretty. Before his demise, his killers impaled him on a meat hook in a local slaughterhouse on the city's southwest side. They brutally tortured him, smashed his kneecaps with hammers, and stabbed his body with an ice pick.

The Cook County Sheriff's Police vice squad was planning to clean up the tiny town and rid it of the illegal gambling and prostitution. But the deputies knew that if the Willow Springs cops were corrupt and heard about the strike, they would tip off the tavern owners and whorehouses that they wanted to close. A Willow Springs patrolman could be fired by the village's crooked police chief or mayor for forgetting to warn the vice dens.

So the sheriff's police needed a diversion for the three cops who would be working the night of the first of several raids. The plan was simple. They would round up the three Willow Springs deputies and take them to the nearby sheriff's department so that the cops couldn't tip off the bar owners while they conducted their surprise attack on the clubs. There would be no charges filed against these Willow Springs policemen.

The roundup began with a phony car chase through the village. County patrol cars screamed through the village in hot pursuit, announcing over the radio that they were chasing a suspect wanted by the county.

Michael Corbitt was a rookie cop working that late shift in 1963 and he and two fellow Willow Springs officers joined the hunt. When the fleeing felon's car was stopped and the three Willow Springs patrolmen came to the scene, the trap was sprung and the three cops were ensnared. A Cook County sheriff's deputy named James Keating carted Corbitt and his two colleagues off to the department's nearby headquarters. When the raids were completed, the three policemen were released.

Willow Springs was home then to twenty-one hundred people, twenty taverns, and two cemeteries. The mayor, first John

Rust, Sr., and later his son, known as Doc Junior, always got a piece of the action. A week after the raid, Doc Junior, with a beer sitting in front of him and smoking a stogie, was interviewed at one of the clubs by a reporter for *Chicago American*. The mayor wore a ten-gallon hat, a cowboy shirt, and a string tie.

First Doc Junior downed a straight shot of brandy. Then he looked the reporter straight in the eye and said:

> I could write rebuttals to all them lies, but I don't need to. I been a round a bit. Nothing to hide—nothing to fear. That's my motto.
>
> You know what kid. Don't be offended; I call most folks that. A grizzly bear is reputedly the boss of the Rocky Mountains. But when Jimmy Skunk comes along, everybody jumps.
>
> All my boys are rallying round the flag, saying if you need any help, Doc, just call on us. Why I've got more friends now than before they started all this. And besides I got real estate around here and I figure the story really put us on the map . . . worth at least $10,000 worth of publicity.

Such homespun yarns didn't hurt Doc's reputation in the community. Doc Rust and his father had been mayor since the 1920s, and despite his daddy's having shot a sheriff's deputy, the Rusts never had any difficulty winning reelection. Doc Rust became one of Mike Corbitt's role models.

Corbitt joined the Willow Springs Police Department in 1963. He was twenty-one. It beat running a gas station, as he had done after leaving his parents' home in Summit at age seventeen. Corbitt had attended a Catholic high school that prepares students for the seminary, and he'd hated it. Public school had not turned out to be any better, so he dropped out. He also had worked for a vending machine firm that supplied many of the joints with the gambling paraphernalia they needed to keep their patrons happy. It was Corbitt's introduction to the underworld.

The taverns and whorehouses paid the cops each time they had to be called out to restore order. Those who didn't pay found out quickly that when they sought help again, the police would not respond. Even in the 1960s, the cops were pocketing referral fees on drunk driving cases from Alan Masters.

Corbitt first met Alan at a restaurant. Corbitt and two other police officers from the neighboring town of Summit were sipping coffee when Alan walked in, and one of the men invited the lawyer to join them. The usual pleasantries were observed and then Alan proceeded to educate Corbitt about his referral and kickback system. Corbitt always thought Alan was pushy, but their relationship blossomed after that encounter.

Corbitt became a quick study in the ways of a small town and its local politics. The rookie cop also was shrewd and daring. He never shied away from a shootout. On April 7, 1967, Corbitt was on patrol when he went to investigate an anonymous tip of a theft underway at a local cabinet shop. The three burglars fired a blast from a shotgun at Corbitt as he stepped out of the car. The shot was errant, but Corbitt opened fire and the burglars returned ten rounds from a rifle. Corbitt wounded one of the men, who dropped a sack of $2,000 in cash and the firm's payroll checks. The thieves fled on foot to a nearby waiting car.

A year and a half elapsed before he killed a Peeping Tom. According to the official version of the incident, Evan J. Torrence, the father of three children who had moved to Willow Springs from Arkansas, was standing on a car hood peeping into a house. The homeowner had called the police, and when Corbitt arrived, he drew his .38 revolver and ordered Torrence off the car. Instead Torrence leaped from the hood, tackled Corbitt, and took his gun away. After a twenty-minute struggle in the rain, Corbitt had the man subdued and was putting on the handcuffs when Torrence allegedly went for Corbitt's handgun. Corbitt drew a second weapon, a .45 automatic, and the gun discharged in an ensuing tussle.

Torrence had important relatives in Arkansas who refused to believe that their loved one was a Peeping Tom. They called in the U.S. Justice Department to conduct a civil rights investigation into the shooting incident. There had been some reports that Corbitt had shot the young man because the home where the viewing occurred happened to belong to Corbitt's girlfriend. But, supposedly, on the night of the shooting, Torrence was peeping four or five houses away from where Corbitt's paramour lived.

Torrence allegedly had a weird habit of peeping only on rainy nights, and Corbitt had mapped out the area where the peeper had been spotted over the last few months in an effort to predict where he might strike again. That evidence, however, did not seem to deter the Justice Department lawyers. Corbitt was within a hairbreadth from being indicted for the shooting when a federal judge intervened and halted the probe.

A few months later, Corbitt joined the Summit Police Department, where his friend Tony Corbo was the chief. He remained there until 1969, when Rust enticed him back to Willow Springs with a tempting offer: he would name Corbitt the police chief. Rust never got to execute the plan. He died prior to the April 1969 election and the new mayor made Corbitt a sergeant.

In 1971, Corbitt killed again. This time he shot a truck driver who was terrorizing forty patrons of a tavern by firing shots into the floor and bar. The thirty-one-year-old man, Jimmy L. Janes, and a friend had been ejected from the bar about a year earlier for fighting, and when Corbitt rushed into the tavern at 3:30 A.M. on September 10, Janes darted past him, heading toward the door. Corbitt yelled and ordered him to stop. The truck driver whirled and allegedly pointed a pistol at Corbitt, who shot Janes once in the chest, according to one report. A coroner's jury ruled the shooting justifiable homicide.

The shootings did not hinder Corbitt's career. In fact, they enhanced his notoriety throughout the area, where he was known as the macho cop willing to risk his life on the job, the man ready to use the pistol he packed in an ankle holster.

In 1973, a Corbitt supporter named Walter Bucki won the mayoral race in Willow Springs, and he named Corbitt the town's police chief.

Corbitt's unorthodoxy differentiated him from his peers. He consorted with mobsters and hobnobbed with Chicago's political bigwigs. He owned a fleet of fast cars and had substantial lines of free credit at various Las Vegas casinos, all of which were compliments of his syndicate connections.

At six feet two and as much as three hundred pounds, he was an imposing figure, preferring gold chains and open shirts or cowboy attire to a uniform. Corbitt oozed testosterone. He was on his second marriage and was trying hard to destroy it by maintaining a long-standing relationship with a waitress.

He also was rich, and getting richer. He worked three jobs, not because he needed the cash, but because he needed the legitimate income to mask the kickbacks he was receiving. He also was investing in real estate.

Corbitt, though, was not greedy. He had seen how the trickle-down system of corruption worked during his stint in Summit, and it kept the troops happy. After court, the police chief called in all of the officers who had cases up and handed out an envelope containing their portion of the day's payoffs from the lawyers. Corbitt, too, would share and share alike.

He reaped unexpected dividends from his friendship with a gangster named Joe Testa. Testa owned a trailer park, Sterling Estates, on the outskirts of Willow Springs. Corbitt first met him in a torrential rainstorm when he stopped Testa's limousine for speeding. According to the tale, Testa and his chauffeur refused to exit the car. For twenty minutes, Corbitt negotiated through a window that had been lowered a few inches so that Testa could respond to his questions.

While the occupants remained dry, the cop was getting soaked and extremely angry. He ordered a tow truck and towed the car to the police station while Testa and his chauffeur sat inside. The relationship may have begun inauspiciously, but the mobster became Corbitt's best friend.

Sterling Estates was part of Testa's diverse financial empire. He owned a savings and loan, stock in a bank, property in Florida, and land throughout Illinois. After various business dealings, including several with the syndicate, his net worth was estimated at more than $13 million. The audacious Testa, who once went to Australia claiming to be a police officer who wanted to invest in gambling in the land down under, had started his career as owner of a gas station.

But Testa also had crossed the mob. Suddenly bombs started erupting at a restaurant that he owned as well as at his suburban home and the trailer park office. A phony explosive device was found strapped to his car. After the bombings, Testa moved to Florida.

On June 27, 1981, he and a friend, James Aquilla, climbed into Testa's Cadillac after a round of golf at a country club in Ft. Lauderdale. The ensuing blast tore off Testa's legs. Corbitt flew to Florida to be at his bedside, where two days later, Testa died. Aquilla survived.

The bomb had been in retaliation for Testa's failure to turn over $2.5 million that he had invested for a mobster named Milwaukee Phil Alderisio. Alderisio had been sent to federal prison for defrauding a suburban bank of $80,000. Before he left, he asked Testa to keep his $2.5 million nest egg and invest it for him, but Alderisio, one of the mob's most notorious killers, never came out of prison. He died of cancer. Testa was advised to return the cash to Alderisio's organization, and he bluntly refused.

There was a crucial meeting at a local mob-dominated country club, where mafioso Marshall Caifano, met Testa in the bar. Caifano demanded the return of Alderisio's investment. Testa told him the money now belonged to him and Caifano could forget it.

Two Chicago underworld figures reputedly were linked to Testa's murder, but no one ever was charged. Testa had been playing golf in a foursome that included Alan Dorfman, an investment counselor who handled the financial dealings of the Teamsters Pension Fund. A few years later, Dorfman himself was assassinated.

Testa's death was bittersweet for Corbitt. He had lost his closest friend. But Testa had named Corbitt and John Hinchy, Chicago's deputy chief of detectives, in his will. Each eventually received five percent of Testa's mammoth estate, which meant a $431,711 windfall for the police chief.

During the years the estate was being probated, Corbitt battled with the executrix over picayune matters. He maintained that the estate was being cheated, because the executrix had sold the Baume and Mercier watch that Testa was wearing, which had thirty-two single-cut diamonds, for a mere $500. The executrix countered that she had sold it to a jewelry store,

Martin and Martin of Oak Lawn, that had been recommended by Corbitt. The jeweler was Chicago's notorious Gino "Blackie" Martin, whom state authorities listed as a member of organized crime. A frequent campaign contributor to the sheriff's campaigns, he was involved with one of Willow Springs' more notorious B-girl joints.

At one point, Corbitt was accused of taking Testa's powerful twenty-nine-foot, oceangoing speedboat back to Chicago. Eventually he was given the two-engined Sea Ray as part of his share of the estate.

Corbitt's inheritance was front-page news. It wasn't often that high-ranking police officers were heirs to a mobster's fortune. Corbitt, though, was accustomed to notoriety. A darling of the media, he always was accessible to the press and willing to be quoted.

His antics as police chief were legendary. One of the more notorious stories dealt with his friendship with Tony Iori, a policeman in a nearby suburb, and their rainy night fun at the expense of a hitchhiker. Corbitt was in his unmarked squad car and was talking to Iori when they spotted a guy trying to thumb a ride at an intersection. Both men wore plain clothes. Corbitt instructed Iori to get into his own car, pick up the hitchhiker, and then lead the police chief on a car chase through town that was to culminate at a local bridge, where their colleagues, who would be in on the joke, would block it off.

Iori picked the kid up and within seconds Corbitt was in pursuit with the lights and siren flashing.

"Hey, the police," the hitchhiker said to Iori. "They want you to pull over."

"Fuck them, I ain't pulling over," yelled Iori, and he reached under the seat and pulled out a carbine with a thirty-round banana clip in it.

"Man, let me out of here." The hitchhiker's eyes were as wide as silver dollars.

"You're going with me," Iori replied. "I ain't going down without a fight."

As Iori's car turned onto the roadway with the bridge, the whole street was blocked off by squad cars. Iori slammed on the brakes. "You don't move," he warned the hitchhiker.

"You stay in the car. I am going to shoot it out with these guys."

By this time, the hitchhiker was trying to climb into Iori's glove compartment. The other squads pulled up and Corbitt fired some shots into the ground, pretending to capture Iori. The hitchhiker was pulled out of the car and brought to the trunk. The guy was begging for mercy. Iori's cohorts dragged him past the hitchhiker, got him into the ditch, and Corbitt fired two shots next to him so that he would appear to have been killed.

Afterward the cops returned to the kid. "Now, you didn't see nothing, did you?" Then they told the guy to go home and never say anything to anyone about the incident.

He took off running across an open field with the policemen laughing as he ran through the weeds. In the meantime, a huge semi turned down the street and saw the police blockade. The driver slammed on his brakes, lost control of his vehicle, and slid his trailer into a parked car.

Sometimes there were genuine duties to perform. One former Willow Springs police officer recalls how a local resident had taken his wife and child hostage during a domestic argument. The police were summoned to the scene, and Corbitt was at home eating dinner when he heard one of his sergeants call for a SWAT team.

When Corbitt arrived, he found his police officers huddling behind their squad cars ready to shoot down the man, who simply had fired a few shots from a .22 rifle out the window into the ground. Corbitt and another officer walked up to the house, entered the garage, and crawled on their stomachs to a door leading into the home. Corbitt opened the door, aimed his service revolver at the suspect, and suggested that it was time to give up, which the man did without a struggle. It hadn't hurt that Corbitt and the suspect had encountered each other before and Corbitt had thrashed him while in custody. The resident knew Corbitt was serious when the police chief said he would kill him if he didn't surrender.

Corbitt's escapades were so offbeat and enthralling that a noted television producer was anxious to base a TV series on the south suburban police chief and his folksy system of justice.

Corbitt was cast as the hero, of course, but the program also would hint that perhaps he was slightly loco. And slightly corrupt. Corbitt, who did not need that type of attention, quashed the show.

But other money-making opportunities presented themselves. When Illinois changed its liquor laws in the late 1970s to allow nineteen year olds to drink, Corbitt and Alan Masters capitalized on it. On a Friday night, as many as twelve thousand youngsters would go drinking at the suburb's taverns.

"You must believe Willow Springs is unique," Corbitt told reporters. "We are loaded with drinking establishments. It's always been a big tavern town. But today, it seems as if 19-year-olds can't hold their liquor. They get loaded and can't control themselves and everybody has problems." Corbitt said that the department was receiving an average of thirteen calls a weekend from taverns to break up fights and the police were ticketing about twelve teenagers a week for drunk driving.

The new liquor law produced a windfall for Corbitt, who bragged that some weeks, he and his men were collecting as much as $6,000 to $8,000 in payoffs. This included the referral fees from Alan and other lawyers for drunk driving cases as well as graft from other scams being run by the department. At Christmastime, they were raking in as much as $25,000 a week. And the town profited, too. Despite its small population and size, traffic tickets issued in 1976 generated $190,000 in income, more than that of any suburb in Cook County.

Yet Willow Springs' infamous reputation made Corbitt a frequent target of state prosecutors. In 1977, he appeared before a grand jury investigating whether he was selling badges. One had gone to an assistant Cook County state attorney who had been the subject of death threats from mobsters for his prosecution of a high-ranking organized crime figure suspected in the fatal shooting of a teamster official.

The grand jury also was interested in Corbitt's private security firm, Swift Security, and how he had landed a job with the Hyatt Regency in Chicago as its assistant director of security. "I've done nothing illegal with Swift Security. This investigation is 100 percent political," said Corbitt.

Corbitt's boss at the Hyatt was then a high-ranking Cook

County Sheriff's Police official, who also worked occasionally as a part-time Willow Springs patrolman, or so the payroll records supposedly showed. The grand jury was trying to determine whether the deputy was a "ghost payroller" and whether the phony job was part of a kickback from Corbitt for the contract at the Hyatt.

But prosecutors did not uncover enough evidence to indict Corbitt. He also survived a subsequent 1978 grand jury investigation into charges of police brutality that focused on Corbitt's brother-in-law, a part-time Willow Springs patrolman, Anthony Barone.

The police chief's reign was about to come to an end, however. He began quarreling with the town's newly elected mayor, Frank Militello, whose primary platform in the April 1981 race had been a pledge to oust Corbitt if elected. He argued that Corbitt didn't even look like a police chief, with his cowboy boots and shirt and blue jeans. Corbitt thought he could defy the odds, just as he had the grand jury investigations. It was his first major political blunder.

"This guy leads a charmed life if he thinks he's got a lifetime assignment," Militello said in May 1981 after firing Corbitt. "The mayor is the people here, and they voted for a mayor who promised to get rid of Corbitt as soon as legally possible. People here are afraid of Corbitt. He has buffaloed and harassed and scared all his life. It's not going to work this time."

Corbitt fought to retain his job. He hired the best attorneys and held a fund-raiser at a south suburban banquet hall. Alan Masters didn't attend, but he bought tickets to the event. Militello, however, was the least of Corbitt's worries. A federal grand jury had been convened, and once again, he was its focus. In June 1981, it subpoenaed Corbitt's financial records dating back to 1975 to try and determine whether he had accepted bribes that he didn't report on his federal income tax returns. Like the other investigations, there was no indictment.

On August 20, 1984, Michael Corbitt became the target of still another grand jury. This one was headed by a relatively new assistant United States attorney, Thomas Scorza, who was looking at Corbitt as a central figure in the dumping of cars into the canal in Willow Springs.

"It is so obvious. How do you dump 70 cars in the canal without knowledge of the police department?" said the town's mayor regarding the investigation. "If they are dumb enough to dump them in their own town, then they deserve to be caught."

There also had begun to be persistent rumors that somehow Corbitt was involved in the dumping of Dianne Masters' Cadillac into the waterway.

Federal agents had been tracking down all of the owners of the cars pulled from the canal and questioning them about how their vehicles got there. One of the people they interviewed was a former Willow Springs tavern owner named Raymond Gluszek, who admitted that he indeed had dumped his 1978 Ford pickup in the canal in order to defraud his insurance company.

He told the agents that the person who had suggested it was a good friend, Michael Corbitt. And, Gluszek claimed, Corbitt had told him the exact place to dump the vehicle in the canal and had followed him there. Corbitt told Gluszek not to worry about the car being found, because nothing had happened several years earlier when a dozen or so cars were recovered from the underwater junkyard.

Gluszek's relationship with Corbitt, however, had started many years earlier, when Gluszek's bar was creating legal and financial problems for him. Gluszek had turned to Corbitt and Alan Masters for help. Masters handled some of his legal battles with local officials over zoning and noise while Corbitt provided a partner for the cash-strapped tavern.

Corbitt's pals virtually took over the entire operation of the business and Gluszek's profits dwindled. In 1975, he went to Corbitt seeking the police chief's permission to burn the place down. Corbitt approved the arson with the proviso that he be given a week's notice. Five years later, Gluszek notified Corbitt and torched the bar with the help of a friend. The subsequent arson investigation, Gluszek told the FBI, was a joke.

Scorza heard several accusations that tied Corbitt to Alan. From the beginning, the prosecutor suspected that Corbitt was probably one of the people whose help Alan would have sought in dumping Dianne's car into the canal. And each time Scorza turned up a tidbit about Corbitt, Alan's name seemed to be connected. The Kuhnkes provided the next link.

Fred and Lorna Kuhnke were two of Corbitt's constituents who came forward. Fred ran a local towing service and junkyard called Community Auto. Corbitt had tried to shake down the Kuhnkes for bribes in 1980. Fred Kuhnke had run into Corbitt and asked why his towing service wasn't getting any of the town's business, and Corbitt told him bluntly that Mr. Kuhnke wasn't paying his dues. An angry Kuhnke told him he would burn his tow trucks in the middle of the town's main drag before he would ever hand over an envelope to the police chief.

Like most salvage yards, Kuhnke's sometimes dealt in stolen automobile parts. And it eventually landed Kuhnke in trouble. In 1981, he had sold a Buick damaged in a car accident that his shop had repaired using stolen auto parts.

On March 25, 1981, the car was brought back into the shop by two crooked Cook County sheriff's deputies. They accused him of using a stolen transmission, which he hadn't, in rebuilding the car and of filing off the vehicle's identification number. They arrested him on auto theft charges. Outside Kuhnke's garage, Corbitt stood and watched as the two sheriff's deputies made the arrest. Corbitt told him not to worry, he would obtain a good lawyer for him.

A few days after making his bond, Kuhnke sat in the law offices of Alan Masters. The fee would be $6,000, but as Kuhnke would learn later, that was just the start. Alan called one of the crooked cops and asked if the cops had "left me some openings" so that he could get the case thrown out of court.

A week or so later, Alan stopped by Kuhnke's garage and told him there was a problem. It was going to cost Kuhnke another $12,000. "He said the policemen and the judges and everybody had to be taken care of. I told him I'd have to borrow the money to start with and I asked him why it was so much. He said: 'Because your old lady has a big mouth.' "

Lorna Kuhnke, the head of the local chamber of commerce, was one of the citizens of Willow Springs who had been an outspoken critic of Chief Corbitt. She frequently attended the town meetings and sharply assailed him in the public forum. Corbitt wanted her punished for a particular remark she had made after a meeting of the town fathers in 1980. "I told Mike that anybody who could afford two Corvettes, a Lincoln, and a Chevy Caprice on a police salary should be teaching economics and not doing police work," she related to investigators.

On April 23, 1981, the Kuhnkes went to court. Lorna handed the lawyer an envelope with $12,000 in cash. Minutes later, the auto theft charges were dismissed against Fred Kuhnke. Conveniently, the sheriff's police had forgotten to bring a search warrant when they made the arrest. Scorza suspected that Corbitt had arranged the entire arrest as a shakedown of the Kuhnkes and to force his critic to keep quiet.

A few months later, the sheriff's police raided the auto shop again. This time the Kuhnkes found a different lawyer, who charged only $2,500. They subsequently sold the business and moved out of state.

Corbitt, though, made the biggest mistake of his life on May 27, 1982. He met with a man he thought was a small-time hoodlum named Larry Wright to discuss opening a bet messenger parlor in Willow Springs like the kind he was running in another suburb. Wright needed to obtain the chief's approval for his venture.

Wright and mobster Joseph Marren pulled up in front of the Willow Springs Police Station and a few minutes later, Corbitt, supposedly wearing his chief's uniform for the first time in years, drove up in a Willow Springs patrol car. Although he reportedly was driving a marked squad car that day, most of the time the police chief tooled around the village in his own vehicles, which he had equipped with lights and sirens.

Marren and Wright entered the squad car. With Marren sitting in the front seat and Wright in the back, Wright began negotiating with Corbitt. "I told him that I was interested in finding out basically what it would cost and to be sure that my protection was there, and I would be taking a risk and things like that," Wright says. "We told him . . . how we were set up. I told him that I set up a not-for-profit corporation, you know, as I had been directed to; and that it was a good front to conceal the activity of the company.

"We didn't discuss specific amounts of money. I told him that I wanted to operate in his town, and that I wanted his OK and his approval. And one of the things I needed to know before we completely got going was how much it was going to cost. He essentially told me that he could work with me, and that once we got going, he'd give me an idea of what it would be."

Wright thought it would cost him only about $600 a month to take care of Corbitt. "He said he didn't think there was any problem working with us. We had to make sure we had some other things taken care of before we could come into his town. But if we did that, it would be no problem." Corbitt, however, wanted to be certain that Wright had already gotten the consent of the Cook County Sheriff's Police. Wright assured him that he had.

Corbitt would swear later that the May 27, 1982, meeting never occurred. It would be an important date to him, one that he never would forget. Because Larry Wright wasn't who Corbitt thought he was.

Chapter Fifteen

August 27, 1984

LARRY Wright was the consummate spy. His looks and demeanor always deceived. At six feet, there was little bulk to his lanky 190-pound frame and his face had an innocence that made him appear much younger than his thirty-four years. His hair was styled and his mustache neatly trimmed. He had a hint of a southern drawl and his speech was peppered with four-letter words. He could gab about any topic.

To those who knew Wright, he was a small-time hood. He had amassed a fortune as a drug dealer in Florida. He had come to Chicago in 1980 to help his partner, Tom Gervais, run their thriving business, National Credit Service. He had met Gervais in California when Gervais was in the Marine Corps. They had kept in touch and gotten to know each other well in Florida.

National Credit was the umbrella for a myriad different companies. There were limousine services, travel agencies, gift shops. But none actually existed, except on paper. The four-year-old National Credit Service, which had been an immediate success, used these firms to launder credit card charges run up at the whorehouses and nude dancing parlors flourishing in the suburbs surrounding Chicago.

A wife tends to wonder when her husband's credit card bill has a $200 charge from a place called the Show Club. But if the charge is attributed to the Acme Travel Agency, few questions are asked. It took more than two years before a state auditor discovered that a University of Illinois administrator had been so enthralled with the services at the Club Taray, a bordello, that he had spent $250,000 of university funds there.

Chicago banks also had barred the vice dens from using the credit cards they controlled. So National Credit Service, which eventually would have more than twenty clients, was a boon to these spots. Each night, it processed thousands of dollars in receipts.

At one time, the clubs had been centered in the mob-controlled suburbs of Cicero, Lyons, and Chicago Heights. But in the 1970s, they expanded into the northwest suburbs around O'Hare International Airport, primarily in the unincorporated areas patrolled by the Cook County Sheriff's Department. At times, the prostitution was so blatant and rampant that women living near the strip joints complained that drivers were soliciting them for sex, thinking that they were working girls from the clubs.

The main thoroughfare of a once peaceful neighborhood had been transformed almost overnight into a glittery row of flashing marquees advertising ALL NUDE DANCERS and twenty four-hour massage parlors. The county's liberal liquor laws allowed them to stay open until 4 A.M., and parking lots were jammed with cars seven days a week. At one point, denizens became so outraged that they staged a massive demonstration, with more than ten thousand parents and children parading down the streets to protest the continued presence of the clubs. But the vice unit of the Cook County Sheriff's Department did nothing.

Wright and his partner, always looking for new opportunities, decided to launch a new venture in unincorporated northwest suburban Palatine. They opened a bookie joint. A mob attorney had found a loophole in the state's gambling laws. While it was illegal to book bets, it was not illegal to collect the bets and travel to the five Chicago area horse racing tracks that ran year-round and place those wagers there.

A plethora of so-called messenger services emerged almost overnight and charged their customers a fee of 10 to 15 percent. However, most of them never actually brought the bets to the racetracks. They simply violated the law and booked the bets themselves.

Wright called his messenger service the Palatine Sporting Fans Club, and it proved to be lucrative. During the thirteen months that he ran the bookie joint, it booked more than $100,000 in bets.

Both endeavors had made Larry Wright lots of new friends. There were the cops, whom he paid off monthly to ensure that his businesses operated smoothly. And he met regularly with the men that Chicago's organized crime bosses had sanctioned to run the vice dens. In the vernacular of the underworld, it was called paying the cops and the robbers. "You have to convince these guys you're a player just like they are," Wright would say later. "There is nothing too crazy you wouldn't do."

On August 27, 1984, the *Washington Post* broke a story about Wright's business partner, Tom Gervais. Gervais told the *Post* that he had gone to the FBI for help in 1981 when he realized that he was in over his head with the syndicate. Two mobsters had approached him, saying he owed $35,000 in back street taxes for his operation. Gervais told the *Post*, "I panicked. I cried: 'I'm broke and there is no way I could do that.' "

The disclosures by Gervais in the *Post* also revealed that Larry Wright wasn't who his friends thought he was. Larry Wright's real name was Larry Damron and he was a veteran FBI agent assigned to work undercover with Gervais. Damron had first met Gervais in October 1981.

For four years, Damron had played the Larry Wright role to the hilt. His daughter was a bubbly eleven-year old when he started the investigation. His undercover existence had meant that he had to talk to his family mostly by telephone, and when he saw them, the meetings were scheduled around his work. While relieved that his life would return to normal, the story had ended the investigation abruptly. Damron, whose FBI career had begun in 1972, was disappointed because the undercover sting was on the verge of something bigger that might have resulted in additional indictments had his identity not been unmasked.

Ironically, some of the people involved in the case with whom he had become friends had called him and asked if it was true he was an FBI agent. In at least one case, he advised them to talk to an attorney and think about cooperating.

Damron's sting had uncovered massive corruption inside the Cook County Sheriff's Department. The bribes and other illegal activities were documented in hundreds of secretly recorded conversations that he'd had with police officers, bar owners, and others, as well as in the hundreds of reports that he had filed. Damron also had kept a journal of his meetings and phone conversations. In those reports and taped conversations were the first clues to the murder of Dianne Masters. The importance of the clues would not be clear until Larry Damron came into the offices of the U.S. attorney to undergo debriefing.

David Stetler, now an attorney in private practice in Chicago, was one of the assistant U.S. attorneys assigned to handle the investigation that Damron had been working on for four years. The FBI had dubbed it Operation Safebet. In reviewing Damron's reports, Stetler and other investigators found that the undercover FBI agent had been paying off Lt. James Keating of the Cook County Sheriff's Department.

Jim Keating was sitting in the Holiday Inn bar at the Ford City shopping center on Chicago's southwest side. At forty-five, he was still a stalwart. His huge body made him look like he could enforce his tough talk. He was balding and his nose was slightly red, the result of numerous rounds of drinks.

The dimly lit bar was Keating's favorite place for meeting Joe Marren, the manager of a club featuring nude dancers and prostitutes in west suburban Lyons. Marren didn't mind serving as Keating's bagman and collecting the payoffs from his fellow club operators and owners, who viewed the thousands of dollars per month that Keating received from them as a good investment. And the glib cop was the kind of guy whom Marren could have fun with. They would sit in the bar and tell jokes.

Keating was never shy or secretive about his purpose. When Marren walked up to the table, he roared in the virtually empty bar, "Well, Joe, did you bring the G-R-A-F-T?" spelling out the word.

By some accounts, Keating was supplementing his sheriff's deputy salary by as much as $4,000 to $8,000 a month, which included the $600 he was receiving from Damron. The Damron cash was called a "six-pack." The monthly payment protected the Palatine Sporting Fans Club from being "hit" by sheriff's police.

Originally Damron had agreed to make payments to one of Keating's underlings. The undercover agent had promised protection money to Sgt. Bruce Frasch, head of the county's vice unit, who had staged a raid on the club. Although he made sure that Damron got advance warning, another operative was arrested on illegal gambling charges during the raid.

Damron told Marren that they were unhappy with Frasch. He was becoming unreliable. Damron couldn't reach him when he needed to. More important, Damron wanted to make sure his employee wouldn't be convicted because of the raid. It was then that Damron turned to his friend and business associate, Joe Marren, for help. Did Marren know anyone who could take care of his acquaintance's criminal case?

Marren, indeed, had a contact in the upper echelons of the sheriff's department. Ten days later, he got back to Damron. "He told us it would cost $1,000 to insure that the court case was thrown out and dismissed, and that the protection money on the operation of the [betting parlor] would be $600 a month." The FBI gladly paid.

For the next six months, the collection of payoffs continued like clockwork. Damron would meet Marren once a month at one of the whorehouses and pay Marren the graft, who then gave it to Keating. But in the summer of 1982, Marren was about to go to jail on federal securities theft charges, and all agreed that a new plan had to be devised.

Marren and Keating arranged for Damron to deliver the bribes through the bartenders at the Holiday Inn lounge. If there were problems, the two bartenders would relay a message to Keating, who would call Damron.

The system was working well, but Damron wanted to meet Keating and deliver the bribes directly to him. He told the bartenders that he needed to talk to Keating. When the cop called, Damron explained that he wanted to meet him to discuss a business proposition. Keating agreed and they decided to meet at the Holiday Inn.

Damron asked Keating how he would know him. "He said he would be easy to spot because he was as big as a squadron," Damron says.

At the meeting in the fall of 1982, Damron told Keating he wanted to open a tavern featuring nude dancing and prostitution in the south suburbs and he wanted Keating's advice on the operation. He would have to know the local authorities to pay off. Keating suggested a lawyer in the south suburbs who could help.

Damron also had brought the $600 monthly payoff to the meeting. "I told him I had the money for the month and I asked him if he wanted it then or wanted it later," says Damron. "I gave him the money. He took it in his hand—he had a windbreaker on—and he put it in his pocket."

Keating encouraged Damron's idea about opening a house of prostitution. He said they would talk more about the plan when Damron delivered the bribes the next month. He also gave Damron some friendly advice. He told Damron to stay away from a crime figure in Lake County who had testified in a federal case involving the corrupt sheriff there. "Once a guy has squealed, the second time is always easier," Keating warned.

At the next month's payoff, Damron met Keating at the bar of one of the nicer south suburban restaurants. It was 10 P.M. on a Monday night. There was a band playing.

Keating addressed Damron as "sir", asking him how his ride to the restaurant had been and how business was going in the bookie joint. When Damron told him that a bettor had scored on a longshot and hit the club for $6,000, Keating was amazed. "How the fuck can you be smiling?" he asked the undercover agent.

Damron sipped a Stoly on the rocks as Keating explained that he had talked to the lawyer and that one of the towns in the south suburbs would be a good locale. Keating told Damron that when he found a club to buy, they would go to the attorney to start the wheels turning and grease the skids with the mayor. Keating said he would set up a meeting with his lawyer friend.

"All right, you go and talk to the guy, OK?" Keating asked. "And he'll tell you what he can do and then, if you feel comfortable, go ahead. . . . If you don't feel comfortable, you walk away."

"OK. I would assume in the first place that if the guy couldn't do it, you wouldn't go to him," Damron told Keating.

"I'll tell ya, I'd feel comfortable with him. But I'm not talking. I feel comfortable, but it ain't my fucking money," Keating replied.

"Well as long as the guy has got the power to do it, then all you can do is go with the guy," Damron said.

"The guy's a lawyer. All right? And he runs that area," Keating emphasized.

A few days later, Keating called and told Damron that the local mayor had given his OK to the operation of the whorehouse. Keating advised him to start off "nice and easy."

Thirteen days before Dianne Masters' body was discovered in the canal, Damron met again with Jim Keating. It was late in the evening when the men sat down at the Holiday Inn bar. Damron didn't wear a recording device that night, but after the meeting, he made out a report on the incident. The undercover agent had given $1,200 in monthly payoffs for November and December to Keating. And the cop was recommending that Damron meet with Alan Masters. "He told me that this attorney could get anybody off of any beef, and that he had connections with all the political people," Damron would say later. "He said that this attorney, his method of operation was that he paid the cops who made the cases, he paid the judges who tried the cases, and everybody else in-between.

"He told me that he had a lot of experience with the guy, that he was close to him. The guy worked with policemen who had referred him cases, particularly drunk driving type of cases, and the attorney would split referral fees with the cops. He said he himself had referred cases to this attorney and gotten referral fees back."

Keating also noted that Alan had been having marital problems but those problems had evaporated with Dianne's disappearance.

"He said that she didn't show up the day before or the day the divorce was to be filed, and he chuckled and thought it was kind of humorous because it was so convenient," says Damron. "He said that Alan Masters had been called in by the police for interrogation, but that he had been released and that he didn't have any more worries, that everything was fine."

Then, a few minutes later, Keating wrote down Alan Masters' home and office telephone numbers on a bar napkin and handed it to the undercover FBI agent.

Over the next two weeks, Larry Damron talked to Alan Masters three times about finding a locale for the whorehouse and obtaining a liquor license for the club. Their conversations were always friendly and Alan invited Damron to his home. Alan told Damron that he had just returned from a vacation but soon would be leaving on another trip.

They talked for the last time on December 10, 1982, at 1:50 P.M. Alan had found someone who would sell Damron the needed liquor license. The attorney had several possible locations for the new establishment, including a restaurant with a large parking lot. The plan was to open after the first of the year. Damron said he would come down to the south suburbs that afternoon to try to negotiate a lease on a building and would then meet with Alan to review the document before he signed it.

"I'll be gone for two weeks," Alan said. "I need vacations. I decided I'm going to leave the practice of law, and if you'd like to come with me, I have a great profession, Larry," Alan joked.

"OK," replied Damron.

"Better than anything you could ever think of," Alan said. "I'm going to become a television evangelist."

"Oh, do those people make money or do they make money," replied Damron. "You know what they say, 'Give your money to God, but send it to my address.' "

Alan said he wanted to set up an operation such as the one run by a television minister who practices faith healing. "If you touched his hand on a television screen, hemorrhoids, leukemia, or ingrown toenails and headaches all go away. He did the counting himself; he opened up the envelopes last year and his count was $38 million Larry."

"Listen, I'll be glad to be your road manager or whatever the hell you need," Damron said.

"I mean it's unbelievable. That's the greatest thing since Wonder bread, you know. He's got the best thing in the world. And he doesn't get arrested for shit, can you imagine?"

Alan told Damron that one of his clients had become a born-again Christian and had given $33,000 to one of the evangelists. Alan had sat her down for a talk: "Honey, I don't tell you to be a Protestant, Jew, a Catholic, or a Moslem, but there are orphanages, there's Mother Theresa who is doing all this work." What she could have done with $33,000 was unbelievable, he told Damron. "You don't have to give it to a guy who drives a Rolls Royce."

Twenty-four hours later, Dianne's yellow-and-white Cadillac was found in the canal. Alan Masters was no longer joking with anyone, especially Larry Damron.

Timothy O'Brien was in the midst of a war and he knew it. For almost two years, the lowlifes running Chicago's highly organized stolen car rings had been battling one another. There were bombings, murders, and shootings over who was going to run the illegal industry. It was lucrative even though operators had to pay the mob a street tax for the privilege of stealing cars, cutting them up for parts, and selling them.

Timothy O'Brien, the owner of Irish Keystone Auto Parts, had become successful in this business by being somewhat of a specialist. He took orders for cars from his not-so-discerning customers.

On the night of May 21, 1979, he had come home for dinner and brought his associate, David "Red" O'Malley. After dinner, O'Brien told his wife that he and Red had to run out to meet someone at a nearby restaurant. O'Brien, a hulk of a man, was not in a good mood when he left the house. He hadn't showered or shaved, as was his normal practice on such nocturnal outings.

Later Mrs. O'Brien received a call from an anonymous person asking where Timmy was and informing her that he was late for a meeting. One hour later, the caller telephoned again. "I can't wait here all night," the person said. "I'm going home. Tell him I'm not going to wait any longer."

Maryann O'Brien then went to bed. When she awoke at 5 A.M. and noticed that her husband had not returned home, she immediately began to worry. In the next several hours, she made a number of phone calls, including one to O'Malley and another to O'Brien's closest confidante, James Keating, who was on the job.

Maryann O'Brien later would tell FBI agents that Keating advised her not to report her husband missing for two days. When she did report him missing, she was to lie to authorities. She was to say that he was last seen at work at the Irish Keystone, which was in a nearby suburban area patrolled by the sheriff's department. That way Keating could run the investigation. Keating said she should remove all of Timmy's business papers and weapons from the house.

Maryann O'Brien reported her husband missing on Wednesday, one day ahead of schedule. Lt. Keating told her not to worry, "we'll take it from here."

When Maryann talked to the FBI a year later, she was a cooperating witness. Her husband's body had been found on June 1, 1979, in the trunk of a two-door 1976 Buick. There were several gunshot wounds to O'Brien's head. Lt. James Keating had been among the police officers assigned to the case. But, Maryann said, Keating was more than just one of the investigators.

She told them how she and her husband had gone to the Manor A-Go-Go Lounge, a nightclub featuring nude dancers near Willow Springs, in March 1978. According to an FBI report, "She indicated that Lt. Keating came over to their table and she saw Timothy O'Brien slip a large amount of money across the table to Lt. Keating, who put it in his pocket."

Mrs. O'Brien said that her husband had traded information with Keating on numerous occasions. He also had run license numbers through Keating on cars that he felt were following him or observing him and in the past, routinely had paid various sums of money to Lt. Keating. She was advised that this was customary, she said. And the payments were made by a number of Timmy's associates who were involved in organized crime and chop shop activities. The Manor A-Go-Go was the usual setting for the exchange of the cash, she said.

A Cook County Sheriff's Police Department source for the FBI later said that Keating and O'Brien were extorting $3,000 per month from the various chop shops for protection from raids. Some of the profits from the extortion racket were going to pay for an apartment in Chicago Ridge that they both used as a place to party.

The street crews that worked for organized crime had not been happy with O'Brien and Keating's little extortion game. One theory offered by the FBI's source within the sheriff's department was that O'Brien had been murdered by mobsters who were angered at the two men's boldness. The snitch also reported that syndicate members had caught Keating one night and threatened to kill him, too, if he did not stop shaking down their chop shops. But apparently, the word had come down from mob boss Joey Aiuppa that the Irish police lieutenant was to be spared, in spite of his indiscretion.

According to an FBI affidavit filed in federal court, Maryann told agents from the beginning that she suspected that O'Brien's friend, Red O'Malley, had set up her husband. The night O'Brien died, he had insisted that he take his son's car. The affidavit said she believed that two reputed syndicate members, Jerry Scarpelli and Jerry Scalise, had killed her husband.

The FBI affidavit stated that Maryann's theory that her husband had been killed by Scarpelli and Scalise was supported by information provided by William "Billy" Dauber, a chop shop owner. Dauber, reputed to be a mob hit man, had been cooperating with the government. According to an FBI affidavit, Dauber said he had learned that Scarpelli and Scalise had murdered O'Brien because they feared that O'Brien would tell federal agents about their robberies of two banks.

According to an FBI agent's memorandum, "Dauber indicated that O'Brien provided the stolen vehicles for both of these armored car robberies and washed the money obtained during these robberies in Nevada." Jerry Scalise was convicted in London for the armed robbery of the famous Marlborough diamond and is serving a nineteen-year prison term there. Scarpelli was sentenced to seven years for the robbery.

Ten months after he told the FBI about O'Brien's murder, Dauber and his wife Charlotte were gunned down in their van as they drove home from a court appearance in Joliet, about forty-five miles southwest of Chicago.

Herbert Panice operated what his lawyer called the best little whorehouse in Chicago Heights, Illinois. The town was home to the men and women who worked in the steel mills of nearby Gary, Indiana, and at the Ford assembly plant on Torrence Avenue. Chicago Heights also is known for its city officials' ties to Albert Cesear Tocco, the south suburban rackets boss, who is now in federal prison. It was Tocco who sanctioned what transpired in his territory, and the owners of such pleasure dens, men like Panice, had to pay him his fair due. The Cook County Sheriff's Police had to be paid off, too. That was always part of the routine.

In the 1980s, Panice suddenly found that some law enforcement authorities didn't think kindly of his Show Club. Then Cook County state attorney Richard M. Daley had his office raid the place. Panice longed for the good old days.

"Thirty fucking years the county has been wide open. All of a sudden, what happens to it? This fucking Dick Daley gets in there and starts raiding establishments," Panice was recorded saying to undercover federal investigators. The beleaguered bar owner even had attempted to reach out for assistance. He had called someone in Chicago's notorious First Ward organization, where historically, the politicians and mobsters have been one and the same, and asked them to try to reach Daley.

Government prosecutors argued that Panice was so upset because for years, he had operated with virtual immunity by making payoffs. "Mr. Panice was thwarting [law enforcement] efforts through the bribery, with both money and sexual services, of members of the Cook County Sheriff's Police Department," prosecutors said.

The Show Club was Herbie Panice's bread and butter. Until 1986, it was a well-known den of ill repute. Taxis from Chicago would bring visiting conventioneers to the club so that the boys could frolic in the upstairs bedroom with the girls Panice was importing from across state lines.

His business acumen failed him, however, when he began working with Larry Damron and his associate, another undercover FBI agent. Panice agreed to process the club's credit card charges through Damron's firm, the National Credit Service. The secretly tape recorded meetings of the three men began to unravel a pattern of massive police corruption in the county.

Panice complained that he was paying the head of the Cook County Sheriff's Police vice unit, Bruce Frasch, $200 a week, but that the money was not well spent. He received no warning of impending raids.

Frasch worked for Keating and the two men became renowned for their shakedowns of the whorehouses that had reemerged suddenly in the 1980s after the earlier crackdown. Panice not only was paying Frasch, he also was well versed on other deputies taking bribes, including Keating. He told the agents that after he was raided for the first time in 1982 by the FBI, his two other contacts in the sheriff's department suddenly were transferred. "They were my contacts and everybody knew it."

Panice told the agents on August 13, 1982, that he was proud of knowing Keating and described their relationship as good friends. Keating had been named the head of the Intelligence Unit of the sheriff's department, and Panice and other operators of the vice dens were thrilled at their good fortune. "Mr. Panice told me that everyone was pleased about Keating's promotion because he wasn't greedy and he would do almost anything," one of the undercover agents said later.

More important, they thought that Keating was well on his way to eventually heading the entire department. Panice told the undercover cops that Keating was certain to be named as the deputy chief when the current one left the post. And when Sheriff Richard J. Elrod retired, they expected that Keating, who had the necessary clout, easily would be slated for the job by the Cook County Democratic party.

On August 29, 1985, two FBI agents armed with a warrant for Keating's arrest knocked on the door of his home in the south suburb of Oak Lawn. They told him that he was under arrest for accepting bribes and engaging in racketeering and advised him of his rights. "Well, I guess this ruins my chances to go to the FBI Academy," Keating quipped.

James Dennis Keating was born on March 10, 1937, to Joseph A. Keating, a Chicago cop, and his wife Myrtle. The couple and their two sons lived on the south side, a neighborhood inhabited by city employees, in a bungalow at Damen Avenue and Marquette Road.

The boys were raised as traditional Irish Catholics and were taught to follow the doctrines of the church to the letter, to attend mass, take communion, and never miss confession. Joseph Keating also instilled in his children that laughter was an elixir. Sometimes his humor was slightly macabre.

According to one story, patrolman Keating was working during one of those cold winter nights in Chicago when the sub-zero temperature makes it seem like the city is near the arctic circle. A captain on the shift had told the troops at roll call that they were to pay particular attention to the homeless that night, as many of the wandering gentlemen had been perishing in the doorways due to the bitter cold.

When patrolman Keating came across a dead man who had frozen in a doorway that night, he knew exactly what to do. Keating took the body to the captain's house and left it on the porch swing of his home. It was the kind of prank that his son would appreciate later.

During his childhood, Jim worked at a fruit stand to help his family. He attended a parochial grade school but went to a public high school. He was known as a serious student. In high school, he was a dedicated member of the school's Reserve Officers Training Corps. The corps drilled in the morning at 6:30 A.M., and Jim Keating was among the most loyal of troops, according to James Mancini, a retired army sergeant. "He was an exceptionally good student who never got into any trouble and always did what was expected of him. His moral standards were quite high,'' Mancini told the *Chicago Tribune*.

Keating was second-in-command of the high school's drill team when it won the city championship in 1955. ''He was never in trouble. When you were an ROTC officer, you were not allowed to get into trouble,'' says a fellow drill team member.

In April 1955, military records show that Keating was serving as a field radio operator in the U.S. Marine Corps Reserves in a unit located on the city's south side. He remained on active duty until January 1958. His father died shortly after Keating graduated from high school.

Following in his father's footsteps, Keating joined Chicago's finest in 1962, pledging to ''serve and protect.'' His record was not one of which his father would have been proud. A month after joining the department, he was bounced. One rumor was that he had failed to meet the department's height requirement. Another was that he had beaten up someone, and that person later complained to Keating's precinct captain and got him fired.

Out of work, he took a job with the Santa Fe Railroad. By some accounts, he was a railroad detective assigned to the rail yards to watch for thieves stealing from the cargo containers. By other reports, he was simply a night watchman.

His big break came in 1964. With the backing of a political sponsor, Keating became a member of the Cook County Sheriff's Police. When he started, he quickly agreed to work the vice and gambling unit. This was the place to be for cops bucking for promotions. Then-sheriff Richard B. Ogilvie, who later became the state's governor, had ordered a crackdown on mob-run vice in the suburbs, and the police were doing just that.

Keating, who became an especially valuable member of the squad, sometimes donned priestly garb in order to infiltrate various fraternal gambling dens. He also quickly became renowned for his wit and humor, earning him a reputation as a gregarious, fun-loving cop who made people laugh. He was dubbed Father Keating, the Don Rickles of the department. ''He was the most personable guy you could meet,'' says a deputy who knew Keating for thirty years. "He was a smooth, funny guy. A talker," says another. "He could have been a great salesman or comedian."

One night, Keating dressed in his robes and was at the police station when a drunk in one of the holding tanks spotted him. The intoxicated inmate begged the clergyman to hear his confession. Keating gave an inspired performance, swearing to the man that his drinking would send him to hell. And Father Keating was going to call the Pope to make sure that the drunk didn't get redemption.

A friend of Keating's related the story about a former sheriff showing off his spanking new Oldsmobile 88, which was then the low-priced model of the expensive family sedan. At the time, Keating was driving the more costly 98 version. When the sheriff spotted Keating's 98, he turned to his underling and asked how Keating could afford such a luxury car on his meager salary. "I steal more than you do," Keating retorted. Fortunately for Keating, the sheriff did not take his admission seriously.

On another occasion, when the sheriff strolled into Keating's office to display his pinky ring, a common fixture among Chicago pols, Keating chided, "Now we can kiss your ring and not your ass."

The Jim Keating sense of humor. It was part of his persona, differentiating him from his coworkers. A guy to know within the sheriff's department.

Keating had worked vice most of his career and it had taken its toll on his family. His wife Agnes left him in 1981, moving to Michigan with their nine-year-old son James and eight-year-old daughter Kathleen. That same year, Keating sold the home at 116 Tupelo in Naperville that he had purchased at a reduced price from Alan Masters. Alan's law firm handled the closing and Keating received $88,000 for the house.

The amiable cop always had envisioned himself as a high roller and he spent most of his cash on wine and women even before he separated from his wife. Despite his 1984 annual paycheck as a sheriff's deputy of $33,909, the bribes Keating pocketed allowed him to play the role. "He'd walk into a bar and order drinks for everybody," one friend recalls.

Keating fancied himself a lady-killer. "The hardest thing about having three girlfriends," he once told an associate, "is Thanksgiving. You have to convince the first one you like having turkey when you first get up in the morning, when you're fresh. Then you have to convince the second one you like the traditional midday celebration of Thanksgiving. Then you have to tell the third one you especially like a turkey dinner in the evening with drinks when you can really relax. Of course, you have to fast for the whole day before."

One of Keating's flings was almost deadly. He was seeing a go-go dancer at one of the clubs he was supposed to try to close down as the head of the sheriff's intelligence unit. As Keating left the club one night, a hunting arrow whizzed past his head and lodged in the front door. The dancer's Wisconsin boyfriend was advising him politely to stop seeing the woman.

Keating's month-long trial exposed much of the corruption in the sheriff's department and particularly in the vice unit headed by Frasch and Keating. Federal prosecutor David Stetler told the jury that the corruption uncovered in the vice unit was so rampant it made him sick. He called Keating's unit a "cesspool of corruption."

Jeffrey Johnson, a former assistant now in private practice, said Keating and Frasch had "fixed cases and took bribes as they saw fit. These defendants violated their sworn oath as police officers. They sold their badges on the street to the highest bidder."

Even during Keating's trial, his sense of humor became well known. His girlfriend said during a recess that she had been reading his horoscopes during his trial. The woman told him, "You don't want to know your horoscope today."

"Go ahead, tell me," Keating replied.

"It says you will be going away for a long time," she told Keating.

Even television was a dangerous pastime, he told the prosecutors. "I wanted to get my mind off the trial and so I turned on a movie and it's *Alcatraz*."

When the guilty verdict was announced in a packed courtroom, Keating was unmoved. Judge James Holderman dismissed the jury and Keating walked over to Stetler, who was talking with his boss, Anthony Valukas, who had come to watch the finale. Keating grabbed Stetler's hand and began shaking it. "Congratulations. You did a great job," Keating told Stetler. Then he turned to Valukas. "Dave Stetler is a great lawyer. He did a great job in this trial."

Federal prosecutors were ecstatic with the conviction. They thought that Keating, the highest-ranking Cook County Sheriff's Police officer to be convicted in decades, now would become a key witness in other related corruption cases. They expected that, faced with the long sentence, the affable Keating would agree to cooperate.

They were totally wrong. "After conviction, he wouldn't cooperate. He was ready, willing, and able to go to jail," says Stetler.

Federal prosecutors subsequently learned that all of Keating's legal bills had been paid by Alan Masters.

Chapter Sixteen

July 15, 1986

JOSEPH Danzl had not been working long for the Cook County Sheriff's Department. The twenty one-year-old deputy was assigned to the county courts building in downtown Chicago, where he made sure that visitors didn't take weapons into the courtroom with them. Now he was scared about losing the only job he had ever really wanted. Just two days earlier, on July 13, 1986, the *Chicago Tribune* had published a story that had stunned him.

It reported that nearly three and a half years after the disappearance of Dianne Masters, federal authorities were investigating her murder. For the past eighteen months, Assistant U.S. Attorney Tom Scorza secretly had convened a grand jury. His probe of Mike Corbitt's activities had produced a separate investigation focusing on Dianne's death.

Randy Turner was elated with the news that the feds were involved. He thought that Dianne's killers finally might be charged with the crime.

In March 1982, when Dianne Masters was killed, Danzl was a teenager unschooled in the realities of life. Nothing was taken too seriously. They were simply two red cassette tapes that his stepfather, Ted Anthony Nykaza, a private detective, had in his possession. Danzl had overheard his stepfather playing the tapes, which contained conversations between two women, in his basement office. Danzl knew the recordings had been wiretapped illegally. A few days later, his stepfather asked Danzl and his brother to destroy the cassettes. So they did.

They pulled the magnetic tape out of the cassettes and broke them apart with a hammer. It seemed innocent then.

Danzl's mother, Sheryl, had been Nykaza's second wife. The couple had one child of their own, Ted Patrick, born on March 13, 1976. Their 1974 marriage had been rocky almost from the beginning and ended in a tumultuous divorce eleven years later. In a petition seeking a protection order from her husband, she alleged that Nykaza, while drunk, had threatened to kill her. It was going to be the sorriest day of her life, he had told her while loading a .38 special handgun and looking for a shotgun. Sheryl said that Nykaza had a number of guns in the house and had abused her physically on previous occasions in front of the neighbors.

Nykaza was one of Alan Masters' friends. The men had first met when Nykaza was sixteen after the police caught him driving while intoxicated. Relatives referred him to an area attorney to handle his case.

A former Chicago policeman with a serious drinking problem, Nykaza's frequent binges had caused him to be late for duty more often than not. Finally he was booted from the force for breaking the department's rule about living outside the city.

He set up shop as a private detective, and since 1977, he had space in Alan Masters' Summit law office. It was rent-free. All Nykaza had to do in return were a few odd jobs—serving summonses, doing background checks, and following errant husbands to take photos of their affairs. And, occasionally, spying on Dianne and her friends.

The headlines, which also noted that the sheriff's department was reopening the Masters case, had frightened Danzl into talking to his supervisor. Danzl said he had seen the stories in the newspaper and he was worried that someone might make a connection between Nykaza and himself. He didn't want to embarrass the department. He also told his boss that he might have some information about the murder of Dianne Masters that could be relevant to the federal investigation.

Almost immediately, the director of the sheriff's department's internal affairs section met with Danzl. The young deputy explained that his stepfather was an alcoholic who, over the years, had discussed several aspects about the case. But

Danzl had ignored them, thinking they were just the ramblings of a drunk.

He told the authorities that among his stepfather's comments was that he had installed, at Alan's request, voice-activated eavesdropping equipment on the telephones inside the Masters' home. On the recordings, Dianne had mentioned her boyfriend. Danzl explained how he and his brother had destroyed some tapes and how he now believed that they were connected to the bugging.

In talking about the case with his stepfather, they had discussed a report in one of the local papers that Dianne might have been stopped by a police car on the night she disappeared. When Danzl asked if it was true, Nykaza raised his hands and shrugged his shoulders in a way that usually meant he knew but would not say.

Asked if his stepfather actually was involved in the murder of Dianne, Danzl said he wasn't sure. He didn't know if Nykaza had any small-caliber weapon like the one used in the slaying. Nykaza, however, was a former Chicago Police Department detective and he had told Danzl that he had killed three people while on the force.

The state police had interviewed Nykaza in March 1983, but he had told them that the only thing he knew about the strange homicide case was what he had read in the papers.

Investigators previously had been told that Alan had requested Nykaza to follow Dianne shortly before her death and that he had taken photographs of her with various boyfriends. They also had been told he had installed wiretapping equipment on the telephones in the Masters' home.

Nykaza denied both allegations. He noted that Alan had found a small bug in a curtain rod in his house after Dianne's disappearance and had reported it to the sheriff's department. The suspicion at the time was that one of the private detectives hired by Randy Turner had placed the device there, which later proved untrue.

Since the discovery of Dianne's body, there had been virtually nothing in the media about her mysterious murder. And, unlike most cases, police had received no information from their snitches about the killing.

A source had tipped the newspaper to the federal grand jury probe. The entire Cook County Sheriff's Police file had been subpoenaed in the case. Investigators told the *Chicago Tribune* that significant information on the Masters case had surfaced and that some of the policemen now convicted or charged with corruption stemming from a federal investigation of the sheriff's department might be implicated in Dianne's death. The paper noted that Damron had testified in Keating's trial that Keating had bragged that the Masters case never would be solved.

The young Danzl was right about the case potentially being embarrassing to the sheriff's department. The *Tribune*'s account once again highlighted the corruption within the agency and it came at the most inopportune time for Sheriff Richard J. Elrod, who was in a surprising political fight for his life against his Republican challenger, James O'Grady.

During the last few months of the campaign, story after story reiterated the point. The trial of Keating and Frasch, once Elrod's two trusted aides, focused on the connection between various mobsters and the sheriff's department. When Keating and Frasch were found guilty of accepting bribes to protect suburban vice dens, a total of seventeen of Elrod's men had been convicted.

When Keating and Frasch faced sentencing, Elrod publicly apologized for the corruption during his long reign as sheriff, admitting that the department's vice unit was permeated with corruption. He accepted the resignation of his chief and deputy chief, political scapegoats to his campaign rhetoric.

For O'Grady, the stories provided the perfect campaign theme. He continually assailed Elrod on the corruption issue, and for the first time in decades, the polls showed that the incumbent Democrat was in jeopardy of losing his job to O'Grady, his onetime aide and a former Chicago police superintendent.

And the challenger publicly pointed to the Masters case as the classic example of malfeasance within the agency. After all, it was O'Grady's private investigative firm, Special Operations Associates, that had been hired by Randy Turner when he suspected that the sheriff's police were covering up Dianne's murder.

O'Grady's staff called Randy and asked for his help. Would he be willing to do a campaign commercial with the candidate about his sister's disappearance and his belief that the sheriff's department had botched the investigation? Randy agreed, but at the last minute, the television spot was canceled.

Given the political climate, Elrod had to reopen the Masters investigation, though it was decided that Danzl's revelations would be kept secret from federal authorities and the public. He ordered his subordinates to assign a detective to review the allegations again.

A young, brilliant investigator, Paul Sabin, was given the task. For assistance he turned to a friend and fellow officer, Sgt. John Reed, who had the reputation of being the best among Chicago's homicide detectives. Like the major players in the Masters case, he was a south sider and knew all of the principals. His knowledge would be invaluable to Sabin, who came from the city's north side. His request for Reed's help was unofficial, so the veteran cop agreed to work with Sabin on his own time.

The men were opposites in almost every respect. The brown-haired, blue-eyed Reed was a giant who resembled a starting tackle from the days of the Four Horsemen at the University of Notre Dame. He stood six feet two and stacked 260 pounds on his broad frame.

Until age seventeen, Reed had planned to be a priest. He attended a Catholic boarding school whose students attended mass daily. The Clorichian brothers, who taught him Greek and Latin, demanded strict discipline and solid minds.

His parents, Honora and James, had started their family on Chicago's southwest side at Fifty-eighth and Lawndale. She was a devout Irish Catholic; James was an Englishman who had farmed in Canada. John was the second of three children. While he was in grade school, the family moved to the far-south suburbs to satisfy his father's yearning for open spaces.

Following high school, he did a three-year stint in the U.S. Marines, serving overseas as a chaplain's assistant. After a variety of jobs, he joined the Cook County Sheriff's Police. Reed, who had a keen sense of justice, believed there were many ways to serve God and country.

Sabin was just under six feet tall and 185 pounds. He had brown curly hair, a nice smile, and was studious. Sabin, who was attending law school, was looking forward to beginning a new career.

Reed was a die-hard cop. Even in street clothes, he looked like a police officer.

The two men's personalities and interrogation styles also differed. Reed was outgoing with a keen sense of humor. He had a mind like a computer and a soothing, disarming interviewing technique that coaxed facts out of witnesses, who frequently found their statements being repeated back to them, almost always verbatim.

Sabin was the serious one. He was a precise speaker who chose his words carefully and was an attentive listener. He quickly discerned discrepancies in witnesses' statements and then asked for further clarification or details, which locked them into their stories.

What the men had in common was veracity and tenacity, both rare qualities among Cook County Sheriff's Department's homicide investigators.

When they pulled the department's original case file, they were both shocked. It was clear from the file that the interviews had been less than thorough. It appeared that some reports were missing and routine steps never undertaken.

Reed knew that there were close ties between Alan Masters and the men initially assigned to the investigation. He had heard the department scuttlebutt about Alan's providing free or low-cost legal services to his colleagues. He also knew that convicted lieutenant Jim Keating and two fellow Cook County Sheriff's Police officers, Jack Bachman and Sgt. Clarke Buckendahl, had once been partners in a private detective agency that operated from Alan's law office.

He and Sabin started investigating the case anew by interviewing all of the principals in the case, including the members of their own department, about their role in the initial probe and their relationship to Alan Masters.

Vanick told the detectives that from the onset, he and Keating had argued about his treatment of Alan as a suspect. Keating had implied that Vanick would be transferred off the case if he didn't stop implicating Alan. "Why don't you give the benefit of the doubt to the client," Keating had told Vanick the day Dianne was reported missing.

Several days after Dianne's disappearance, Vanick told the detectives, he was ordered to meet with Deputy Chief Richard Quagliano. The deputy chief said that Alan had called to complain about the way Vanick was focusing the investigation on the attorney. Quagliano warned him not to try the case in the newspapers.

Vanick told Reed and Sabin that he believed that Keating had been reading all of the police reports on the case and passing on witnesses' statements to Alan, because witnesses had complained that what they were telling the cops was getting back to Alan.

Ted Anthony Nykaza lived just three miles southwest of Dianne and Alan Masters. When his subdivision was first being built in the late 1970s, it was plopped down in the middle of what was once a farmer's field. Nykaza had bought the lot and the adjoining one as well and had hired a builder to construct the house, which sat at the crest of a hill.

Reed and Sabin made their first visit to Nykaza's home on October 20, 1986. It was 2 P.M. when their unmarked squad car pulled up in front of 13650 South Santa Fe Trail in the unincorporated neighborhood. In the driveway was a black Cadillac Eldorado belonging to Nykaza's wife Sheila.

The deputies did not know how Nykaza would react to their unexpected presence. They had been warned that he always carried a gun—and might use it—so they were not taking any chances; they wore bulletproof vests under their plainclothes.

At the front door of the eight-year-old, off-white trilevel, was a dog's bowl and a large chain, which was attached to the house. When the two police officers rang the bell, the pet started barking. Rusty, an Irish setter, had once belonged to Dianne Masters. From inside, Nykaza asked, "Who is it?"

After the men identified themselves, there was a momentary

delay; then he swung the door open and led the detectives through his five thousand square foot house, which featured cathedral ceilings and a gigantic family room and was decorated with expensive, modern furnishings and artwork. Near the wall phone in the kitchen was a montage of cryptic messages and notes the private eye was saving.

Nykaza was a chronic alcoholic and the disease had taken its toll on him physically. He was only forty-one but looked years older. He was six feet tall and a mere 150 pounds. His blue eyes were bloodshot from frequent binges and long nights of surveillance. He often watched the sun rise during stakeouts of a cheating spouse when Alan needed evidence for one of his divorce cases. Nykaza used a special camera that reportedly could take pictures in embarrassing detail, even through curtains.

There was a hint of alcohol on his breath as he led Reed and Sabin to his basement office. When Nykaza had the house built, he had made sure that the carpenter, an Irishman, had made the concrete walls taller than in most homes. As a result, the basement had eight-foot ceilings, and it was carpeted and paneled.

Inside his office, the walls were covered with as many as fifty commendations from his career as a Chicago policeman. He had been a savvy street cop who never shirked his duty. His awards served as an admonition to Reed and Sabin: he must be taken seriously. And gaining his cooperation was going to be tough.

Nykaza displayed all of the tools of his trade—old phone books, a criss-cross directory, which lists the names of individuals by address and phone number, copying machines, and numerous filing cabinets. Reed recognized him as a pack rat and hoped the private eye had saved a tape.

Nykaza knew that the policemen had been to see his ex-wife, Sheryl. She had reported to him that she had told the detectives everything she knew, and she hoped Alan got what he deserved. Nykaza wasn't aware, though, that Sheryl's son, Joe Danzl, had told the police months earlier about destroying the cassettes.

Nykaza told his adversaries to ask specific questions. He

volunteered little during the two-hour conversation, but often his answers were provocative. He did not want to get involved, he told them. He said he had no theories about Dianne's death, but then he would tease Reed and Sabin with tidbits.

Alan Masters was living with another woman now, said Nykaza. Her name was Jan and she was Anndra's governess.

The lawyer wouldn't discuss the case, he told Reed and Sabin. Nykaza was convinced that Alan knew nothing about his wife's slaying. He said that when Dianne's body had been discovered, a sobbing Alan had called him and asked him why anyone would have killed such a beautiful woman.

Twice during the interview, Nykaza told the detectives that even if Alan had confessed to him, he would never inform on the attorney. Nykaza theorized that Dianne had been grabbed on her driveway the night she came home. He never identified who had attacked Dianne, but he referred to her killers in the plural.

Nykaza explained to the detectives that Alan could not have planned his own wife's disappearance, because it would have gotten screwed up if he had been involved. Alan, he told them, did not do well under emotional pressure. Once, when Anndra accidentally fell into the pool, Alan became so befuddled that he tripped over his own feet in trying to rescue his daughter.

Nykaza told the detectives that Alan had done everything he could to save his marriage to Dianne. He had gone on weight-loss diets, he had purchased fur coats for his wife, and he had seen a hypnotist to stop his snoring. Nykaza had overheard Alan begging Dianne to stay with him. He was crying and pleading with Dianne not to divorce him.

When the detectives asked how Alan had learned about Dianne's boyfriend, Nykaza simply replied that Alan would go crazy if he found out that Dianne had been seeing someone else.

Nykaza suggested that a possible suspect could be a husband of one of Alan's former clients. The man had become so enraged at Alan that he had attacked him outside a courtroom and broken Alan's arm.

Reed asked Nykaza if he was familiar with the test of a true friend: "Call your friends at 2 A.M. and tell them you just murdered your wife and ask them to help you dispose of her remains. A true friend will be right over; all others will beg off."

Nykaza just smiled.

For Reed, it was just the reaction he had been hoping for. Jim Keating had originated the test question and it was something he had always talked about. Keating had said that a true friend was one you could take on a bank robbery with you or someone you called about the murder of your wife and they responded. The smile was an indication that Nykaza realized that the two detectives knew of his relationship with Keating. Left for the private eye to decide was whether Reed and Sabin were friends or foes of Keating.

Nykaza knew of Mike Corbitt but said he would be hard-pressed to recognize him. He did tell the detectives, however, that one of Alan and Dianne's friends, Arlane Yoways, had told him that Corbitt had been following Dianne before her death.

Nykaza claimed that he had been involved in four fatal shootings while he was a policeman and Reed made a mental note to check whether the shots had been fired to the head—like those that killed Dianne.

When Nykaza was fired from Chicago's ranks, he joined a suburban department, but he hated being in uniform, so he opened his own private detective agency, Ted Anthony and Associates.

With the help of Alan Masters, it became much more than a private detective agency involved in domestic disputes. It obtained contracts to provide guard services for large trucking terminals on the southwest side of Chicago. Nykaza hired off-duty sheriff's police officers and Chicago cops to guard against cartage thieves. (Reed himself had once been employed by the firm, although he had never met Nykaza until now.)

Alan gave Nykaza space in his Summit office. Another agency, run by James Keating, Clarke Buckendahl, and Jack Bachman, also was headquartered there. The three Cook County Sheriff's Police officers moonlighted as private detectives. Originally it had included Robert Cadieux. Using the first names of the men, the detective agency was called J.

Robert Clarke and Associates. But Cadieux, who later was convicted of interstate fraud and extortion charges, dropped out, and Bachman then joined. The three cops split the annual $2,000 insurance premium they paid for their private detective liability insurance with Nykaza. They maintained their own operation but worked under his license.

Nykaza told Reed and Sabin that Alan used his company exclusively. He knew, he said, because he rifled through Alan's desk drawers at the office, on occasion, looking for evidence to confirm whether he was hiring someone else.

Nykaza's private detective business was a prosperous one. By the time of his 1985 divorce from Sheryl, he had accumulated more than a dozen utility stocks, a half dozen certificates of deposits, various individual retirement accounts, and brand new cars. The divorce case indicated that the couple had amassed the large portfolio, although Nykaza grossed just $30,000 a year and Sheryl worked as a clerk in a J.C. Penny store.

Actually, Nykaza's earnings were much higher. When he was hustling, he made $250,000 a year just serving court papers. No wonder he told the detectives that one of his greatest fears was the tax man.

His ex-wife had run up big charges on his credit cards—all twenty-five of them—and left him with the debts. Officially, he agreed to pay $40,000 in credit card bills, $50,000 in cash and $300 a month to end the marriage to Sheryl. He got the house and adjacent lot, the stocks, and the bank accounts, if there was anything left in them. He also had a $56,000 mortgage to pay on the house.

Within months after the divorce, Nykaza married Sheila Mikel. They had originally met in 1976 at a bar where he was drinking and she was serving. She was now a dispatcher in a local police department, but she had once been employed in Alan's law office. She also had been Alan's lover.

The affair had started just six months after she became Alan's secretary in 1978. As he had done with Dianne, Alan had lavished gifts on her during their relationship. There was jewelry and cash, and he had given Sheila $5,000 to buy a house.

This was the affair Dianne had learned about when she

returned home from a European vacation and found a pair of underpants in her car along with a gas station receipt showing that Sheila had been using it. Supposedly she had demanded that Alan fire the woman; Sheila left his employ in March 1981. However, in June of that year, Alan gave Sheila a ring for her birthday. Their half-hour to one-hour couplings ended around the time of Dianne's disappearance.

Five years later, Sheila turned to Nykaza. They wed in August of 1986.

When Reed and Sabin ended their lengthy session, they followed Nykaza upstairs. At the top of the stairway, Reed started playing his bumbler role. As he talked to Nykaza, he opened the door to the garage for a peek at what was stored inside. It looked accidental and innocent, but Nykaza knew differently. He had quipped that Reed would find no bodies inside his garage. Nykaza laughed at the antics of the detective. He knew exactly what Reed was doing.

When Reed and Sabin left, Sheila, who was at home and had remained upstairs during the interview, called Alan Masters and told him that the two detectives had just interviewed Nykaza.

Unbeknownst to the deputies, the marriage of Nykaza and Sheila was almost over. But their relationship with Ted Nykaza was just beginning.

A week after the two detectives interviewed Nykaza, they sat down with Alan Masters at his Summit office.

The lawyer reviewed the night of Dianne's disappearance and how she had told him in January that she was preparing to divorce him. He asked the two detectives what they had learned about her murder and asked if they had interviewed a suspect in a local homicide.

Alan blamed the department's lack of objectivity for its failure to solve Dianne's abduction and homicide. He told the two detectives that Lt. Vanick had focused on him rather than two men suspected of killing women in the area. Alan was certain that Dianne had never made it to the driveway the night she disappeared. His bedroom was located next to the garage,

Dianne was very feminine from an early age, always the perfect little lady.

Both Dianne and Randy had inherited their father's musical ability.

In high school, Dianne was extremely popular and a perfect student, combining both beauty and brains.

Dianne at her first wedding, to Ronald Mueller. They appeared to be the all-American couple. *(Courtesy of Sally Mortenson)*

Dianne was a bridesmaid at her brother's wedding. Her new sister-in-law Kathy proved to be a valuable friend and confidante.

Dianne and Alan's rambling ranch-style house was set far back from the street, offering seclusion.
(Photo by Karl Baumrucker)

Dianne befriended all animals. Her dog Baron was one of her favorites.

Five months before her death, Dianne was honored for her work as founder and outgoing president of the Crisis Center for South Suburbia. This photo of Dianne, Alan, and Anndra was the last formal picture taken before Dianne disappeared. *(Photo by* Star-Herald)

Dianne's distinctive yellow-and-white Cadillac became her coffin. (Chicago Tribune *photo by Chuck Barman)*

James Keating was a well-liked cop whose good nature hid a darker side. (Chicago Tribune *photo by Carl Wagner)*

Michael Corbitt's derring-do was renowned throughout the Chicago area. (Chicago Tribune *photo by Quentin C. Dodt)*

Alan pleaded innocent at his arraignment. (Chicago Tribune *photo by Carl Wagner)*

Thomas Scorza wanted justice for Dianne Masters and would not rest until he found it. *(Photo by Mark Alan Dial)*

Sergeant John Reed was viewed as a "Serpico" by his brethren on the force. Here, he is honored as the hero of the Dianne Masters investigation.
(Chicago Tribune *photo by Don Casper)*

Jan Bower secretly wed Alan before his trial began and gained legal custody of Anndra. *(Courtesy of Janet Masters)*

Randy Turner will not be satisfied until Alan Masters is charged and convicted with his sister's murder.

and either he or a neighbor to the north would have heard something if she had been attacked outside.

When the detectives asked if Alan had ever employed deputies to work for him in his law office, he said he had never hired sheriff's police or allowed any of them to work out of his law office.

He denied owning or operating a bordello. When he was told that the tax bills went to his legal secretary, Alan explained that she was the beneficiary of a land trust for the property and that the two detectives should talk to his secretary, who already had testified about it before a grand jury.

Alan told the detectives he couldn't understand why the name of his longtime friend Michael Corbitt always surfaced as a possible suspect in the murder. Corbitt had nothing to do with Dianne's death, he assured the two detectives.

And he was irate that Reed and Sabin had interviewed Robert Rosignal, a Cook County Sheriff's Police officer who occasionally housesat for Alan when he went on vacation. Alan wanted to know why they considered Rosignal a suspect and accused Lt. Vanick of siccing the detectives on his friend. "Rosignal would not hurt a fly," Alan declared.

Rosignal had told Reed and Sabin that the night Dianne was murdered, he had called in sick. He was working a night shift and attending school during the day. Rosignal said that he was either too tired to go to work or was studying that evening and offered to take a polygraph test to clear his name.

Alan proudly told the police that he had fired a handgun only once in his life, but then he produced two handguns from his desk drawer. One was a .38-caliber revolver with a two-inch barrel and the other was a .38-caliber chrome revolver with a four-inch barrel. Masters also showed the detectives a .22-caliber Winchester rifle that had belonged to Dianne's father.

Alan told Reed and Sabin that he believed there was still an eavesdropping device in a vent in his home, because he frequently heard something emitting a beeping sound. He compared the noise to a weak battery in a smoke alarm.

Alan told the men that he had contemplated hiring a noted attorney to file lawsuits against the *Chicago Sun-Times* and

Chicago Tribune for stories inferring that he was a suspect in Dianne's death. Then he turned to the investigators and said that he hoped to read that he was uncooperative during his interview.

"Mr. Masters was cooperative and may be re-interviewed at a later date," the detectives wrote. But Reed and Sabin realized that Alan was implying that his contacts in the department soon would be providing him with their report for his review. And that Alan was boasting to the investigators about his clout in the sheriff's office.

Chapter Seventeen

November 13, 1986

It was lunchtime at the criminal court complex, a series of buildings on the city's west side that covered several blocks and included the courtrooms, jail, and offices, all part of the country's largest criminal justice system.

The cases being tried in this facility were often some of the most gruesome tales of man's inhumanity to man—parents senselessly beating their babies to death; teenagers killing rival gang members over flashing hand signals; brutal rapes. The list was endless. So at lunchtime, people usually streamed out the doors on California Avenue seeking a respite from the harsh realities of life in urban America.

A few blocks east was an enclave of Italian restaurants that served some of the best food in the city. At noon, the establishments were filled with prosecutors, defense attorneys, and judges. Other workers headed toward the nearby fast-food eateries.

Inside the courthouse cafeteria, a place rarely frequented by any criminal justice system employee, Sgt. Jack Reed was having soup, the only thing he relished on the cafeteria's menu. He was meeting with a fellow Cook County Sheriff's Police officer, Jack Bachman.

Reed had let it be known in the department that the investigation needed the help of his coworkers. He knew that some of them had been corrupt, but they were still police officers. His message to them was simple: "Draw the line at murder. Cooperate in this investigation."

And that was what he reiterated to Bachman perhaps a hundred times on November 13, 1986. The men had come to the second-floor cafeteria from the courthouse's subterranean basement, where Bachman and Reed worked in the sheriff's department's warrant section. It would be three weeks before Reed was pulled out of the unit and officially assigned to investigate the Masters case with Sabin.

The men sat at one of the tables in bright-blue and orange plastic chairs. Reed spoke quietly, but there was an urgency to his tone. "Jack, I need some help on this case," the detective said. "I think you can help me."

In fact, Reed was certain that Bachman could help him—if he could convince his colleague to draw the line at murder. There had been talk in the department about Bachman's past. He was close to Corbitt and he had a relationship with Keating, who was the godfather of one of Bachman's children. Reed knew that the men ran a private detective agency out of Alan's office. But the ties between Bachman and Keating went well beyond friendship and legitimate business. The two men had another kind of association, the kind where money exchanged hands to protect crooked gamblers and whorehouses.

Reed didn't care about such bribes or corruption. He wanted the deputy's help on just one case: the Dianne Masters murder. "I don't want to know anything about anything else," he told Bachman. "I am not interested in the gamblers in Cicero. The corruption in Lyons. I am not interested in nose picking at stoplights. I am only interested in the murder."

Bachman was good looking and serious about physical fitness. A weight lifter and black belt in karate, he had a muscular build and a face that could catch any woman's fancy. Like Reed, Bachman had joined the force in 1966. He, too, had been in the Marine Corps prior to joining the sheriff's department. Bachman also had worked for the phone company, an occupation that reportedly served him well when he and Keating operated their private detective agency business. Bachman had developed a reputation as one who was adept at wiretapping telephones.

Over the years, Reed and Bachman's careers had crossed

paths on several occasions. In the 1970s, they worked for Intelligence and Investigative Support Services, a unit headed by Lt. Jim Keating that helped small and poor suburban communities by providing them with detectives who were experienced in murder investigations and major crimes. Reed and two deputies worked out of Maywood, a blue-collar suburb on the west side of the city. It had been undergoing rapid racial integration, and consequently, the crime rate had soared. One suburb to the east, Jack Bachman was working for the unit in predominately white Forest Park.

So Reed and Bachman were acquainted with each other's reputation. After Reed finished his sermon, it was clear from Bachman's demeanor that he was going to help. He said he would tell Reed only what he *thought* had happened, but Reed knew instinctively that what Bachman was telling him was much more than educated guesses. He suspected that Keating had told Bachman what had happened.

Bachman knew all about the illegal wiretaps Ted Nykaza had placed on the telephone at the Masters house. He described Nykaza as an expert at the art of wiretapping, no small compliment from someone of Bachman's reputation. Nykaza had told Bachman that he was sorry that he had bugged the phones, because it had contributed to Alan's decision to kill his wife.

Bachman said that the taped phone calls had recorded Dianne talking to her boyfriend, Jim Koscielniak. During one of their conversations, the lovers had discussed a sex act they had performed. Alan had become enraged upon hearing the tape.

Before Dianne's murder, Alan had treated Nykaza as a gofer. After her death, Alan went out of his way not to offend the private detective.

Bachman said the talk was that Dianne had been ambushed at her home when she stepped outside of her car the night she disappeared. He asked Reed if there had been a flat tire on Dianne's car when it was found. Bachman also said he doubted that Corbitt had shot Dianne, unless there was a gun pointed at him.

He thought that his onetime business partner, Keating, was now cooperating with the U.S. Attorney's Office. Keating could fill in a lot of the blanks, he told Reed. And he knew that Lt. Vanick was worried that the press would discover that he had gone swimming in Alan Masters' pool.

Like a priest hearing confession, Reed did not question Bachman. The veteran detective knew that Jack Bachman would reveal only what he wanted to. Other than indicating that he had spoken to Nykaza, Bachman would not divulge who had provided him with any of the details. Reed also was keenly aware that Bachman was an insider in Alan Masters' cadre and that he would provide answers only if he trusted Reed.

When Reed finished his soup, they returned to the basement. A coworker, who was a close friend of Bachman's, noticed Bachman's demeanor when they walked into the room. "He's real upset about something," the coworker said to Reed.

"I didn't say anything to him," he replied in self-defense.

Bachman had provided Reed with the motive for Dianne's murder. Alan had discovered Dianne's infidelity and was so outraged, he had her killed. The evidence, of course, had been destroyed. But now the detective clearly understood that her death involved a conspiracy. Ted Nykaza wiretapped the phone, Alan was responsible for his wife's death, and Corbitt supervised the disposal of the body. Reed realized that Bachman knew much more.

In his reports, the investigator dubbed Bachman a confidential source with the code name EOL. The acronym stood for "end of the line," as in the end of the line for Dianne's killers. Or so Reed hoped.

CHAPTER EIGHTEEN

November 23, 1986

JACK Reed and Paul Sabin sat in one of the booths at the Purple Steer in Calumet City, a working-class suburb on Chicago's south side. On one side of the off-white formica-covered table, Reed and his brown leather coat occupied much of the blue-green vinyl seat. Sabin sat wedged into a corner opposite him. The two policemen sipped coffee, munched on sweet rolls, and waited for Jim Koscielniak.

It was 10 A.M. Sunday, November 23, 1986, and at that hour, a trickle of customers began patronizing the twenty-four-hour eatery, their weekly stop for breakfast following church services. The Purple Steer typified many of Chicago's suburban restaurants. Owned by Greeks, it provided decent food, reasonable prices, and quick service. It featured a bar, counter service, and room for 230 or so diners. But the eatery rarely was filled. It had been Jim's choice for the interview; he lived just eight blocks south of the place.

The two detectives saw a 1984 Dodge van pull into the restaurant's parking lot at 147th Street and Torrence Avenue. When a man they thought was Jim emerged from the van, one of them made a note of the make and model of the vehicle and recorded its license plate, FSN 577. That was part of the investigators' routine. They already had pulled Jim's driver's license, which described him as five feet eleven and two hundred pounds, with gray hair and hazel eyes. When he entered the Purple Steer, one of the detectives got up, went over and introduced himself, and led Dianne's former lover back to the table.

Jim probably had been interviewed by authorities as often as had Randy and Kathy Turner. His brown hair was grayer now, but other than that, he looked the same as he did the day Dianne disappeared. During the next few hours, he provided Reed and Sabin with an extraordinary flashback of the months before Dianne's murder.

They often had taken wine and cheese with them when they went to a motel, and on February 24, 1982, they used the libation as part of their frolicking. Jim had brought along a white French wine, poured it into Dianne's vagina, and then engaged in oral sex.

He had gotten the idea from a particularly provocative newspaper column written by Reverend Andrew M. Greeley, a Chicago priest, novelist, and *Chicago Sun-Times* columnist, which had appeared on February 13, 1981. Entitled "Love and Sex: Truths the Bible Teaches Us," Greeley discussed pornography and *Penthouse* magazine's interview of the Reverend Jerry Falwell, and mentioned a church decree that declared "it was all right for married people to have sex as long as they promised not to enjoy it very much."

Greeley had pointed out that the Bible celebrates sexual love, including oral sex, and that in the old versions of the Song of Solomon, one of the chapters describes an oral sex scene. He noted that there was no indication that the couple was married; the woman is naked through most of the story, and the lovers celebrate each other's sexual organs and skills in detail. One translator, in an effort to clean up the words, went so far as to describe the woman's vagina as "a goblet filled with spiced wine, surrounded by wheat and flowers," Greeley wrote.

The column had impressed Jim, and he had clipped it for a philosophy class. Later, he was going through his files, spotted the article, and decided to share it with Dianne.

She thoroughly enjoyed it. She sent a letter back to Jim quoting from Greeley's work. "One might say that God reveals himself/herself to humans through the power of sexual passion," Greeley had written. "When the lovers in the Song are frolicking joyously, reveling in their taste and smell, when all lovers delight in one another, they are hearing the beat of angels' wings, the pounding feet of the hound of heaven, the taste and the smell of a passion which is never daunted, never given up and never ends." She told Jim that she, too, believed that their passion never would end.

Their mistake, he explained to Reed and Sabin, had been to discuss their lovemaking on her wiretapped telephone. She had complained that Jim had inserted the bottle into her vagina. "Why did you do that?" she asked him during their telephone tête-à-tête.

Jim thought it odd that Dianne had mentioned the incident. After all, she suspected that the lines were bugged, because Alan had repeated her private conversations to her. To Jim, it seemed sometimes as if Dianne were trying to make sure Alan knew she was having an affair.

He also told the detectives that on one occasion, they stayed together at a motel all night. When Jim suggested that he should take Dianne home, she replied, "I want Al to know it's over between us." Also, for several weeks in February, Dianne and Alan had separated and Alan lived at his brother's home. On one occasion, Jim spent the night on the couch with Dianne and left at 6 A.M. She had wanted him to stay in the house, although to Jim, it had seemed risky.

That same month, a day after Jim's birthday, he and Dianne met for lunch at a local restaurant. She had learned that it was his birthday and rushed out to a department store to buy him a sweater and some cologne.

He recalled that it was a late lunch, because he had a class that ended at 3 P.M. and another that started at 6:30. Dianne ate something spicy and then complained that her ulcer was acting up. He chided her, but she said she loved the spicy food.

After his birthday lunch, he walked her to her car and kissed her good-bye.

"Stop, we can't do that," Dianne told a confused Jim. She said they were being watched by two Orland Park police officers whom Alan was defending on departmental charges. But Dianne had been mistaken about the men's identity. And Jim, unknowingly, had passed on incorrect information to Reed.

Later, another source would tell Reed the truth. It had been

Howard Vanick, the lieutenant in charge of Dianne's investigation, and his companion who had spotted Jim and Dianne necking that day. Vanick copied down the license plate number to learn Jim's name and the information was passed on to Alan.

One of Alan's pals in the sheriff's department also had checked Jim's criminal history and discovered that he had pleaded guilty to battery stemming from a minor incident with an old flame. In 1980, the girlfriend told Jim that the relationship was over. She tripped, hit her head, and pressed charges. Jim was sentenced to court supervision, which meant that the conviction would be erased from his record if he was not found guilty of another criminal offense for a year.

On March 2, 1982, Dianne's college board had met to hire a new president. Jim had called Dianne at home and arranged to meet her after the board meeting at a local pub frequented by both board members and organized crime figures. Afterward, they would go to a nearby motel.

At the tavern, there were about a dozen people from the college. It was a busy night and service was slow. Rather than wait at the table, Jim went to the bar to get two glasses of Chablis for him and Dianne. There sat Lt. James Keating, dressed in a brown three-piece suit and smoking a cigar, which he immediately extinguished.

"Are you from the college?" Keating asked.

"Yes," replied Jim.

"What do you do there?"

"I teach economics," Jim said.

Keating again grabbed his cigar, crushed it in the ashtray, then asked the professor his name. Jim told him and returned to the table to join Dianne and the others. When he sat down, Dianne touched him gently on the leg, but the two avoided holding hands.

"I look up and this guy was staring at me. The next time I see him is on television and he's being arrested in Operation Safebet," Jim related to Reed and Sabin.

That night, a three-and-a-half-inch snowfall blanketed the city. As is common with such March storms, it was a wet, clingy snow that stuck to the trees. The kind that makes the outdoors look pristine. When they walked out of the tavern and got to the car, Dianne remarked how lovely the pine trees looked in the snow. Instead of going to the motel, she suggested that they drive and park somewhere.

They found a secluded side road and made love in the car. Jim told Reed he believed that he and Dianne were to have been slain that night. The investigators would discover later that apparently, the killers were waiting for the couple at the motel. It was supposed to look like a murder-suicide, but a scenic snowfall, or perhaps Dianne's identification of Keating at the tavern, had saved their lives.

Reed and Sabin also learned from Jim how deeply Dianne feared for her life. He and Dianne had joined Bénédicte for dinner in Chicago one night about a month before her disappearance. When she called home to check with the babysitter, Alan, who was supposed to be attending the fights with friends, answered. He told Dianne, "I am going to destroy you."

Alan reportedly had made other threats as well. When he returned to the house after staying with his brother, he reinstated daily deliveries of flowers to the home. He then told Dianne, "You are going to need flowers soon" and "Flowers are appropriate for you at this time," followed by a knowing wink.

When, during their discussions over the divorce, they argued about possession of the house, Alan yelled at Dianne, "You want this house? You will live in this house until you die."

Jim told the two detectives that in the last few weeks of her life, Dianne had been on guard constantly. It seemed that wherever she went, she felt watchful eyes upon her. When she and Jim rendezvoused at the La Grange Motel that day in March, she took special precautions. Before she pulled her yellow-and-white Cadillac Coupe de Ville into the parking lot, she drove through the nearby White Castle twice to stop and look for the car she suspected was following her. She didn't see it, so she drove into a furniture store parking lot and waited for Jim to drive to the motel.

When the two detectives interviewed Bénédicte, Dianne's best friend, she recalled how Dianne had trembled when she discussed Alan and what he could do to her. Bénédicte told the two investigators that two weeks before Dianne's disappearance, she had told Bénédicte that a handgun she carried had been taken as well as some jewelry.

She said that when Cook County Sheriff's Police officers had come to talk to her during the initial investigation, they had told her that they were having trouble with Dianne's friends. "You know, people don't want to talk to us because we are friends of Alan," she quoted the police as saying.

"Well, aren't you?" Bénédicte had responded. She described her interview with the police as superficial. She told Reed and Sabin that she had no faith in the 1982 investigation. "Alan Masters always said that nothing could happen to him, because he had too many big people and judges covering for him and looking out for him," she said.

Both Bénédicte and another friend, Teri Swanson, said that Dianne had accumulated important papers that could put Alan in prison. Teri had been asked by the detective agency hired by Randy Turner to check out the Masters home about three weeks after Dianne had disappeared. She did, and reported that Alan knew Dianne was never returning. He already had removed her furs, clothing, and shoes from her bedroom and hall closets.

Two weeks before Christmas, John Reed telephoned Randy and Kathy Turner and requested a formal interview. For the last four years, it seemed that during almost every yuletide season, some investigator from one police agency or the other had turned up on their doorstep asking them to repeat the tale they had told the police since Dianne's body had been discovered. The Turners had no reason to trust Reed or his partner, Sabin. After all, the two investigators were from the same department that the Turners believed botched the initial investigation into Dianne's death.

Randy called Dan Davis, one of the partners at SOA, and asked whether Davis thought they should talk to these detectives and his evaluation of the two men. After reassurances from Davis, Randy called Reed back and invited him over.

Sitting on the couch in the Turners' living room, the two detectives began the interview at 7:00 P.M. Sabin played the straight man and asked the majority of the questions. He was always the serious one. Reed, on the other hand, joked and kidded. He put the couple at ease. He was also one of the most talkative policemen they had encountered, willing to share with the couple numerous details that they had unearthed in the case.

Reed's obvious concern startled the Turners. They had not expected such solicitude from a Cook County Sheriff's Police officer. He also talked openly about his disgust with the corruption he was uncovering within the department and how he and Sabin had become outcasts because of their investigation. But there still were good police officers on the force and they were stepping forward, he told the Turners.

Reed reminded Randy of Francis X. Delaney, the crackerjack detective in Lawrence Sanders's novels. He was an investigator who diligently researched every detail and clue, and he was confident and reassuring.

Sipping coffee, the detectives and the Turners discussed Alan's violence, how Dianne had left him and then reconciled, and Dianne's fears about being followed and her statement to Kathy the week before her disappearance that Alan was capable of getting rid of Dianne without a trace.

Why hadn't Alan changed the locks on the house after Dianne disappeared? the Turners had asked. Alan had responded that he wanted Dianne to be able to walk right in when she returned. But the Turners felt that any prudent person would have changed the locks, because the keys to the Masters' alarm-protected home would have been in the hands of the killers.

They told the two detectives that about two weeks before Dianne disappeared, Alan had borrowed Dianne's Cadillac for the day. Dianne had found it so strange that she had mentioned it to the Turners. Randy told the detectives that Dianne's trunk was always jam-packed with tennis gear and other junk, so there would have been no room for a body unless someone cleaned out the space. Randy also told them about Alan's sleazy whorehouse (as he had done in a 1984 interview with an FBI agent).

The interview ended after five and a half hours. Reed and Sabin had given the Turners the best Christmas present ever: hope that Dianne's murder would be solved.

CHAPTER NINETEEN

February 22, 1987

TED Nykaza had been a very good cop, but he was an even better private detective. He had a knack for playing the games that went with the profession—acting macho and displaying a facade of confidence that assured clients he could get the job done. Despite years of drinking, his mind was brilliant. He was adept at sparring with the detectives who had visited him recently.

Over the past few weeks, Jack Reed and Paul Sabin had been investigating Nykaza. The picture that emerged from those interviews was complex and contradictory. The two detectives had been told this was a man who easily could have pulled the trigger and killed Dianne. His soon to be ex-wife, Sheila, had told them that Nykaza, in a stupor, had once mumbled that he wasn't going to kill anyone ever again.

But he also was being described as a puppy dog. Be firm and fair with Nykaza, he's incapable of harming anyone, Reed and Sabin were told. They didn't know if they had a suspect or a witness. What the men did realize, however, was that they had found someone who possessed knowledge of the crime.

Nykaza's stepson had told them more about the recording device. It was a special order, and Nykaza had gotten a very slow speed, voice-activated tape recording device to tap the phones. Some of the tapes had been played repeatedly to try to decipher the telephone numbers that Dianne was calling. Nykaza also had sought the help of a connection who worked for the phone company to try and decode the dialing tones.

Usually the private investigator was armed. He carried a loaded .38-caliber Colt revolver in his combination-lock briefcase. When Nykaza had car problems, he solved them by torching the vehicle. In 1983, his Camaro was pushed to a secluded cul de sac, and a rag was placed in the gas tank and ignited. He walked home and with a can of spray paint scrawled, YOU'LL BE NEXT on his garage door. The car was reported stolen.

Sheila told Reed that she had become deathly afraid of her husband in the months since their separation. She claimed that Nykaza had constructed a dartboard in the basement with her picture on it. She was very worried that if he had killed Dianne, it would be easier for him the second time around to kill her. Every day, Sheila prayed that Nykaza would kill himself before he killed her.

Reed wanted to determine whether Ted Nykaza was the killer or the witness they had been searching for. At 2:33 A.M. on Sunday, February 22, 1987, Reed stopped by Nykaza's residence. Officially, his police report would say that he had just been driving by. What he had been told was that it was worthless for him to stop by in the afternoon or early evening, because Nykaza was nearly always still at work. Or still moderately sober. It was better to catch Nykaza in the early morning hours when he had been drinking.

Once again there was a buzz on the intercom and barking from the dog. Nykaza opened the door, but this time he was carrying a fully loaded chrome-plated Colt snub nose revolver in his right hand. He let Reed in and unloaded the revolver. He claimed that he had answered the door with the gun because he thought someone had come to kill him.

Nykaza was without wheels and asked the patrolman for a lift to a local liquor store, where he purchased a bottle of J & B Scotch. While en route, he asked if it was safe to talk in the car.

When they returned to Nykaza's home, it was evident that his wife had left him. The place was unkempt and reeked of dog urine. Dishes were piled in the sink.

Nykaza was on a drinking spree, and he skipped from subject to subject. And he was playing mind games with the detective.

The men first sat in the kitchen and and then moved to the family room, where there was a huge fireplace, a couch, two chairs, and a television set.

Nykaza began the histrionics. He pointed to Rusty, the Irish Setter who had once belonged to Dianne, laying nearby, and said that the dog would tell Reed what had happened the night Dianne was murdered. "Mommy came home one night all happy and got popped twice and never came home again," said Nykaza, speaking for his pet. "That dog is smarter than me. He knows enough not to talk about Al."

Nykaza then began a series of reenactments of his experiences as a Chicago cop. They were little dramas played out for the sergeant about his alleged shootings. "Halt, stop or I'll shoot," Nykaza shouted. He was crying and grabbed his left side above the belt. He told the detective that he relived the incidents by regularly viewing the morgue photos of the persons he shot. He prayed for forgiveness from the people he had killed.

Nykaza looked straight into Reed's eyes. "I shot one child in the forehead three times. I'll never forget how the child's eyes rolled back inside his head." That shooting supposedly had occurred during racial unrest on Chicago's west side after the assassination of Dr. Martin Luther King, Jr.

Nykaza recalled another time when his wounded suspect walked out of a darkened alley all bloody, holding his head and saying how badly it burned where he had been shot. Nykaza claimed to have cut another suspect in half with a shotgun.

Shortly after the theatrics ended, Reed went to work. What about the Dixmoor whorehouse? he wanted to know. Masters, Nykaza said, had wanted to run the profits through his detective agency. Nykaza told him it would be all right as long as someone paid the taxes, but Alan never mentioned another word about the idea.

Had Nykaza seen the reports on Dianne? He told Reed to ask Keating, Buckendahl, and Bachman about whether they knew who had provided Alan with the signed copies of the sheriff's department report. "See if Al asked for them or if they were just being provided as a courtesy," he suggested.

Nykaza turned to the detective and said bluntly, "Tell me what you know and I'll tell you what I know."

Reed did. He told him that they knew Alan Masters had requested Nykaza wiretap the phones. Nykaza had agreed and used a slow-speed, voice-activated tape recorder. The tapes had been destroyed.

"You've got a lot of it," Nykaza replied. "Why do you need me? You guys did your homework."

Reed asked whether there were any tapes left. Nykaza answered that all of the tapes had been destroyed.

Was a silencer used?

Nykaza claimed he never saw one.

"I'm not going to jail," he told the detective. "You said you were just interested in the murder . . . I'm through killing people, but I could kill Sheila."

Where did the murder occur?

"Dianne was hit on the driveway while Big Al stayed inside the house," Nykaza replied.

Pressed about how he knew that scenario, Nykaza responded, "That's newspaper stuff." Then he shouted for Reed to leave. "Talk to my outfit lawyer if you want any more. I've said too much already. Get out of my house if you don't have a warrant or something. Come back tomorrow after I get some sleep. You can search my house and I will even give you a key and you can come in anytime."

Nykaza proceeded to pass out. He slept for a few minutes on the floor of the family room and then suddenly awoke. He sat up and blurted out, "I know what you want. If I give it to you I could get killed. Corbitt is your guy. Corbitt told me."

He said that the two men had been attending a fund-raiser in 1983 or 1984 and Corbitt was mad at Alan. Corbitt told Nykaza that she was killed "over some shit."

Why was Dianne killed? was Reed's next question.

Nykaza couldn't remember what Corbitt had told him the motive was. "Hey, buddy," Nykaza said to Reed. "I'm half in the bag. I could be just making it up. I guess Alan wanted the kid very badly."

Suddenly Nykaza told Reed to forget everything he had just

said. "My big mouth just got me in trouble again. Just say I was half stiff and didn't know what I was saying." Nykaza feared Corbitt.

Nykaza, upset by his own indiscretions regarding Alan, blasted Reed. "You bastard. How can I face Alan tomorrow? After spilling my guts to you today, I'm in the middle. You bull-shitted me to get Corbitt. I can't testify. You will have to go another way. All you want to do is pick my brain; then it's good-bye Teddy. I've done it and now you're doing it to me. Buddy, if this was my case, I would put it together in a day."

There was more banter from Nykaza, but he was getting tired. He passed out again on the floor and Reed couldn't awaken him. An hour after his arrival, Jack Reed departed, locking the front door behind him.

He still didn't know if he had a witness, at least a reliable one. But at least now he was convinced that he wasn't dealing with a murderer.

John Reed and his wife Arlene were sound asleep when their telephone rang at 4:00 A.M. It was two weeks since Reed's middle-of-the-night interview with Nykaza.

Arlene was accustomed to phone calls at all hours. It was like this whenever her husband totally immersed himself in a case. And over their twenty-year marriage, she had become his sounding board, sharing theories and analyzing suspects. An elementary schoolteacher, she even helped type his reports. She knew the details of the Dianne Masters investigation as well as her husband did. And like Reed and Sabin, she was anxious to solve the case.

A patrol officer was calling to say that he had spotted Nykaza walking along the roadway toward his home. He was carrying a bottle in his hand and he looked suspicious, or at least that is what would be written in the police report. In actuality, Reed had sought out the deputy assigned to patrol the area near Nykaza's home.

Reed had told him that if he saw Nykaza, he should be aggressive and inquire what the private investigator was doing. When the deputy stopped and searched him, Nykaza was armed with his Colt revolver and a .38-caliber over and under, two-shot derringer that he carried in a zippered pocket in his jacket. Nykaza was walking home from the Masters house, he said.

Nykaza might be having legal difficulties, the deputy suggested. Did he have a permit to carry concealed weapons? Did he have a firearm identification card?

Reed drove to the scene where Nykaza had been picked up, ostensibly to help the beleaguered private detective. It was a classic example of good cop–bad cop. Reed waited while Nykaza showed his identification verifying that he could carry the two guns. Nykaza fell for the ploy. He asked if Reed would take him home, stopping at the store first to get some milk.

Reed agreed, and when they reached Nykaza's house, Reed was invited in. As they entered, making their way past the dog, Nykaza warned him not to talk, his house was "all wired." "I don't know nothing about any tapes," he told Reed without being asked, and then he winked.

They sat in the family room. The games began anew.

Nykaza told Reed that Alan had been letting him use one of his cars and that Nykaza had just dropped it off. He and a date had accompanied Alan and his new girlfriend, Jan Bower, and Illinois state trooper Chuck Yoways and his wife Arlane to a fancy restaurant for dinner.

Nykaza said he feared that Corbitt would kill him if he ever learned Nykaza had disclosed the former police chief's role in the murder. Corbitt would stuff him under his swimming pool cover and he would be found in the spring.

"I know what happened, but I can't tell you. Now or ever." Nykaza claimed that he had not been at the Masters' home when Dianne was killed, but he knew the details. He would write them down for the detective and give them to a friend for safe keeping in case Nykaza was killed.

"I play the best mind games. I'm the best cop around," he bragged to Reed. "For all I know, Alan paid you big bucks to come over and find out what I know and if I'm talking." Then he admitted that he had slipped and told Alan that Reed had been by his house two weeks before. Alan wanted to know what questions the police sergeant had asked.

Then Nykaza said to Reed, "I'm not talking anymore. Leave me alone. Let me get some sleep. One of your guys took eight of my silver bullets and I want them back. OK, Tonto. Just because I drink doesn't mean I lost all my marbles, pal. I might not be here the next time. I'm about ready to end it all . . . run to Canada. You got me in this mess. Coming over here talking shit. Alan is pissed that I talked to you. I know what you want, but you're asking too much. Alan loved Dianne and he's too soft-hearted to do it himself. Go away. If Al sees you here again, I'll get in more trouble. Don't fuck with it anymore. They will screw things up in time."

After Nykaza fell asleep on the couch in the family room, Jack Reed left and locked the front door.

Six weeks later, on April 14, 1987, Reed again called Nykaza at 11:45 P.M. to chat. Nykaza, who had just returned home from the grocery store, invited him over.

It looked as if it would be another night of Nykaza's mind games. He played loud music all during the interview and every half hour would get up and, for no reason, go into his file room. "You know Alan is not beyond paying you big bucks to come here and see what I would say about him. I don't trust you 100 percent yet," he said.

He added that a sheriff's police officer had warned him about Reed—that Reed was on Alan Masters' payroll and that Reed had attended parties at the Masters home and had been seen working around Alan's office.

But later he admitted to Reed that he was testing him to see his reaction.

The homicide detective stayed for hours, listening to Nykaza talk about himself and his life. His divorce case was coming up on May 1 and Nykaza hinted that after it was over, he might become even more cooperative.

After Dianne had disappeared, Alan called Nykaza to sweep his home for electronic eavesdropping devices. Nykaza told Alan that he had located a small transmitter in a curtain rod in the home. (For reasons that were never clear, he would later confess to having placed it there.) After the discovery, Alan went to Keating and asked whether the sheriff's department had installed the listening device in his house. Keating said they hadn't and suggested that perhaps Nykaza was working with the federal government. Since then, the relationship between Alan and the private detective had not been the same.

Then, with little prompting, Ted Nykaza provided Reed with some amazing details about the murder of Dianne Masters. Alan had heard the tape of the conversation between Jim and Dianne about the lovemaking involving the bottle of wine. "Al Masters went berserk when he listened to the recording," Nykaza told Reed. "That's it," Alan had said. "It's going to be a home invasion. Everything gets killed. The dogs, cats, Dianne. Every living thing will be dead and I'll be off somewhere with Anndra when it happens."

It seemed that Dianne was supposed to be killed two weeks before she actually disappeared. Alan had called Nykaza and others and told them to have an alibi for that night. During the next two weeks, Alan called him again—at least two or three times—telling him again to arrange an alibi for his whereabouts.

"This is a test for you not to give me up," Nykaza informed the startled Reed. "Come back in ten days to two weeks. I want to see how much of this gets back to Al from his pals," he told Reed as he was leaving.

This time Nykaza was fairly sober.

Two weeks later, Reed received a call from Sgt. Clarke Buckendahl. Nykaza had telephoned the department looking for Reed. It was a few minutes before 10 P.M. "Some guy named Nykaza called for you," Buckendahl told Reed. "You got the number, right?"

Nykaza's recently divorced wife was at the house moving some of her belongings in accordance with a court order. Nykaza wanted Reed present.

A few days later, Nykaza again asked the detective for help. He wanted Reed to give him a ride to pick up a truck he owned. As Reed drove, Nykaza made another astonishing revelation. He confided to Reed that he had not been alone when Alan had gone crazy after hearing the tape. There had been at least one other person present, Joe Hein, a Cook County sheriff's deputy.

On Thursday, March 19, 1987, the fifth anniversary of Dianne Masters' disappearance, Reed conducted a surveillance at St.

Adalbert Cemetery. The headstone at that location was engraved:

Wife–mom
Dianne G. Masters
1946–1982

He noted no unusual activity at the gravesite and the only noncemetery vehicle to come near the area and stop was driven by an elderly female. Reed also learned that every Christmas, a woman from Alan Masters' law office ordered two twenty-inch green fall and winter wreaths at a cost of $12 each. St. Adalbert's allows only one wreath per grave. Masters' employee told St. Adalbert's to keep the extra $12.

Chapter Twenty

March 12, 1987

REED and Sabin had been summoned to the U.S. Attorney's Office in the federal building in Chicago. Tom Scorza's federal grand jury investigation of Dianne's murder had been calling witnesses for nearly two years. The two FBI agents assigned to the case, Ivan Harris and Roger Griggs, had informed Scorza that two detectives from the sheriff's department were developing significant leads.

The federal agents had heard through the grapevine that the deputies had acquired a solid new clue. Reed and Sabin's reputation in the law enforcement community was excellent, top-notch. Perhaps the two men ought to be working with them instead of at cross-purposes.

Scorza had to be convinced. He and his fellow federal prosecutors found the sheriff's department's corruption so widespread, it was hard to believe that the agency employed any honest people. A number of deputies whom Scorza was calling to testify before the grand jury seemed to find truth elusive. They evoked their Fifth Amendment right against self-incrimination so often that he had become repulsed. If there was actually a Diogenes among them, it was news to Scorza.

But the information that Reed and Sabin had gleaned from their interviews with Nykaza, Scorza knew, was the key to an indictment. If the government could develop a conspiracy count relating to the murder of Dianne Masters, it would be a coup.

On March 12, 1987, Sabin and Reed walked into the fifteenth-floor office of Assistant U.S. Attorney David Stetler.

The office looked out over Chicago's lakefront and skyscrapers and provided one of the most breathtaking views of the city. The tall, blond-haired Stetler had been the prosecutor whom Keating had congratulated when Stetler convicted him. Now it was he who was handling the case of corruption in the sheriff's department. He, too, wanted to hear what the detectives had to say.

Scorza was more diminutive in stature, but he had a reputation as a feisty prosecutor. He was atypical of the lawyers who had joined the office, traveling a circuitous route to reach the job.

Scorza was an Italian from the Brooklyn borough of Bensonhurst, the fictional home of television's Ralph Cramdon and the real-life home of one of New York's famous mafia dons, Carlo Gambino. Until he was sixteen, he thought that when you grew up, you had to either be a barber, a dentist, or a bookmaker, the chief occupations of his neighbors, Sicilian Italians and conservative Jews. A rite of passage for boys in the community was the ability to discuss horse racing and sports scores with the men at the local luncheonette and newsstand.

Scorza attended a Catholic high school in Brooklyn called Xaverian. It was famous for its tough, brilliant brothers who opened the minds of their pupils to new vistas. He was one of the students whose life was affected deeply by his schooling.

The first in his family to graduate from college, he was accepted by Harvard Law School. But with a low draft number in the lottery, he expected to be called into military service to fight in the Vietnam War. He opted for graduate school at Claremont University in California. There he became Dr. Scorza after obtaining a degree in classical political philosophy and American government. Seven years and two university teaching jobs later, he realized that he was disenchanted with the meager salaries and politics of academe.

Having chosen the wrong profession, he returned to law school at the University of Chicago. In September 1983 he joined the U.S. Attorney's Office. Scorza's cohorts described him as a somewhat Machiavellian figure—cunning, attuned to the politics of the office, and willing to wage war to achieve victory.

Joining Scorza and Stetler in the meeting was FBI agent Ivan Harris, who looked like an aging power forward on a professional basketball team. On the desk in front of Scorza sat Sabin and Reed's reports on the case. There were more than two hundred pages representing literally dozens of people the two investigators had interviewed. The question of how the federal prosecutors and FBI had obtained them wasn't clear.

"You guys got a lot of it here," Scorza told the sheriff's policemen. "It needs some more work. This is what we are going to do."

To share any information on the probe could be disastrous to the federal investigation. Scorza and the two detectives knew that the department was a sieve. They knew that somehow, their reports were being read and their contents disseminated to members of the department who were targets of the probe or at risk of losing their jobs as a result of the investigation.

Bachman had called Reed just days earlier to inform him that there was a leak. Everything he had been telling Reed with regards to the investigation was being repeated back to him by Sgt. Clarke Buckendahl.

Reed traced the leak to a deputy in the state attorney's office downtown. The deputy had met with Buckendahl at a local pub and apparently passed on some of the details of the investigation.

To prevent such disclosures, Scorza proposed that Reed and Sabin be made agents of the grand jury. This was done infrequently but was not all that unusual. As agents of the grand jury, their reports would become secret and would protect them from being scrutinized by sheriff's department employees. Also the detectives could review the grand jury testimony of witnesses and follow leads.

Scorza would attend to the particulars and the two detectives would work for him. Sabin and Reed liked the idea and immediately began funneling their reports to Scorza.

But for reasons that remain unclear, the sheriff's department balked. Apparently, it wanted to keep reading Reed and Sabin's reports.

A month later, Scorza had another idea, one of the most

frequently used investigative techniques of federal agents. He asked if Reed and Sabin would be willing to share everything they learned with the bureau and the grand jury without being appraised of what the federal government had uncovered. The detectives agreed, as did the sheriff's department.

With the addition of Reed and Sabin, Scorza now had four veteran investigators assigned to the case. On the team, along with FBI agent Ivan Harris, was Roger Griggs, a slightly balding blond man, who was concentrating on the Corbitt investigation.

Harris had taken over the Dianne Masters investigation earlier that year, when agent David Parker, who had been working the case for almost four years, was reassigned. During Harris's ten-year career, he had seen lots of corruption of all types. He helped the bureau incarcerate some of the nation's most re-known underworld figures, including several of Chicago's top organized crime bosses, who were convicted of running a skimming operation that had stolen millions from casinos in Las Vegas.

As he reviewed the Masters file, he was amazed. Alan Masters was the center of a vast venal circle of friends that included police officers, judges, and lawyers. When he first read the reports, he knew that Alan was suspected of murdering Dianne, but by 1986, it did not appear that there were any new leads worth pursuing. "It looks kind of like a dry hole. It may never be solved," he said to himself at the time.

Months later, he decided to review some of the reports and transcripts of the four-year undercover investigation of Larry Damron (known to the underworld as Larry Wright). Harris knew that some of Damron's conversations with individuals like Corbitt had not been discovered until months after the agent's investigation ended. He wondered if additional conversations had been overlooked between other principals in the Masters case.

It was fairly difficult to locate the masses of material Damron had compiled, but Harris persevered. Damron had been working out of an FBI office in the northern suburbs and some of the records were there; others had been used in trials. Harris's efforts were rewarded. Reading through Damron's reports, he discovered that Damron had tape recorded telephone conversations with Alan Masters. This provided more evidence for the case.

Now he felt optimistic. There was a tape recording between an undercover agent and Alan. In reviewing those tapes and transcripts, he felt reassured that this was one more piece of the puzzle that could be used in a racketeering investigation.

Reed and Sabin provided another key to the conundrum—Ted Nykaza.

Nykaza's admissions that he had wiretapped the Masters' telephones and his story about Alan listening to the recording of Dianne and Jim discussing the use of the wine bottle in their lovemaking was so remarkable that the FBI agent was stunned. "My initial reaction was [that] it was almost unbelievable that this had occurred. Knowing just a little about Nykaza at the time, that he was an alcoholic, I tended not to believe that story when I initially heard it. Sure it would be easy for Ted to say that he did this and [that] Alan and he were the only ones privy to this conversation."

Harris needed proof that the conversation actually had occurred. When he discovered that Joe Hein had been present too, it added credibility to the whole story. Harris now thought the government had a chance to make its case.

Scorza, the assistant U.S. attorney, was enthralled with the new information supplied by the private investigator. He came to the conclusion that Nykaza was being honest about the details leading up to the killing of Dianne Masters when Nykaza insisted that Alan's original plan called for a home invasion in which Dianne, her dogs, and her cats would be killed. "The acorn from which the tree grew were the statements by Nykaza," Scorza would say later.

Despite Nykaza's character flaws, he was considered an important potential witness in the case. The federal prosecutor never really viewed him as a suspect. He had no evidence against him. And the more he talked to Nykaza and the more information he got from him—and other individuals—it seemed that Nykaza wasn't capable of committing such a crime. In Scorza's mind, he was the one person who gave him hope that a case could be made.

* * *

Tom Scorza was not the only assistant U.S. attorney trying to indict Alan Masters. Down the hall from Scorza's office, Sheldon Zenner was immersed in Operation Greylord, a massive federal investigation of corruption in the courts. And Alan Masters was one of his targets.

Using undercover agents placed in the court system, federal agents over the years had infiltrated a good-old-boy network of bribery and corruption. Most of the corruption that was uncovered was in traffic and misdemeanor courts, where the reigning judges had been appointed by the politicians. Here justice was sold cheaply. A lawyer could get a case fixed with a $50 handshake to a judge's baliff, a courtroom aide, or a venal prosecutor willing to fix the case. Alan's handshakes had become notorious.

When Operation Greylord ended, more than eighty judges, lawyers, sheriff's deputies, and court personnel had been convicted of various bribery schemes and income tax fraud charges. Only two judges had been acquitted. Among those caught in the snare of federal prosecutors was Alan's former law partner, Arthur Zimmerman. He was convicted of income tax evasion two years after being acquitted in state court of charges of paying a $7,000 bribe to a Cook County Circuit Court judge on behalf of a client accused of rape.

Alan became a focus of Operation Greylord in 1985, when the federal probe expanded into the twenty-four courtrooms in the Fifth District, located in Bridgeview, where Alan practiced most frequently.

The investigation in the suburban courts had begun with one of Alan's former De Paul Law School classmates, attorney Joseph E. McDermott. McDermott had been one of traffic court's miracle workers, a group of lawyers with an astonishingly successful rate of acquittals among their clients. Actually, the lawyers had been part of a bribery club.

In November 1986, while McDermott was under investigation by the grand jury, the voters of Cook County elected him a judge. McDermott previously had been identified during federal trials as one of the attorneys who paid a judge a number of $100 bribes to fix drunk driving cases, and for seven years, he had delivered $2,000 Christmas presents to the magistrate.

At the time of his election, McDermott had been granted immunity from prosecution in the ongoing grand jury investigation of corruption. But he had declined to testify and was facing a prison term of up to eighteen months for his refusal. Later he was jailed for contempt, resigned his judicial post before he was sworn in, then agreed to cooperate in the federal investigation.

McDermott's cooperation led prosecutors straight to a labyrinth of corruption in the Fifth District. McDermott told federal investigators that he had paid off five different judges in the district on various drunk driving and other minor criminal cases. Among the judges McDermott named was Roger Seaman.

Seaman, once described as one of the meanest jurists who ran a courtroom, agreed to cooperate. Seaman told federal prosecutors that most of the payoffs he received came from lawyers, who were thanking him for steering defendants lacking representation their way.

Alan Masters didn't need any such referrals, he told the federal agents, but according to Seaman, Alan knew how to reward his friends for favorable dispositions. Alan would put the money inside the coat pocket of Seaman's jacket, which hung in his chambers. He estimated that he had received from $50 to $200 on about twenty occasions from Alan.

The prosecutors also had netted a former assistant Cook County state attorney who was now willing to testify. Carey Polikoff was a University of Chicago Law School graduate who matriculated with former U.S. Supreme Court nominee Douglas Ginsburg. Federal prosecutors described Polikoff as a nice Jewish boy who looked like a tax accountant and whose father was a judge. And he paid everything that moved, authorities noted.

Before going into private practice, Polikoff was a corrupt prosecutor who started out in Chicago's downtown traffic court and later was assigned to the Fifth District.

He was there less than a week when Alan Masters came up

to him after a pretrial conference and asked if he could say thank you.

"Certainly," replied Polikoff.

He then received a $50 thank you from Alan. Thereafter, he took Polikoff under his wing and asked if he could show him around. Alan wanted to introduce him to trustworthy people.

Through Alan, Polikoff met a succession of defense attorneys working in the Fifth District, all of whom would gladly pay Polikoff to help their clients resolve their legal problems. Alan paid Polikoff on at least twenty occasions.

Based on what the federal prosecutors had learned, they went to retired judge Francis Maher, the father-in-law of a high-ranking Cook County politician. Maher was one of the judges who visited the Masters' home frequently, and he had attended Dianne's funeral.

Federal prosecutors drafted an indictment. Polikoff's accusations were well beyond the statute of limitations. To charge Alan, they needed Maher to testify.

Rather than cooperate, Maher decided to go on trial. He subsequently was acquitted of accepting payoffs from the attorneys—only the second judge to be exonerated in the history of Greylord.

With Maher's refusal to cooperate, Sheldon Zenner tried another tact. He subpoenaed a lawyer working in Alan's office, Diane Economou, to appear before the grand jury. "I was turning over every rock I could think of and I thought maybe she would have something on Masters," he would say later.

After Economou received the subpoena, she hired an attorney, who called Zenner to ask if the prosecutor would be willing to interview his client in his office rather than drag her before the grand jury. Zenner agreed and made an appointment to see Economou.

When she arrived, she appeared outwardly to be composed. A massive woman with jet-black hair and a powerful voice, her career path had taken her from De Paul Law School to the tax department of Arthur Anderson and Company in Chicago. Economou then joined the juvenile division of the Cook County State Attorney's Office and soon was appointed to the rape task force. Later she received one of the toughest, most brutal assignments in the country—the homicide sex courtroom.

In her five-year stint as a prosecutor, she had seen virtually every type of atrocity. It was the kind of legal work that could burn out the best. In 1978, Alan Masters offered her a lucrative job as an attorney in his Summit office. Having seen enough violence for a lifetime, it was a great opportunity.

Her session with the tall, handsome Zenner, who looked like he would be just as comfortable in a corporate boardroom as he was in a courtroom, lasted four or five hours. He fired question after question about Alan's relationship to judges and lawyers suspected of corruption. Economou told Zenner that she had no knowledge of any corrupt activities regarding Alan or others.

Zenner knew that Scorza was conducting an investigation into the murder of Dianne Masters. On a long shot, he decided that with Economou sitting in his office, he would question her briefly about Dianne's disappearance. His queries were of the softball variety, nothing accusatory.

When he asked the first question, Economou's demeanor changed noticeably. She began acting skittish, frightened. Her attorney asked for a brief recess and they disappeared into the hall.

After they returned to Zenner's office, Economou's attorney told Zenner that although Economou was reluctant, she had something important to tell him.

In the next few minutes, Diane Economou told Zenner that she had been in the back room of the law office one day talking with Ted Nykaza. She and Nykaza were discussing how Alan was having someone tail Dianne and how Alan would learn eventually that Dianne was having an affair with Jim Koscielniak.

As they were talking, Alan came storming into the room. He was angry as hell. He had been meeting with Jim Keating and had apparently just learned about Dianne's infidelity. "That's it. I've had it. I'm going to have her killed," Economou quoted Alan as saying.

Zenner was a veteran prosecutor. He had tried numerous

federal cases, interrogated more than his share of witnesses, and had heard several confessions. He watched as Economou began to erupt emotionally. Her secret finally had boiled to the surface. With each word she uttered, tears streamed from her eyes. She had lost any semblance of self-control. Nearly hysterical, she couldn't stop crying. Zenner handed her a box of Kleenex tissues.

Then he went down the hall to fetch Scorza. In the course of just a few minutes, Economou had given one of the most incriminating statements yet against Alan Masters.

CHAPTER TWENTY-ONE

May 15, 1987

WHEN Jack Reed was a rookie in the Cook County Sheriff's Department, one of his first partners had been Joe Hein. The two men had followed divergent paths in the agency, but during those months they had ridden together in the south suburbs, they had an innocent kind of fun. There had been those times when they were cruising on patrol and had gotten so engrossed in their conversation about their new life that they had actually driven out of state.

"Hey Joe, there's a lot of Indiana plates all of a sudden," Reed would tell his partner.

"Yeah. I think we're out of Cook County," Hein would laughingly reply.

Hein took the department's political route. He got to know those who could help him. Alan had done legal work for Hein, handling a worker's compensation case and some matters involving Hein's divorce. The sheriff's deputy was also a good friend of Mike Corbitt and had stood up at his second marriage.

Since Dianne's murder, he had been working for the Cook County State's Attorney's Office. It was one of those jobs that isn't very demanding and offers regular hours. The friendships forged there are what matters. Now Hein was a sergeant in charge of protecting the Cook County state attorney, whose father, Richard J. Daley, had been Chicago's most legendary and politically powerful mayor. His son, Richard M. Daley, wanted to follow in his father's footsteps.

Reed had heard through the department grapevine that when

Dianne was killed, Hein had acted strangely. He had lost a lot of weight. And he was nervous, especially any time someone mentioned the Masters case.

Reed was asking his former partner to draw the line at murder. He found Hein on May 15, 1987, at 1:24 A.M. They were standing in the parking lot at a White Castle hamburger stand on Chicago's southwest side.

The man was scared; pacing back and forth as Reed questioned him. He was sure that government agents were sitting in a nearby van recording the meeting between the men.

He swore then that he had never been told to have an alibi by Alan, who he admitted was a close friend. In March 1982, he had obtained a loan from the police union and flown to Ireland, taking his mother and father with him. "How's that going to sound? The guy who never takes a vacation and he's off in Ireland when Dianne disappears," he asked Reed.

It was obvious that Hein thought the federal government had either been wiretapping some of his telephone conversations or that somehow they had obtained a tape recording of him mentioning to someone that he had overheard the tape between Dianne and Jim. There had been talk that Ted may have secretly recorded Alan playing the tape using a small, voice-activated tape recorder that he sometimes carried.

"Do they have me on tape?" he asked Reed that night. "Maybe I walked out of the room when they were planning it. Would the tape show that? Keating or Nykaza had to testify or both, right?" Hein inquired. "If people say I was there, I'm not going to call them liars; I just don't remember.

"I'm not going to lie to you. I really don't know if I was present when plans were discussed. Maybe I was around or maybe I stepped out of the room."

He gazed at the van suspecting that men inside were taping the conversation. Then he complained to Reed that he had probably already said something he shouldn't have. "If I go in before the grand jury and say I wasn't there and they play a tape with my voice on it, I'm screwed. What should I do?" he asked Reed. "I would never lie to the grand jury. I believe in the oath."

Joe Hein knew that his police career was doomed. He admitted as much that night in the parking lot to Reed. "I'm finished. This is the end."

Within weeks, FBI agent Harris and Scorza began talking with Hein. He hired one of the best criminal defense attorneys in Chicago, William Kunkle.

Kunkle told Scorza his client would be willing to make a proffer, a statement to authorities that outlines what an individual knows and what he can offer prosecutors in return for a deal.

Hein and his attorney were summoned to Scorza's office in the federal building to make the statement. It was an agitated and frightened Hein that Scorza and Harris confronted.

Hein told the investigators that he was, indeed, in the room when Nykaza had played the telephone conversation between Dianne and Jim Koscielniak. He verified what the private detective had told authorities. Up to a point. But then he declared that Alan had made no boast that he would have Dianne killed for her indiscretion. Subsequently Hein failed a polygraph on that question.

"Hein claimed Alan was very calm; noncommittal about the tape, which I found very hard to believe," Harris would say later.

As Kunkle listened, Harris and Scorza interrogated Hein for several hours about the tape recording and the circumstances of how he came to be at Alan's house that day.

"We went over what we had been told," Harris said. "I recall very clearly that on a couple of occasions, Joe was going to come clean and tell us a little more about when he was listening to that tape with Alan. Maybe something else we didn't know. I recall just having a feeling that Joe was going to do the right thing."

As the session dragged on, there were breaks in the intense and emotional conversation. Those recesses gave Hein time to convene with Kunkle and collect his wits. Each time, Scorza and Harris were hoping that Hein would come back into the room and be candid with them. Willing to tell more of the secrets they believed he was hiding.

"The bottom line is he didn't say anything more than that he was present with Alan and Ted when the tape was played.

While that was significant by itself, I thought Joe was going to tell us more,'' Harris said.

When Hein next saw Reed, he was a broken man. With tears streaming down his face, he told his ex-partner that his police career was over.

Jack Reed once describe himself as a Dunkin' Donuts kind of guy. Which aptly applies both to his waistline and one of his favorite places for meeting confidential informants. The night after Reed had interviewed Hein, he met Bachman for lunch at the Dunkin' Donuts in Forest Park.

Bachman was worried about his future with the department, he told Reed during their brief lunch. What would happen to a guy, he asked rhetorically, who knew details of a murder and did not come forward until now?

From the beginning, Reed had promised that he was only interested in the murder. But there were other forces at work of which Reed was unaware. Bachman was the target of a federal grand jury. He had been fingered as a crooked cop by Bruce Frasch, the former sergeant in the vice unit under Keating, and Bachman's former boss. After serving just several months in one of the worst federal penitentiaries, Frasch was ready to talk. Federal prosecutors were shocked that he was agreeing to cooperate with the government's investigation of the sheriff's department. Gossip columnists were reporting that both Keating and Frasch were being hauled before a federal grand jury.

Over the next few months, Reed met with Bachman more than a dozen times. Their favorite spot was the Dunkin' Donuts on Chicago's north side and it was here that Harris was introduced to Reed's most confidential informant.

At the meeting, Harris mentioned to Bachman that he had just returned from Atlanta where he had been assigned to a federal prison in the aftermath of a major riot. The uprising had been caused by Cuban prisoners who had been sent over on boats to the United States by Fidel Castro.

Harris was trying to be chatty. And he made an offhand remark about how horrible it would be to have to go to prison.

For some reason, Bachman thought Harris was sending a message to him that unless he started to cooperate completely, Bachman would spend time behind bars.

Although that wasn't the case, the remark had shocked Bachman. Suddenly he began having second thoughts about helping Reed. He became reluctant to share any information with Reed about Dianne's murder, especially about his friendship with Keating and others.

Months later, the U.S. Attorney's Office began its squeeze play on Bachman. He called Reed and told him an FBI agent, not Harris, had asked for a meeting. The agent had wanted to talk with Bachman about his knowledge of corruption in one of the suburban courts. Bachman wanted to know why he was being whipsawed by Reed and the FBI.

Frasch had confirmed what authorities had always suspected. For years, he, Keating, Bachman, and other deputies had been shaking down the very people they were supposed to arrest: car thieves, gamblers, and pimps. Some authorities characterized the group of deputies as operating in much the same way as an organized crime street crew handled the business for mob figures—extorting protection payments from individuals.

"They were a group of people that were running roughshod over a lot of criminal enterprises where they could take advantage of the people who were involved in some criminal activity," Harris noted.

Bachman was no angel among such thieves as would later become evident in court. But his cooperation was essential in the Masters case.

"Jack Bachman was the key to unlocking the Alan Masters case," said David Stetler, the former assistant U.S. attorney who negotiated the government's deal with Bachman. "When he cut his deal, then we knew that we were real close to being there. It was the whole key to the Alan Masters case."

Bachman made his decision to fully cooperate and testify against his friends and associates. Some believed he might never have cooperated had Jim Keating not made a miscalculation. Keating had been at a bar celebrating the birthday of one of the women bartenders from the Holiday Inn. He had pulled

Bachman aside. He asked if one of Bachman's closest friends on the force could cause him a problem with the federal government.

"Maybe," Bachman replied.

Keating formed his right hand into the shape of a gun with his thumb extended as the trigger. "Should we get someone to pop him?" Keating asked, snapping his thumb down as if firing a weapon.

Bachman was agreeing to tell all. He admitted not only to being a bagman for Alan, Frasch, and Keating, but had also been solicited by Keating to murder Dianne. And he was willing to go on the stand and testify about it.

Scorza maintained that it was Bachman's guilty conscience that caused his conversion to informant. Bachman was a person who could accept taking payoffs from the scum who ran strip joints and whorehouses, but there was a fine line crossed in the Masters case. "I think he was shocked about how far it went," said Scorza. "I read him as a guy who had made a choice. He could fight us and end up like Keating, or make a deal and get it behind him." He opted for the latter.

Bachman had pleaded guilty to income tax evasion and racketeering charges, but sentencing would be delayed until after he testified in two trials. His first test as a government witness came in the federal trial of a south suburban attorney, Frederick Aprati, Jr.

Bachman took the stand and told a hushed courtroom how, in August 1982, he was paid a $1,000 bribe by Aprati after a prostitution case he testified in was dismissed. Aprati was representing Jerry Cooley, the manager of Plato's Palace South, a brothel in the far south suburbs. Frasch and his vice unit had raided Plato's and charged Cooley on prostitution-related charges.

Bachman described how, after his testimony helped to acquit Aprati's client, the lawyer followed him into a bathroom at the courthouse and stuffed an envelope into his pocket. When Bachman opened the envelope later in his squad car, he found ten $100 bills inside, he said.

Under cross-examination, Aprati's attorney asked if Bachman had ever taken bribes before 1982.

His reply shocked the spectators. He told the court that for eleven years, starting in 1970, he had been the bagman for his supervisors, Lt. James Keating and Sgt. Bruce Frasch. Bachman would pick up the money from the law offices of Alan Masters, the middle man in the transaction, and deliver it to Frasch and Keating to be split. The bribes were monthly payments from five bookmaking operations in west suburban Cicero.

With Bachman as a key witness, Fred Aprati was convicted in federal court of racketeering and tax fraud charges, which included paying bribes to sheriff's police and providing prostitutes for assistant state attorneys during a party he held at a brothel.

When Reed and Sabin had first interviewed Lt. Howard Vanick, he admitted that over the years he, too, had developed a personal relationship with Alan Masters. Vanick had never disclosed his relationship to Alan during the initial investigation which he headed. When Vanick had filed for divorce in 1981, Alan had represented Vanick for free. The couple had reconciled, but divorced two years later. Vanick didn't hire Alan then, but used another attorney well known for his handshakes, Frederick Aprati, Jr.

Reed had been bothered that two Orland Park police officers were unjustly accused of spotting Dianne and Jim on February 16, 1982, kissing at a local restaurant and reporting it to Alan. Reed had heard that it had actually been Vanick who had seen the lovers. He had a note that indicated that Vanick himself had called Keating and tipped him to the tryst between Dianne and Jim.

Reed confronted Vanick at a country club about the allegations that it was Vanick, not the two Orland Park cops, who had seen Dianne.

Vanick recalled that he and investigator Ron Bennett were entering the Charlie Horse Restaurant in Orland Park for lunch to visit Vanick's girlfriend who worked there, when they saw Dianne leaving with a young man. Vanick told Reed that Dianne was arm-in-arm and quite chummy with her apparent boyfriend. "What a cunt," he thought to himself at the time for cheating on Alan. Vanick wouldn't admit to Reed whether he copied the license plate on Jim Koscielniak's car, but he vehemently denied trying to find out if the car's owner had a criminal record.

Vanick told Reed that he recalled that back in 1982 many of Alan's police pals were snickering about the big-time divorce lawyer having a wife who was cheating on him. He claimed that he did not hide the fact that he had seen Dianne with her paramour.

He offered to take a lie detector test to prove that he had never called Alan to tell the attorney about Dianne's rendezvous with her boyfriend.

Vanick insisted that Reed contact Bennett in order to verify his account of the incident. The lieutenant telephoned Bennett and asked him to come to the country club to speak to Reed.

It was Vanick who began the conversation when Bennett arrived. "John here has some allegations that we followed Dianne Masters, which, of course, is not true!" Vanick told Bennett. Reed, at this point, had never said anything to Vanick about following Dianne.

Reed asked Vanick to leave so that he could interview Bennett alone. Vanick made a fuss but finally agreed.

Bennett said that when they were entering the restaurant, they had spotted the two lovers and that Vanick had called Keating to advise him that Dianne was with Jim Koscielniak. Bennett said he did not know who had copied the license plate.

A few minutes later, Vanick returned. "Well, what was said?" he demanded. Reed told Bennett he was free to tell Vanick what he had said. Bennett repeated his story and when he got to the point where Vanick had called Keating, Vanick exploded.

"Come on partner," Vanick told Bennett. "That's not what happened."

"Well, you called somebody," Bennett replied.

Vanick demanded that Reed show him the evidence that had indicated Vanick had called Alan about Dianne and Jim's lunch. He followed Reed from the country club to his home a few miles away. When Reed walked into his tri-level, Vanick was screaming and yelling. He was angry. The shouts woke Reed's wife, Arlene.

For weeks, there had been threatening phone calls and Reed had made sure that when he was out of the house she had a weapon. She quickly slipped the .38-caliber revolver that was underneath her pillow into the pocket of a nearby robe and walked down the hallway from the bedroom, down the small flight of stairs, into the living room. Thinking Vanick was attacking her husband, she was ready to shoot. Only Reed's intervention prevented her from actually pulling the trigger.

Vanick saw the evidence. "That did not happen that way," Vanick pleaded. "I'm going to the FBI and tell them what happened to save my reputation," he told Reed.

The next night, Vanick called Reed at home at 9:37 P.M. Vanick admitted that he had run a check on Koscielniak's license plate to learn the identity of Dianne's boyfriend. He had thought to himself at the time: "What a shame; we all have our problems."

He had never made any official report of his observations either when Dianne disappeared or when her body was recovered. And when the two Orland Park policemen were implicated as the ones who had spotted Dianne and Jim, he had never stepped forward to acknowledge the mistake in identity.

Vanick told Reed that he had believed that a high-ranking sheriff's official had taken the Dianne Masters file and sanitized it, purging it of interviews and leads that would incriminate Alan.

Vanick ultimately expressed his disdain for Reed. He felt Reed was trying to ruin his reputation.

A few weeks later, Reed met Bachman at the Dunkin' Donuts in Melrose Park. Bachman said that a few weeks before Dianne had disappeared, Vanick had called him and related that he had bumped into Dianne and Jim. Vanick gave Bachman the license plate information on Jim's car.

Vanick had said to Bachman, "Give this to Al. Maybe this will help me with Al. I am going through a divorce myself."

Vanick told Bachman that he had followed Dianne from the

restaurant. She had headed north from there and gone to her home.

Bachman informed Reed that later in the month, Vanick called again and told Bachman to remind Al that it was Vanick who had copied down the license plate for him.

Bachman said he had passed the information on to Jim Keating. It was Keating who ultimately told Alan that his wife was out with another man, Bachman said.

Weeks later, Vanick called Reed at home again. It was 11:30 P.M. on a Sunday night. Vanick said two fellow deputies had approached him and inquired whether he had a problem with the federal grand jury. Vanick demanded that Reed somehow stop the departmental gossip that was occurring.

At the end of the conversation, Vanick issued a warning. Reed, who was viewed as a Serpico by many in the sheriff's department, might find himself in trouble in the future when he needed the help of his fellow officers.

CHAPTER TWENTY-TWO

May 20, 1987

MIKE Corbitt sat in a Chicago restaurant sipping his second cup of coffee. Across the table were two FBI agents. They talked; Corbitt just listened.

It was a balmy spring day in Chicago, which is when the city is at its best, before the summer's humidity makes walking the streets unbearable. It was late afternoon and Corbitt had driven during rush hour to meet the agents. He felt angry and perhaps even a little scared.

Earlier that day, Tom Scorza had indicted Corbitt on federal charges. He was accused of racketeering and trying to extort payoffs from undercover FBI agent Larry Damron. Corbitt also was accused of conspiracy in connection with the firebombing of a Willow Springs tavern owned by Raymond Gluszek. Gluszek contended that Corbitt took $7,000 worth of pinball machines in return for Corbitt's cooperation in quashing the ensuing arson investigation. The indictment also charged that he had sold Willow Springs police badges, extorted $6,500 in fees and discounted carpeting from a south suburban merchant, and extorted two handguns from a businessman.

Corbitt had gone to court that afternoon, pleaded innocent, and been released on bond. A sympathetic federal judge had allowed him to retain his handgun because of minor threats against him, despite the objections of prosecutors. Since his firing as Willow Springs' police chief, Corbitt had obtained a ghost payroll job as an investigator for the clerk of the Cook County Circuit Court. It was a payback for his efforts on behalf of the clerk who had become a political boss in the south suburbs. The title gave him a badge and, more important, the right to carry a concealed weapon.

After the court appearance, Corbitt walked over to the nearby office of James Marcus, his attorney, and they chatted briefly about trial strategy. Then Corbitt left to face the drive home to Willow Springs. He was barely out of the Loop when his car phone rang.

It was Marcus. His attorney had received an urgent telephone call from Scorza. The prosecutor wanted Corbitt to meet immediately with the FBI agents. Scorza wouldn't say exactly why, but it was urgent.

The two agents were from a south suburban office, and they arranged to meet Corbitt at the restaurant because it was equidistant from their office and downtown.

The investigators had more bad news for Corbitt. Federal authorities had overheard a conversation during a wiretap that organized crime figures had put out a contract to kill the former police chief. Authorities suspected that the mob was nervous that Corbitt wouldn't keep his mouth shut. He might consider cooperating with the government rather than go to prison. The two agents then made Corbitt an offer: tell them what he knew about organized crime and the Masters case, and they would place him in the federal Witness Protection Program.

Corbitt pondered the proposal. He would have a new identity and his family would be protected. But he was a man of affluence. He had cars, boats, and vast real estate holdings. How would he adjust to an austere life? For Corbitt, the deal was not sweet enough. He left the two agents, went home, packed his bag, and kissed his wife and son, Joey, good-bye. Until his trial, he lived in an apartment under an alias.

Joey was his pride and joy. The small boy suffered from Down's syndrome. Although he was only mildly affected by the disability, it had caused other health problems for the youth. While in hiding, Corbitt visited or talked to Joey daily, but he always took extreme precautions so that his family's safety would not be jeopardized.

As the trial date approached, Corbitt came up with an alibi.

He maintained that he had not met with Larry Damron on May 27, 1982, as the government had charged. He even produced a rental car receipt to substantiate that he was in Ft. Lauderdale, Florida, on the day in question. Corbitt contended that he had been in Florida from May 27 through June 4, 1982, handling some business in conjunction with the estate of his friend, Joe Testa. If this was true, all of the charges against Corbitt would have to be dismissed.

But the day the trial was to begin, Scorza told Judge Prentice Marshall that the government would prove that the rental car receipt was a forgery—and a bad one at that. According to village payroll records, Corbitt's time cards for the day indicated that he had gone to work at 9:34 A.M. and put in an extraordinarily long day, ending at 1:05 the following morning. "Unless he owns a Concorde, he wasn't in Florida," Scorza told the judge.

Further, Scorza noted that Corbitt's credit card records showed that he had checked into a hotel on Christmas Day, 1981, and flown home on January 4. He argued that the rental car receipt simply had been doctored by writing in a "6" so that it appeared Corbitt had returned the car on June 4, 1982, instead of January 4, 1982. The car rate on the receipt also indicated that he had paid the Christmastime rate.

The evidence impressed Judge Marshall. He told Corbitt that he "would have a real uphill battle to get this document introduced into evidence. It is evident to the untrained eye that the date has been written over."

Corbitt's attorney asked for a recess, and a few hours later, Corbitt pleaded guilty to the charges. Scorza argued that Corbitt was a flight risk, and Marshall ordered Corbitt jailed pending sentencing.

Corbitt's attorneys sought his release from jail prior to his sentencing. At one of the hearings, Corbitt was linked publicly to the Dianne Masters investigation for the first time. Scorza said that Corbitt was a target of a federal investigation involving a 1982 murder. "There is an active investigation arising out of the murder of Dianne Masters," Scorza told the judge.

He urged Marshall not to release Corbitt on bond. And he

revealed that in the month before his trial, the former police chief had purchased a $300,000 oceangoing yacht, which Scorza said indicated that Corbitt was preparing to flee.

Corbitt had also recently purchased a $35,000 Corvette, which was spotted by DEA agents conducting surveillance on a Florida restaurant where drug deals were being made.

His attorneys contended that Corbitt was not a flight risk. They noted his four-year-old son's disability. Since his birth, Corbitt had been trying to build a loving home for the child, Marcus said. Corbitt wanted to put his house up for bond, arguing that he would never disappear and risk his son's being without a home.

Scorza viewed the introduction of Corbitt's disabled child into the proceedings as despicable, and he taunted Corbitt. "Why wasn't Mr. Corbitt thinking of his boy when he put $35,000 into a Corvette Stingray?" he asked. Scorza's remark started a bitter battle between the two men that would last for years, for Corbitt, elevating the prosecutorial fight beyond the courtroom.

Judge Marshall was not swayed by the arguments of Corbitt's attorneys. He called the former police chief an unstable member of society and expressed disbelief that Corbitt, facing a certain jail sentence if convicted, would go out and buy a sports car and a boat in the weeks before the trial. "These are not the transactions of a man who plans to suck in his gut, do his time, and return to his wife," the judge said.

In the next few weeks, there were frequent court hearings for Corbitt, who suddenly had second thoughts and denied some of the government's charges. Specifically he contended that he had not sanctioned the arson for Gluszek and never had received any pinball machines. But later, he conceded those charges and admitted seeking approval for Damron's operation from two known organized crime street bosses and the Cook County Sheriff's Department vice unit.

When Corbitt came before Marshall for sentencing, the judge was sympathetic. Marshall, unaware that Damron's meeting with the police chief had not been reported to federal prosecutors for four years, chided Scorza for waiting so long to indict Corbitt, noting that the case against him had been made in

1982. "A delay in prosecution always troubles me," Marshall said.

He mentioned that Corbitt was a first-time offender and the father of a disabled boy. And Marshall took special notice of the deluge of letters he received on behalf of the former police chief. "Not just ordinary folk, but elected public officials, appointed public officials" were vouching for Corbitt.

There were forty letters, including those from ten public officials, two priests, schoolteachers, and his family. Marshall was astonished at this reaction, saying later, "I would have to struggle to remember a time when a public official, in the role of the office they hold, has written a letter on behalf of a person convicted of a crime."

Corbitt, dressed in a blue prison jumpsuit, cried openly and requested leniency. "I don't have any excuse for what I've done. When I took over as police chief in 1972, there were three policemen, a rundown shack for a police station, and 4,000 people in Willow Springs. I didn't have the best of guides. I should have been a leader, not a follower. I want to apologize to the court, my family, my children, my mother, my community, to the government. I am very sorry, Your Honor."

Scorza refuted Corbitt's image as a community leader. "He was a prostitute wearing a badge," he told the judge. Scorza characterized Corbitt's reign as police chief as a riot of corruption and noted that Corbitt's crimes were enough "to take your breath away." He said that Corbitt, despite his background in law enforcement, had refused to cooperate with ongoing investigations, and he asked that Corbitt receive a lengthy jail term.

Marshall sentenced Corbitt to only four years in prison. He would be eligible for parole in just sixteen months.

Scorza, however, vowed that Corbitt would not be freed.

CHAPTER TWENTY-THREE

October 19, 1987

JACK Reed pulled the unmarked county squad car into the parking lot of a local forest preserve. The sporty off-white 1983 Malibu had a distinctive-style wheel, which usually attracted glances from passersby, but no one imagined that its occupants were police officers.

It was just a little before 1 P.M. on Monday, October 19, 1987, when Reed and his partner, Bob Colby, arrived. There were just one or two other cars there, workers from nearby offices who had come to eat their lunches amid the peaceful setting. On weekends, the place might have been filled with picnickers, lovers, and other outdoor enthusiasts flocking to watch the change of seasons. The colors on the maple and oak trees were at their peak, a brilliant blaze of red-and-orange foliage.

Since September, Bob Colby had been assigned to work with Reed on the Masters investigation. Paul Sabin had left the department to practice law and was now a prosecutor with the Cook County State Attorney's Office.

If there were spectators, it didn't matter. Reed and Colby got out of the car and walked to the rear. Donning surgical gloves, the two plainclothes detectives pulled two green plastic trash bags out of the trunk. Reed and Colby had just completed a raid on the four fifty-five-gallon garbage cans in the alley behind Alan Masters' law office. A tipster had advised that Alan had been housecleaning on the weekend, discarding odds and ends that he had accumulated over the years.

They had checked with Scorza to see whether they needed a search warrant to seize the rubbish and rummage through it, but he said that previous court rulings made it unnecessary. Several months later, a U.S. Supreme Court would uphold such practices.

Alan was tossing not just old correspondence and records, but a conglomeration of ephemera—messages, notes, newspaper articles, business cards from dozens of police officers, including Reed and Sabin, and scraps of paper he had saved.

The deputies sifted through the contents of each bag, looking for clues. Among the clippings was a story about then U.S. attorney Anton R. Valukas and his father, Cook County Circuit Court judge Anton J. Valukas, who had been honored by a Lithuanian organization in Chicago. On a sheet of paper decorated with an antique stove in the top left corner and stamped with the heading "From the kitchen of Dianne Masters" was a name and address in Alan's handwriting. Another scrap contained Jim Keating's new address, the federal prison in Seagoville, Texas, where he had been sent following his conviction in Operation Safebet. Reed and Colby also found a copy of the penitentiary's rules for visiting inmates and a map detailing how to get there.

There was a note from Alan to someone named Emil urging him to hire his friend, Jack Bachman, who cleaned rugs and paved lots. He also pointed out that Bachman was competent and cooperative. Among Alan's telephone messages were ones to call U.S. Congressman William Lipinski and to phone Judge Thomas Walsh at home. In Dianne's handwriting, there was a page listing the names of two books on domestic violence: *Scream Quietly or the Neighbors Will Hear* and *Conjugal Crime: Understanding and Changing the Wife Beating Pattern.*

The informant had been true to his word. The detritus was a gold mine. The most interesting find was a bar napkin imprinted with the phrase "I've got rhythm," which started across the top and danced down the right side of the square. On it Jim Keating had written a reference for Larry Wright indicating that Wright wanted to purchase a bar in the Summit-McCook vicinity. He also had written his telephone number in Michigan at the top. Keating had given the napkin to Alan after meeting with Larry Damron, the undercover FBI agent posing as Larry Wright, at the Holiday Inn in 1982. Coincidentally, on a crumpled piece of paper from one of Alan's office memo pads, Alan had written "Larry Wright" and his phone number at his Palatine office.

The detectives were thrilled with their finds. It wasn't the first time Reed had gone through garbage in the Masters investigation. He had dug through Nykaza's refuse on several occasions in the event that the private eye might discard a tape or other evidence. Instead he had learned that Nykaza was an epileptic by finding prescriptions that were used to control his seizures.

The two detectives logged in the evidence and drove the bags down to the federal building where they turned it over to Assistant U.S. Attorney Scorza. Because Reed was not privy to the grand jury testimony, he was not aware of the significance of the bar napkin. But for Scorza, Keating's note to Damron would become a crucial piece of evidence in the Masters case.

For months after the discovery, Reed and Colby continued to make almost nightly searches through Alan's office trash, hoping that their forays would glean more evidence. They also began delving through the refuse at Alan's house.

They would ask the garbage man to pick it up and drive it around the corner, and then they would get it off the garbage truck. Using Colby's Mustang, they would back the unmarked squad car right up to the garbage truck and load the trash bags into the trunk. Reed noted that the sight of two men transferring trash from a garbage truck into a car trunk drew strange looks from passersby.

Alan eventually learned of the men's forages. To his garbage at home, he added a special mixture of dog feces in some kind of solution. "It was a terrible odor. A terrible odor," says Reed. The raids on the trash soon stopped.

Tom Scorza was a perfectionist, the kind of person who couldn't tolerate carelessness or incompetence. He had a temper and often exploded at underlings, because he understood that little mistakes could turn into major blunders when cases were presented to juries.

In the fall of 1987, he was reviewing the file on the Masters case. He was perusing the records that the Illinois State Police had compiled during its 1983 investigation of the homicide, and among them were the logs of all of the police radio dispatchers from the surrounding suburbs the night Dianne Masters disappeared.

Scorza waded through the records of the Willow Springs Police Department. The logs were in police shorthand: "1949, Car 53, Park & Shop, 10-25, Park & Shop. Unknown problem," read one of the entries. The radio dispatcher had assigned a squad car to visit a local store that night at 7:49.

As he poured over the entries, Scorza sensed that there was something wrong with the reports. Suddenly it dawned on him. There were huge gaps in time, as if there were pages missing. Indeed, in copying the documents, someone had been careless. They had copied only one side of a two-sided police log. Scorza couldn't believe the stupidity.

He drafted a subpoena. He wanted to see what was on the other side. An FBI agent was sent to Willow Springs to retrieve the crucial records. Scorza hoped that the logs would not have been destroyed after all that time. But he was in luck. The village had maintained all of the records and they were filed by date.

When the box arrived in Scorza's office, he pulled the logs for the eighteenth and nineteenth of March 1982. On a page that he hadn't seen before, he noticed a startling entry. Dispatcher Joe LaRocca had written: "2203, shots fired west of station." LaRocca had heard the gunfire himself and had written down the time. It was 11:03 P.M. on March 19, almost twenty-two hours after Dianne's disappearance. LaRocca had written in police shorthand that six squad cars had responded. Among them was Michael Corbitt's.

Corbitt and his men were investigating shots fired at the canal at exactly the same spot where Dianne's Cadillac would be found nine months later.

Scorza recalled an FBI report by Dave Parker, the former

agent on the Masters case. In it there had been something about a Willow Springs police officer spotting Corbitt at the canal during an investigation of shots being fired. The report, however, was fuzzy on when the shooting had occurred.

Scorza and his investigators started wondering about the earlier assumption that Dianne's killers had immediately disposed of the body and the car in the canal. What if something had happened that delayed the plan to dump the Cadillac until the next night? Hadn't Bachman mentioned something to Reed about a flat tire on the car?

In some respects, that theory defied logic. Why would Dianne's killers risk storing the car overnight? Where could it have been kept? Every police agency in the south suburbs was looking for Dianne's car the next day. How could anyone have risked transporting her car to the canal with police looking for it?

Scorza and the investigators believed that the answer to some of those questions could be found in the police logs and through new interviews with those Willow Springs police officers who were on duty that night.

They also realized that their new theory began to make sense when they considered who was on the scene. Mike Corbitt, the police chief who could do virtually anything he wanted in the town of Willow Springs. Scorza believed that Corbitt's police acumen had enabled him to devise a solution. Hide the car overnight and dump it in the canal the following evening. Change the clock in the car and the time on Dianne's wristwatch to make it seem that she had been killed the night she disappeared. Remove her underwear to make it appear that she had been assaulted, so that if the body was ever found, it would not look like a domestic homicide.

Parker had interviewed former patrolman Robert Olson in January 1983 about his recollections of the night Dianne was murdered. Reed and Sabin repeated the interview in late 1987. They asked Olson to recall the night he had heard the shots. Olson was uncertain about the exact date and time, but he remembered heading toward the canal after hearing the shots fired.

Olson had been on patrol and had stopped a gray Chevy on

one of the streets leaving the canal area. Much to his surprise, it was Chief Corbitt and another man. Corbitt told him that he had checked out the shots and couldn't find anything.

Olson was one of the police officers fired by Ross in 1982 when Ross took over the department. Shortly after he informed the new police chief of meeting Corbitt near the canal, Ross rehired him.

Checking the police duty roster for the night of March 20, 1982, Harris found another witness, former patrolman George Witzel.

Witzel told Harris that just before the shots were fired that evening, he spotted Corbitt in his squad car at a local tavern. Earlier the chief had called in to the dispatcher that he was assisting a person locked out of his vehicle. Witzel said that when he saw the chief, Corbitt was sitting in the squad car with another individual, not assisting anyone with a lockout. Witzel said that the chief then ordered him to go to the canal before he went off duty and make sure no one was there.

Scorza and his agents concluded that the call from Corbitt saying he was assisting a motorist had been a ruse. They believed that the two men had been preparing to take Dianne's car from an underground garage at the tavern. The other man in the car would drive Dianne's Cadillac to the canal complete with an escort from the chief of police. It was the perfect time, because at 11:00 P.M., the shifts were changing in the Willow Springs Police Department.

For John Hess, a telephone repairman, a story in the *Chicago Sun-Times* had jolted his memory. After Dianne's disappearance, Hess had been in the Masters home because of complaints about problems with the phone lines. He had gone down into the basement troubleshooting and had entered a crawl space to check the wiring.

He had noticed one or possibly two .22-caliber rimfire brass shell casings laying in the dirt. Using his needle-nose pliers, he moved them out of his way and placed them to the side. The repairman had thought nothing of the discovery until a coworker told him that the woman of the house had been murdered. Then Hess had forgotten the incident until he read the newspaper account about the ongoing federal investigation, which prompted him to contact the sheriff's department.

Around Christmas, the FBI visited Alan Masters' house armed with a search warrant. Alan, Anndra, and her governess, Jan Bower, were preparing to leave that day on vacation. Alan was in the kitchen when he saw the federal agents pull into the driveway. "Maybe we're not going to Florida," he kidded Jan.

The lawyer answered the door and greeted the search party. Jan shuffled Anndra off into a back room with a game and ordered her to stay put. Before the agents entered the home, Jan requested that they take off their muddy shoes. They looked at her as though she were crazy.

FBI agent Ivan Harris led the expedition, which was confined to the basement. Alan accompanied them and cracked jokes as he watched the proceedings. Soon Jan was overwhelmed by curiosity and went downstairs to see what was happening. After more than an hour and a half, the agents finished their task. And as soon as they departed, Alan, Anndra, and Jan got into a limo and left for Florida.

The agents had indeed discovered a .22-caliber shell casing in the crawl space.

Days passed before FBI scientists could make the comparisons between the shell casings found in the trunk of Dianne's car and those retrieved from the basement of the home. Finally it was determined that the shell casings did not match. Reed and Colby learned later that one of the previous owners of the house had a small firing range in the basement. Apparently the brass for the bullets had been discarded years before Alan and Dianne had moved into the home.

Reed had urged the federal agents to look inside a file cabinet in the house for the minutes from the college board's meeting. He was optimistic that Dianne had come home that March night and placed the minutes in a file cabinet supplied by the college. If the papers were there, it meant that Dianne definitely had arrived home. Like Alan's mistake of dumping incriminating evidence in his trash, Reed was hoping that he had made another error and kept the minutes.

Apparently no such search was ever conducted. The warrant did not authorize the agents to look for the minutes.

When the sheriff's department originally had investigated Dianne's disappearance, they had done at least one thing correctly. They had obtained phone records.

Alan and Dianne had what Illinois Bell Telephone called Call-Pack Unlimited. At the time, a subscriber to that service paid a flat monthly fee and received unlimited calls within Chicago's 312 area code. Other telephone customers pay for their local calls based on the number of units used each month. The police call those phone records MUD sheets—multiple unit dialing sheets. Using phone company MUD sheets, the authorities can determine the telephone number called, the length of the conversation, and the date and time.

But because Alan and Dianne had the special unlimited telephone call package, the phone company could not provide any lists of whom the couple had called in the days before Dianne disappeared. The only calls that could be traced from the house were outgoing long-distance calls. That night, while Dianne was at the college board meeting, Alan called his sons on the East Coast at 8:52 and 8:54 P.M.

At Alan's law office, however, every call was itemized. With Nykaza and Bachman telling authorities that Alan had called and told his friends to have alibis in the days before Dianne's death, the telephone records obtained during the original, 1982 investigation took on a new meaning.

Reed and Colby began reviewing the records retrieved from a county warehouse. There were literally thousands of telephone calls. Alan's was a busy three-lawyer office.

Using phone directory services and telephone company lists that provided the subscribers of unlisted telephone numbers, the two detectives began pouring over the MUD sheets. The detectives discovered a series of phone calls between Alan and Nykaza, Alan and Bachman, and Alan and Sgt. Buckendahl. Were these the calls from Alan telling his cohorts to have alibis?

The two detectives had traced the call to Buckendahl by

sheer luck. Bob Colby, a certified flight instructor, had given several of the department's police officers flying lessons. Buckendahl had been one of his students. At the time, he had given Colby his home phone number. Colby had discovered that the number for Buckendahl in his phone directory at home did not match the telephone number that Buckendahl had given to the department. Buckendahl had installed two telephone lines into his home: one was his official residential line; the other was his private line, which he mistakenly had given out to Colby. The records showed that three days before Dianne had disappeared, Alan had called Buckendahl on his private line.

Reed and Colby also found an intriguing call to the home of a judge, which Alan had placed fourteen minutes after phoning Buckendahl. Alan had talked to the magistrate for twenty-nine minutes.

Several weeks later, Reed met Buckendahl at the sheriff's department headquarters. During the original investigation into Dianne's disappearance, Alan's calls to Buckendahl's private line conveniently had been omitted from departmental records. Buckendahl couldn't explain the discrepancy. And he swore that none of the calls from Alan had pertained to arranging an alibi.

He then turned to Reed. "What would happen to a person who received such a call and did nothing about it?" Buckendahl informed Reed that Bachman had told him that a friend had, in fact, gotten such a call from Alan.

It was a Tuesday, Reed's day off, around noon when the calls began. Every few minutes his telephone rang. After he answered, the party would hang up. Finally, at 3:30 P.M., Reed heard a male voice.

"Watch your step," the caller warned. "These guys are crazy. You're making some people nervous."

Chapter Twenty-Four

June 13, 1988

FOR Randy Turner, it was a routine workday—making follow-up calls to clients, checking on shipments, writing letters, contacting buyers about their purchases of Chicago Cubs T-shirts. His business was housed in a stately old home that had been converted to offices and apartments. His desk was in the former living room and he looked out on a busy suburban roadway. Kathy had a desk in the dining room and her father had a small office in the kitchen.

Shortly after 3 P.M. on Monday, June 13, 1988, Randy received a phone call from a local television reporter asking what his reaction was to the indictments of Alan Masters, James Keating, and Michael Corbitt in connection with his sister's murder.

Randy was stunned. What was the reporter talking about? He quickly collected himself and said he couldn't comment until he had a chance to confer with his lawyer, former U.S. attorney Dan Webb. He wanted to make sure that Webb, whom he had retained only recently, approved of his talking to the press. The reporter, Rich Samuels from NBC, said he would drive out to the office anyway. The crew would be in the area and would call Randy soon about going on the air. Samuels wanted a live shot for the five o'clock news.

Randy also was angry. Why couldn't Tom Scorza, the prosecutor, have given him a clue that the indictments were imminent? After all we had been through and all we had done, why

couldn't he have even given us a hint, any idea? Randy s.
to himself.

The Turners' only knowledge of the grand jury investigation had come months earlier, when Jim Koscielniak was asked to testify. He had called Randy and told him that he had gone before the grand jury. A friend of Dianne's had informed them of her appearance as well.

Over the last few months, Randy had called Scorza, trying to elicit from him some indication as to how the case was progressing. Would there be an indictment? "I constantly called to bug him," says Randy. Scorza would say only that there might be something forthcoming. For Randy and Kathy, it was the same rhetoric they had heard for years. "Forthcoming could have meant another eight years in my mind," he says.

Now Randy was recalling some of the things that the assistant U.S. attorney had said in their dozen or so phone conversations. He had explained to Randy that he couldn't provide him with any information about the investigation because of secrecy laws dealing with federal grand juries. But he had emphasized: "We have never gone after a guy we didn't get. We don't waste our time."

Randy's office lacked a radio or a television, so there was no way to learn what actually had happened. So he called Scorza and then Dan Davis, the president of SOA.

Scorza apologized for not having told Randy that the indictment would be returned that day but said that violating the secrecy of the grand jury would have been illegal. Earlier that afternoon, U.S. Attorney Anton Valukas, Scorza, James McKenzie, the special agent in charge of the Chicago FBI office, and others had stood before a packed room of reporters and announced the indictments.

It was a complicated list of charges that accused Alan, Corbitt, and Keating of plotting Dianne's murder. The indictment contended that they had engaged in a criminal enterprise in planning Dianne's murder, soliciting killers and covering up the crime. This was not a novel legal theory. It was the same kind of indictment used by federal authorities to charge organized crime figures involved in murders. In effect, the indictment alleged that Alan and his associates were akin to a mini-Mafia.

Keating was accused of offering Bachman $25,000 to kill Dianne, which Bachman refused. Corbitt was charged with dumping the car in the canal. Alan was charged with mail fraud for collecting the $100,000 from Dianne's life insurance policy.

Another count alleged that Alan, Keating, and Corbitt had participated in a long-standing bribery scheme. Alan was accused of paying Corbitt for referring cases to him. Keating was charged with splitting bribes with Alan that were derived from the county police department's protection of a Cicero gambling operation.

When Randy called Dan Davis, the president of the private detective agency said he knew nothing about the indictments. Davis had become one of Randy's closest contacts over the past six years. They had talked every few months. Sometimes Davis would call just to see if Randy had heard of any new developments. While his firm really had uncovered few clues in the case, he had offered Randy and Kathy something far more important: hope that justice would be served.

"I remember him saying once, 'You are going to like the outcome, but you are going to have to be patient,' " Kathy recalls.

"He always maintained that some way, somehow, these guys would be caught," says Randy.

Attorney Dan Webb returned Randy's call within the hour. He had just learned of the indictments from the news broadcasts, and he told Randy that it would be all right to talk to the press but urged him to choose his words carefully. He was to say only that he was elated and that he had retained Webb as his attorney to seek custody of Anndra and investigate possible legal action against the sheriff's department for their coverup of the murder.

Randy had barely hung up the telephone when the NBC television crew appeared at his door. Inside the office, Rich Samuels questioned Randy about his reaction and Randy replied exactly as he had been instructed. The interview also gave him the opportunity to praise Sheriff O'Grady, O'Grady's detective agency, and the U.S. Attorney's Office for their work on the case.

When the TV crew left, the Turners' phone began ringing. ABC wanted him live for its 5:30 newscast. Randy sidestepped the request, saying he had an important business meeting. In reality, his son Sean was playing in a Little League game. He told the television station that they could interview him at his house at 7:30 that evening.

The station's minivan was already outside when Turner pulled his Chrysler into the driveway following the game. A small crowd of neighbors had gathered and were watching the crew work.

One of the television stations used a portion of Randy's interview as a promo for the upcoming ten o'clock news. And that night, the telephone continued to ring incessantly. Newspaper reporters were asking the same question again and again: what was Randy's reaction?

Watching the news, he realized that this was just the beginning. It might be a year before there was a trial. He began wondering how strong the prosecution's case was. No one had told him that Jack Bachman, the crooked cop, or Ted Nykaza, Alan's private eye, were cooperating. And what would prosecutors allege was the motive?

On Friday, *Chicago Sun-Times* reporter Art Petacque, whose career had started in the "Front Page" days of journalism, called the Turners. Nearly two years earlier, after the federal grand jury had been convened, Petacque had contacted them promising that he was going to solve Dianne's murder.

He had won the Pulitzer Prize years earlier for a series of stories about the abduction and brutal murder of the daughter of former U.S. Senator Charles Percy. His stories linked a man, who subsequently was imprisoned, to the horrible tragedy. Petacque had said that he would do the same as he had with the Percy murder—he would break the case—and asked if they could provide him with whatever they had on the investigation. The Turners agreed to lend him the scrapbook they had assembled that had an extensive collection of news stories, pictures, and other related items.

Petacque, whose contacts in the law enforcement community

are both extensive and infamous, had dispatched a state trooper to pick up the scrapbook. Petacque never returned it. Now he was promising to give back the scrapbook and to write a Sunday story that would be a chronicle of the murder. Randy was hooked again.

On Saturday, when the Sunday paper hit the street, Randy was infuriated. Petacque's chronicle had metamorphosed into Jim Koscielniak's torrid three-month love affair with Dianne.

"I could not believe I was taken in by this sleazy journalist a second time," Randy says. He was equally mad at Jim for talking to Petacque about his affair with Dianne.

"Did I do something wrong?" Jim asked when an incensed Randy called him that Saturday.

"I told him that he had turned the case into a sleazy sex scandal and that he had ruined everything we had worked for. He had insinuated that my sister had been murdered because of their affair, and it was a travesty of the truth. She was murdered because she knew too much," says Randy. "To this day, I believe Dianne was murdered because Alan and his friends were afraid [of] what would come out in a custody battle."

He had slammed the phone down angrily while talking to Jim. The college professor had tried to call back, but Kathy hung up the phone after realizing it was Jim. They would resolve their differences over the next few months, however.

Sunday was Father's Day, which Randy was to spend with relatives. He was dreading the outing because he knew everyone would have read the *Sun-Times* story or heard about it when the television stations and other newspapers picked it up. But family members helped convince him that sooner or later, the affair would have become public. It was going to be presented at the trial. Randy, though, thought the forum—a newspaper story with its screaming headline—was offensive. He began sipping beers, and by the end of the afternoon, he was slightly drunk.

Soon after he walked through the door of his Buffalo Grove home, the telephone rang. Randy had agreed earlier that week to go on the radio show of Ray Hanania, now a *Sun-Times* reporter, who had covered Dianne's disappearance extensively back in 1982. He had forgotten about it. Randy asked Hanania not to mention the *Sun-Times* story or Jim's affair with Dianne during the program, and Hanania agreed.

Cook County State Attorney Richard M. Daley had been quoted recently as saying he was considering convening a grand jury to investigate Dianne Masters murder, and Randy relished the idea of taking a verbal jab at the prosecutor: "Where was he six years ago?" Randy didn't know it, but the state attorney had played a major role in the indictments of Alan, Corbitt, and Keating. Scorza had obtained special permission from the presiding judge of the federal court to allow Daley's office to review the federal grand jury's case.

Scorza, a friend of Daley's, had worked with the state attorney and an assistant in the office. Scorza had written a sixty-page memo outlining the case and the men had had extensive discussions about the possibility of trying Alan and the two policemen in Cook County on murder charges.

"Their judgment was it would be very difficult to win a murder case," Scorza says. There also were problems with admitting some of the evidence gathered in the federal investigation in state court.

There was yet another reason for not making it a state case. "We were dealing with fixers and we wanted this in a forum where nothing could be fixed," emphasized Scorza.

Unlike Randy, Alan Masters knew that the indictment was forthcoming, thanks to Patrick Tuite, one of the city's top criminal defense attorneys, whom he had hired to represent him. Tuite's reputation in the legal community is that of a brilliant lawyer whose zeal for his clients sometimes goes precariously close to exceeding the bounds of the law. He was one of the few lawyers to beat the federal prosecutors in court on their Operation Greylord cases, successfully defending one of the two judges acquitted in the probe.

As a result, his rates are steep. He is among a handful of lawyers in Chicago who commands a six-figure legal fee. And most of his clients pay it gladly.

Two weeks before the indictments were disclosed, Alan

pulled Anndra out of her private school and sent his daughter and Jan Bowers to the condominium in Long Boat Key, Florida. He wanted to protect them from the barrage of cameras that he knew would descend upon his home when the indictments were made public.

Anndra, who was now nearly eleven years old, was upset about leaving school so suddenly, and Jan tried to explain it to her. She reportedly told Anndra that her father might have to go to jail and that some people suspected that he had killed her mother.

While Anndra and Jan stayed in Florida, Alan went to the June graduation of his son Douglas on the East Coast. From Boston, Alan flew back to Florida and waited until the indictments were announced before returning to Chicago.

Tuite had arranged for Alan to surrender the following day at the Dirksen Building, the federal courthouse in downtown Chicago. That saved Alan the embarrassment of being handcuffed and led away from his home or office by the FBI and police.

Tuite's cocounsel, David Mejia, handled the arraignment held on the twenty-first floor of the courthouse before U.S. District Court Judge James Zagel. Zagel had once headed the state police agency that conducted an investigation into Dianne's death. Mejia later would seek to bar Zagel from hearing the case, citing his earlier involvement in the murder probe.

Alan, who had grown a bushy mustache and sported wire-rimmed aviator-style glasses, wore a light-gray suit, blue shirt, and white tie to the hearing. After each count was read, he responded in a firm voice, "Not guilty."

Scorza argued that Zagel should set a high bond, $200,000. The judge agreed and gave Alan a week to obtain the required 10 percent, $20,000.

Afterward, at a press conference, Mejia called the allegations against Alan a desperate legal shot, saying that the federal charges had been filed only because of the lack of progress in a state murder investigation.

A few minutes later, Alan walked into the FBI's offices on the fifth floor of the courthouse, where Ivan Harris was waiting for him. It was a moment that the agent had been anticipating for months. He was going to fingerprint Alan and take his photograph for the FBI file.

The bureau's fingerprint room is only slightly larger than a janitor's closet. There is a small area for rolling the suspect's fingers in black ink and, within easy reach, a can of Glop to remove the stains. To the left of the fingerprint area is a camera and a backdrop where the suspect stands to have photographs taken.

While Harris was fingerprinting the attorney, Alan was cracking jokes. He told Harris an off-color story in which the punchline usually involved a doctor or lawyer, but Alan substituted an FBI agent. "Here he was being fingerprinted for the murder of his wife, and he's telling jokes," Harris recalls.

CHAPTER TWENTY-FIVE

October 18, 1988

JAN Bower was a pretty, buxom strawberry blond with green eyes and a preponderance of freckles. Her outgoing, straightforward personality and down-home charm obscured the fact that she was extremely bright and shrewd.

When she started working for Alan in the summer of 1982, she had just turned eighteen. She was in the midst of looking for a new job, and Alan, a good friend of her mother's for more than a decade, wanted to help. He offered to find her a position in a law office, but when that didn't materialize, he had another idea. Would Jan be willing to care for his young daughter? They tried it out to see if she and Anndra would get along with each other.

From the beginning, there was a magical chemistry between Anndra and her governess. Jan took her miniature golfing and taught her how to bowl. They went to the parks, zoos. What started as a governess job evolved into a role that was far more complex.

Jan, who also was going to college part time, was quickly immersed in the family. And it didn't take long before she became the most important person in Anndra's life besides her father. She had been present when Alan told his five-year-old daughter that her mother was never coming home.

Soon everyone depended upon Jan. When Alan's own mother, Esther, became sick in 1983, she briefly moved into the Palos Park home until Alan and his brother Leonard were able to find a nursing facility for her. Jan started staying overnight at the house to care for her and Anndra because it was useless to try to go back and forth between her house and Alan's. On weekends, she worked at Leonard's currency exchange.

Alan began doting on the affable young woman who was caring for his child, and they did almost everything together. His favorite hobby was shopping, and he pampered both his daughter and her governess. There were gifts of expensive jewelry, fur coats, trips. "Alan liked to spoil people; he liked to try to make you happy," Jan notes. "When I had a cold or Anndra got sick, he liked to take care of you. He was very compassionate and caring. There were so many nice qualities about Alan."

Yet at the onset, she never envisioned him as anything but her friend and employer. But after spending so much time together, their platonic relationship eventually changed.

The nearly thirty-year age difference between them was not an issue, because Jan had always dated older men. There was never a generation gap, and Alan was easy to get along with. She liked country music, so he liked country music. They were very compatible.

Jan wanted to move from the rambling, ranch-style home, but Alan refused. Surprisingly, the house looked virtually the same as it did the day Dianne disappeared. Jan had made only minor changes; she felt that the familiar environment provided Anndra with stability.

So Anndra grew up surrounded by her mother's possessions. Dianne's bedroom, which Jan occupied, was still lavendar, pale yellow, and white. On the east wall hung a stunning portrait of Dianne sporting a page boy and bangs, with Anndra, then three years old, beside her. "I don't think Anndra would remember what Dianne looked like, if I took it down," says Jan.

Near the portrait, there was a small table containing numerous photographs of Dianne, of Dianne and her parents, and of Dianne and Anndra. To this grouping, Jan added snapshots of her own family and the German shepherds she raised.

Against the wall in the dining room stood Dianne's baker's rack filled with her brass and copper treasure troves, including a cannister with the monogram DGM. On the refrigerator were many of the dead woman's magnets, among them a picture of a pig, which she had needlepointed. It said "kitchen closed."

Many dog and cat figurines from Dianne's vast collection were displayed on shelves in the living room. And Dianne's portrait of Baron, her beloved Irish setter, hung above the fireplace. A bookcase held her beloved clarinet as well as a mantle clock that had belonged to Dianne's parents. Once Anndra, who played the flute and piano, had spotted the instrument on the shelf, she was determined to master it.

"Can I play it?" she asked.

"We have to buy a reed," Jan replied.

"No," Anndra told her. She had brought one home from school. Anndra's first musical rendition on the clarinet was less than perfect, Jan recalls. "She sounded like a sick duck."

Although Jan claims she had never met Dianne, she gained insight into the dead woman's personality by reading her diary as well as notes, letters, and poetry she had written. "I feel like I know her. Living with all her things. Looking at pictures of her. There was a lot of her left around the house."

In her diary, Dianne had ruminated about her daughter and her plans for the child's future. And Jan reread those portions often. "That's how I get an idea of how she would have raised Anndra." She saved Dianne's writings so that Anndra could read them when she got older.

With her charge gone for most of the day, Jan wanted other employment. Like Dianne, she adored flowers, so she decided to become a florist. After completing the three-month course, she received several job offers, but Alan did not want her working outside the home. Instead he sent her flowers daily to hone her skills—six dozen a week, which she arranged and displayed throughout the house.

However, he later encouraged her to take an income tax preparation course. The couple then opened their own business, Tax Masters, Inc., in his Summit law office. "He really did it so I would have something to do," Jan says. "He let me do income tax [as opposed to being a florist] because the tax business was in his office."

Their lives had become irrevocably intertwined. They lived together, worked together, and were raising a child together.

Jan's devotion to Alan was tested, too. Tom Scorza, the assistant U.S. attorney, saw to that. Through her mother, he arranged a meeting with Jan in a Chicago restaurant.

She thought it was in her best interest to attend. She went because she wanted to see what the government had on Alan. And the prosecutor hoped that she would consider cooperating if Scorza could prove to her that Alan was responsible for Dianne's murder. But she never had to make that decision.

Over cocktails, the prosecutor pleaded with Jan to become a federal witness. "I am going to tell you how your husband killed his previous wife," Scorza told her. He talked nonstop for nearly forty minutes, offering his entire theory of how Dianne was murdered. He continually referred to Alan as Jan's husband, and that irritated her.

Finally, she stopped him. "I don't think much of your investigation if you don't even know I'm not his wife," she told him.

Scorza tried to scare Jan by implying that she might be charged with withholding evidence unless she cooperated.

"Give it your best shot," she challenged.

He told Jan he was sure that she had information that she didn't think was important but that was, in fact, important to the investigation. The prosecutor tried to convince Jan that if she cooperated, she would be safe. She would be placed in the Witness Protection Program. No one would ever find her.

What would happen to Anndra if she went into the Witness Protection Program? she wanted to know.

"She would go with you," he replied.

"Now I know you're nuts," she retorted. "The fastest way I do know of to get in danger is to take his daughter and run away."

Throughout the meeting, which lasted several hours, Jan listened attentively. At one point during the conversation, she told Scorza that she had mentioned to Alan that she was seeing the prosecutor.

Scorza had a fit when he found out that Alan knew Jan was

there. "You're in great danger," he told her. "You can't be here doing this," he said.

Jan remained adamant. She would not cooperate.

"If you change your mind, here's my card. If somebody's following you or you're in danger, call immediately," Scorza implored.

The young woman had stood by her man and there was nothing anybody could say to change her mind. She was not going to turn against Alan.

With his original trial date set for September, Alan decided to legitimatize his relationship with Jan, and the precariousness of his situation changed her thinking about matrimony. She never had been concerned about observing the formalities. Ultimately it was Anndra's welfare that influenced her decision. Anndra needed security. Whatever happened at the trial, Jan would be there for her, but no longer as her governess. She would become Anndra's mother, and Alan's wife.

On October 18, 1988, Alan and Jan were married in a clandestine ceremony in Indiana. She was twenty-four; he was fifty-three. Jan had hoped for a traditional wedding with a horde of spectators filling the church, but the marriage was in a judge's chambers with little fanfare. She regretted the way they got married. Jan had wanted her father and one of her girlfriends present and she had wanted to wear a long white dress.

Anndra was ecstatic about the union. She had wanted them to get married for a long time. Alan arranged the paperwork for his new bride to legally adopt his eleven-year-old daughter.

For several years, Jan had displayed a gift from Alan, a pear-shaped, 2.58-carat diamond mounted on a wide gold band, on her left ring finger. She had worn it for so long that no one would suspect that she and Alan had wed. It would remain their secret until after the trial.

CHAPTER TWENTY-SIX

May 18, 1989

THE courtrooms in Chicago's federal building were modern and austere. Plain, dark wood paneling lined the walls. And the recessed lights in the thirty-foot ceilings did nothing to brighten the drab interior. The building's heating and air-conditioning system never had functioned properly, so the courtrooms were nearly always uncomfortably warm and filled with stale air, which has lulled some jurors to sleep during boring testimony.

From the back of the long room, Judge James Zagel's bench and the witness box appeared to be miles away, often making it difficult for spectators to hear the proceedings. The jurors sat on the right-hand side of the courtroom in plush office-type chairs affixed to the floor. In the back, there were five long rows of wooden benches flanking the double doors that led into the hallway. Reporters and artists from the city's newspapers and television stations occupied the front row. The federal building's court buffs, a ragtag assortment of primarily retirees, grabbed the remaining seats.

The habitués had come to see the day's best soap opera: a criminal trial featuring Chicago's top legal eagles. The stars that Thursday, May 18, 1989, were Thomas Scorza, a young assistant U.S. attorney who had quickly developed a reputation as one of the best in the office, against Patrick Tuite, Alan Masters' defense attorney. Both men possessed a flamboyant courtroom demeanor that promised fireworks when they clashed. Each was also a natty dresser, but that was where the similarities ended.

Their appearances differed vastly. The distinguished-looking Scorza, who was just five feet seven and 145 pounds, wore a full, neatly trimmed beard and gold wire-rimmed glasses. Tuite was five feet ten, had jet-black hair streaked with touches of gray, and possessed a five o'clock shadow even in the morning.

Tuite had a young attorney from his office, Brent Stratton, at his side. Corbitt's attorney, Dennis Berkson, and William P. Murphy, who was representing Keating, also had assistants working at the defense table.

James Zagel was a no-nonsense judge who had earned a reputation as a law-and-order advocate as a result of his reign as head of the state police force before ascending to the bench. During his tenure, his agency had investigated Dianne's death, a fact that led to the defense team's efforts—albeit unsuccessful—to remove him from hearing the case. In legal circles, he was known for his brilliant mind and his wit. Among defense attorneys, he was considered a judge who favored the prosecution. Zagel was about the same height as Scorza but considerably heavier. Dressed in his black robes, his olive complexion and black hair looked even darker.

Kathy Turner's parents, Rick and Virginia Hawley, had positioned themselves in seats where they could look directly at Alan. Scorza had subpoenaed Randy and Kathy as potential witnesses, which precluded them from attending the trial until they were called. He wanted to maintain a long list of possible witnesses so that the defense attorneys would be wondering continually what the Turners and others might disclose under oath.

Alan's new bride, Jan was there with one of Alan's sons. So was Marilyn Hastings, Jim Keating's girlfriend. Corbitt's wife Sherry was sitting in the back row behind the defense table with her five-year-old son Joey, who was afflicted with Down's syndrome.

The morning session already had erupted into a donnybrook of sorts, as Scorza had objected to the presence of Corbitt's son in the courtroom. He believed that the presence of the young boy was designed to tug on the heartstrings of the jury and to attempt to get unjustified sympathy for the defendant.

Judge Zagel didn't bar the child from the courtroom but asked that Corbitt's wife and Joey move to the back of the room. That way, if the child looked at his father, it wouldn't be so apparent to the jury.

Scorza and a young assistant, Patrick Foley, had spent countless hours readying themselves for trial. As is the custom in the U.S. Attorney's Office, the prosecutors' calender, which usually is filled with routine court appearances, was cleared a month in advance so that they could prepare their case.

One of Scorza's most important lessons while serving as a clerk to U.S. District Court Judge Milton Shadur had been trial organization. He had seen trial attorneys enter the courtroom arguing multimillion-dollar cases who never had focused on the basic story they wanted to relay to the jury or judge.

As Scorza prepared for the trial, he had written out what he called "Our Story," a summary of the case in terms the jury could understand. It emphasized the points the prosecutors wanted to underscore and what each witness probably would say on the stand. In effect, it became the outline for the government's case, from the opening remarks to the closing comments.

For Scorza, who had lived with the case for years, the summary was what he had told his wife while he sat in the living room of their Hyde Park apartment. He would toss a theory out and get her reaction. "Our Story" was also how he related the workings of the case to his fellow prosecutors. And it was the combination of all of the memos to the U.S. Justice Department and the Cook County State Attorney's Office outlining the case.

"Our Story" was ingrained in Tom Scorza's head. He did not need any notes. For two hours, the one-time college political philosophy professor delivered his opening remarks.

> This case is about three defendants. Alan Masters, whom you will learn, was a corrupt attorney practicing law, if that's the word, in Summit, Illinois.
>
> It's about the second defendant, Michael Corbitt, whom

> you will learn was the corrupt police chief until June 19, 1982, in Willow Springs.
>
> The case is also about the third defendant back there, the man in the gray suit and the gray tie, James Keating, whom you will learn was a corrupt police officer on the Cook County Sheriff's Police Department. In fact, a very high ranking officer, a lieutenant and a commander.

Scorza described Alan as the master fixer, the ring leader of a corrupt association between the defendants that engaged in bribery, the murder of Dianne, and the subsequent coverup of the homicide. He told the jurors, "It is a case about an unholy trinity of greed, corruption and murder."

After the discovery of the body on December 11, 1982, Alan Masters learned for the first time that his wife had a life insurance policy in the amount of $100,000 as a result of being a trustee on the board at Moraine Valley Community College. After Alan Masters heard about the policy, he went ahead and collected the insurance by lying to the insurance company about his role in the murder, Scorza told the jurors.

Undercover FBI agent Larry Damron would be the first witness and he would explain the criminal association between Alan Masters, Keating, and Corbitt. They would hear how Corbitt and Keating had referred cases to Alan for years and how they had received illegal kickbacks. The scheme would be discussed by Keating in his own words, those taped by Larry Damron on November 27, 1982.

Scorza continued, quoting Keating: " 'My guy, my lawyer, his name is Alan Masters. He pays all the cops. He pays all the judges. He can fix any beef. He gives me money to refer cases. He refers cases. He gives money to other cops. He's your man.' "

Four witnesses would tell the jurors that Corbitt had a similar deal with Alan. One of the witnesses, the current Willow Springs police chief, Herman Pastori, would take the stand and admit that he, too, was receiving such fees from Alan.

Scorza knew that of all his rhetoric that morning, the most compelling would be what he told the jury about the killing.

He started with how the couple had met in 1969 because of Dianne's divorce. "Fatally, her divorce attorney turned out to be the defendant, Alan Masters. That's how they met. She was obtaining a divorce. He was her divorce lawyer." For many years, Dianne was Alan's mistress, he told the jurors. He had an apartment for her. Then later he bought a house. Dianne was subservient in their early relationship. Scorza continued:

> Somewhere in the period, 1977, 1978, you will see Dianne Masters undergoes something of a late blooming. She has a child, a girl named Anndra. She begins to take a role in the community. She becomes very heavily involved in what was called the South Suburban Crisis Center for Battered Women. And she becomes active politically.
>
> The crisis center is interesting because you will be able to conclude where her interest in that matter came from, because you are going to learn from her friends that in the 1970s and then again in about 1976, the friends directly witnessed Alan Masters strike Dianne Masters when he discovered that she had been unfaithful to him; in other words, had gone with another man even before they were married.

Scorza explained to the jury that in 1981, Dianne met Jim Koscielniak. They fell in love and began an affair. The couple saw each other on Friday nights, when Alan was usually at the fights, and after the college board meetings, they would go to one of the local motels.

Alan and Dianne had begun feuding in the summer of 1981, related the prosecutor. Alan first approached Sgt. Clarke Buckendahl and asked who would investigate if there were a crime committed in Alan's home. When Buckendahl told him that it would be Vanick, Alan asked why Keating wouldn't be involved.

The conversation with Buckendahl, Scorza contended, was the beginning of the murder plot. Alan's original idea was to kill her at the Palos Park home.

The jury listened intently as Scorza outlined Dianne's divorce plans and how she had hired Gretchen Connell to represent her. As that divorce date neared, Dianne told her friends that she had been threatened by Alan and was growing more fearful of him and that she suspected she was being followed.

In January 1982, Alan asked Ted Nykaza to place recording devices on the couple's home telephones. And a month later, on February 17, Lt. Howard Vanick spotted Dianne and Jim at a restaurant and passed on the license plate number that eventually reached Alan.

On February 24, Dianne went to a college board meeting and saw Jim afterward for a session of lovemaking. Scorza told the jurors:

> For their meeting on February 24th, you will find may be the most memorable part of the evidence in this case, human nature. It involved some very, very sensitive and graphic sexual matters.
>
> I apologize to you, if I need to. Ten years ago, I would not be able to tell you this in open court. These are the kind of things we see more and more on television and movies, so I am going to go through it with you.
>
> The story begins in the Bible, believe it or not. Many of you mentioned that you went to church regularly. Some said you even studied the Bible.
>
> You may remember one of the books of the Old Testament called the Song of Solomon. If you read it in school or in church or had your minister or your rabbi read it to you in English, you would see or hear a very pretty poem about the love between a husband and a wife.
>
> And the usual interpretation of it is this is an allegory about the love of the God of the Old Testament for his people, the Israelites, and that's the way it's always interpreted and I have always seen it interpreted.
>
> What you can't tell from the English translation is what you'll be able to see if you read Hebrew or Aramic or even St. Jerome's Latin. If you read the original Song of Solomon, it turns out that it is an extraordinarily graphic description of sexual activity. The description of the sexual activity is very graphic and involves in one place the man pouring wine on the body of the woman as part of their sex play, including pouring wine on her vagina prior to oral sex.

Scorza said that Jim had seen a column in the newspaper written by novelist Reverend Andrew Greeley about the Song of Solomon, and he had saved it. During his affair with Dianne, he had sent her a copy of the article.

All of this brought Scorza back to the night of February 24.

> When Dianne Masters and James Koscielniak got together after leaving a board meeting, after going out for drinks with the board members, after going to their motel, they did what the Bible told them . . . and they went ahead and engaged in that exact sexual activity.
>
> That episode would have been a private matter forever between James Koscielniak and Dianne Masters. The day after, apparently, or the next day, James Koscielniak called Dianne at home to talk about their next meeting and the fun that they recently had.
>
> What Dianne Masters and Jim Koscielniak did not know was that the telephone had been tapped. Alan Masters caught the conversation that he was looking for. Alan Masters managed, through the work of Ted Nykaza, managed to capture the record of his wife not only talking to her boyfriend, but talking about this very graphic sexual activity of the night before.
>
> That day, the day after their sex play, began the final period of the life of Dianne Masters. On the next day, Alan Masters was talking to a lawyer who worked for him, Diane Economou, who had learned, by the way, about the tape from Nykaza.
>
> Alan Masters said to Economou that day: "I'm going to Nikko's restaurant. I'm going to get Jim Keating. I'm going to get him to kill Dianne and make it look like an accident."

Later, Jack Bachman met Keating, and Keating told Bachman that Alan had a tape recording of Dianne talking to Jim Koscielniak about the sex act.

A couple of days passed, and something more startling occurred, Scorza told the jurors. Bachman went to Keating's office and asked, "How is Alan doing? Has he calmed down?"

"No," Keating told Bachman. "He's committed. I can't get him—he wants to kill Dianne. Alan wants Dianne murdered.

He wants to make it look like a home invasion. He's willing to pay $25,000 and Mike Corbitt doesn't want to do the killing, but he's ready to dispose of the body."

"Bachman, who is a corrupt cop, is not a killer," Scorza said. He made a little joke: "Well, I've got $25,000. I don't need the money that bad."

On March 1, 1982, Keating approached Bachman at work and out of the blue told him to make sure he had an alibi for that night. "By the way, Jack, I hope you have something to do with your bride tonight," Scorza quoted Keating as saying.

That night, the college board went to its usual watering hole, Artie G's, after the meeting. Dianne and Jim Koscielniak were there together, and when Jim went to the bar to get drinks, a cigar-smoking James Keating confronted him.

"What's your name?" Keating asked Koscielniak. Jim told him. "Where do you work? Are you a teacher?" Keating inquired.

Scorza continued:

> On March 2nd, 1982, James Keating was stalking Dianne Masters and James Koscielniak. He was confirming their routine. Maybe by premonition, maybe by luck, maybe by at the end of this case you will even suspect divine intervention, on that night, Dianne Masters suddenly changed her mind. Jim Koscielniak and Dianne had arranged on that tapped phone that they were going to go to their regular hotel, the Budgeteer or something like that.
>
> But Dianne said, "It's a snowy night. Let's not go there. Let's park on the side of the road." They made love in the car on the side of the road on March 2, 1982.

The following day, Scorza told the jury, Bachman and Keating met at work. Keating told Bachman that Dianne had not shown up and that she had not been killed as planned. The murder was then set for the night of March 16, when the board scheduled another meeting. But at the last minute, the board changed it to Thursday night, March 18. "The third night was the fatal night, Dianne Masters' last night on earth."

On March 17, fate intervened for James Koscielniak. When he saw Dianne, she was very upset and scared. She gave him a picture of Alan. "You might be seeing him soon," Scorza quoted Dianne as saying to Jim. "I want you to know him. I'm asking you something else, Jim. Don't come to the board meeting. My divorce lawyer says we shouldn't be together so close to the filing of the papers. Don't come. Please don't come."

Scorza noted that on March 18, after the meeting, the board members decided to try a new restaurant, the Village Courtyard, rather than go to Artie G's. At 1 A.M., Dianne left the restaurant. He related how Genevieve Capstaff followed Dianne home.

"At this stage, a curtain falls across the stage," Scorza explained.

> It's a peculiar kind of curtain. It's not one of those real thick red ones you see in downtown theaters where you can't see through at all.
>
> Unfortunately, it's not one of those transparent curtains you sometimes see on a shower stall. It is a curtain which you can see through partially, like St. Paul says, as through a glass. You will be able to see certain things because circumstantial evidence is so strong. But at first you're going to realize that there are going to be certainties and uncertainties.
>
> For instance, it's going to be certain beyond a reasonable doubt that Dianne Masters drove into her driveway that night. You won't be able to be certain whether she goes into the house. It's possible that the defendants who have been plotting her murder are lurking in the driveway. One of them strikes her as she gets out of the car. That's possible.
>
> You will find in the end that maybe you won't believe that's too likely.
>
> You will know for certain that Dianne Masters, sometime after 1:10 A.M. on March 19, 1982, was brutally struck with a blunt instrument at least once, possibly twice. You will know that for certain.
>
> You won't know, as I say, whether that takes place on the driveway or in the house.
>
> You're not going to know for certain whether the blows themselves were fatal. They certainly were enough to cause

her immediate death, but it's possible that she lingered. And you will find that . . . raises the question of why there is a curtain there at all.

The reason for that is like in all secret conspiracies, the defendants take precautions against being found out. The special factor here, of course, is look at the defendants. One is a criminal lawyer. He knows the system. The other two are cops. They know what policemen look for. They know how to arrange things. That's what Masters had been talking about the whole time to his friends. Have his friends, the cops, help cover it up. Make it look like an accident. Make it look like a home invasion.

There will be an uncertainty on the two points about when exactly Dianne Masters died and what is the actual cause of her death. The reason for that is a horrifying action committed by the chief of police in Willow Springs, Michael Corbitt, at 11 P.M. on March 19th, 1982, 22 hours later. Michael Corbitt and an unknown accomplice drove his car and Dianne Masters' car to the canal. Mike Corbitt and/or that accomplice shot two bullets into the head of Dianne Masters as she lay dead or maybe just dying in the trunk of her car.

You will hear how Mike Corbitt then sunk that car in the canal right at the point where, of course, it would be found on December 11, 1982.

Scorza told the jurors that Mike Corbitt had been on injury leave from the department the week that Dianne disappeared. But a strange thing happened at about 10:30 P.M. on March 19. Corbitt called the police department requesting assistance for a person in a tavern parking lot who had locked himself out of his car. When patrolman George Witzel responded, there was nobody in the parking lot except Corbitt, who was sitting in his car with a companion. The police chief told his subordinate to clear out the canal, often a teen hangout, and radio him when he was done. Witzel did as he was told and then returned to the police station. It was nearing 11 P.M., the end of his shift.

A few minutes later, shots were heard coming from the canal. The police station was just blocks away from the waterway, and even the department's radio dispatcher had heard the blasts, noting them in the log.

Willow Springs policeman Robert Olson, who was just starting his tour, heard the shots and raced to the canal.

Scorza continued:

> He drives around heading toward the canal under the Willow Springs bridge and whom does he see? Mike Corbitt. Not going down to the canal, but coming out from where he was when those shots were fired.
>
> And Mike Corbitt says to Officer Olson, "Don't go down there. I took care of it." Two shots. It was from exactly the place where Dianne Masters will be found on December 11, 1982, with two shots in the head.

Like Keating, Scorza said, Corbitt found it funny that Dianne had disappeared. He told a friend that authorities had as much chance of finding Dianne Masters as they had of finding Jimmy Hoffa's pinky.

Scorza explained that Corbitt and Keating had intervened in the planning of Dianne's death. "What they decided the best thing to do is make it appear that she just disappeared. Make it appear that she just was swallowed up off the face of the earth." Alan would be home asleep. He would know nothing about any such plan. But when Dianne didn't show up at Artie G's restaurant, the plan went awry.

"Dianne Masters made it home that night. She very much surprised the man who was there that night. She got undressed, after maybe kicking off her shoes and putting away her papers, taking off those uncomfortable panty hose. That's when Dianne Masters, you see, met her fate and was struck by the same man who had struck her twice before, her husband, Alan Masters," Scorza told the jurors.

There was an underground garage at the tavern where Witzel had met Corbitt on the night of March 19. Scorza suggested that Dianne's killers had been forced to park her car in that garage because the car sustained a flat tire.

Corbitt, Scorza said, also took a precaution that night. He changed the clock in the car and Dianne's wristwatch to make it appear that she had been abducted after leaving the Village Courtyard restaurant and taken immediately to the canal, where she was killed and her car dumped into the waterway. It was a move that only a policeman like Corbitt would think of. The car clock had stopped at 1:50. Dianne's watch had stopped at 1:54.

FBI experts examining the car clock and watch believed that Dianne's watch had run down and stopped because it hadn't been wound during the time she was laying dead or wounded in the trunk, Scorza said. The experts suspected that Dianne's wristwatch had been reset to synchronize it with the car clock.

Scorza's opening remarks were drawing to a close. He told the jurors that at the end of the case, he and Pat Foley would argue that they had accomplished exactly what they had promised to do. After hearing all of the evidence and listening to the tapes, the jury would be able to conclude beyond a reasonable doubt that all three defendants were guilty as charged.

Like Keating, William P. Murphy was an Irishman with a homespun sense of humor. Murphy, Keating's attorney, had the unenviable task of following Tom Scorza. Using a bit of self-deprecation, a common technique employed by some attorneys to get jurors to identify with them, he explained that he was no Tom Scorza. "I know I'm not a particularly eloquent person and I know that a lot of times I appear a little nervous; and if I do that I apologize. I'm not a real polished person," Murphy said.

He talked to the jury as though they were his neighbors. He was representing a law enforcement officer, he told them.

> Some of them can be brave and intelligent, dedicated and earnest. Some can be conniving and rotten and evil. And they're just like everybody in today's society.
>
> Jim Keating was a patrol officer, a member of the Cook County Sheriff's Department for about 22 years. He's a gentleman now in his 50s.
>
> Lt. Keating was an excellent cop, an excellent commander. He was smart, congenial, personable, a leader at times, afraid at times, but he also possessed the frailties that all cops and all human beings really possess. He made mistakes. He let himself down. He let the people that looked up to him, the people he led, he let them down.

He told the jury how Keating had been convicted of accepting bribes from Larry Damron. He admitted that Keating had accepted money from the undercover FBI agent and said he had been severely punished for that.

Murphy warned the jury not to believe Jack Bachman, Keating's onetime friend, whose son was Keating's godchild. Murphy provided a description of him: "A convicted racketeer, a cowardly vice cop who is facing sentencing in federal court right now and has been for almost the last year for racketeering and tax evasion." He continued:

> I believe that the evidence will show that Jack Bachman is a conniving individual, cunning individual. A desperate man. Not a stupid man at all, but a person who would do anything and say anything to protect himself.
>
> He is an actor, ladies and gentlemen. I think you will see that. And, I think he will fit right into the play that Mr. Scorza talked about in his opening statement.
>
> Through his own mouth, I think he will say that he was a thief, a pimp, a purveyor.

Murphy noted that Bachman had pleaded guilty to federal racketeering charges but that he had yet to be sentenced. They were waiting to see how Bachman testified, holding the sentence over his head to win his cooperation. Keating's attorney argued that the government was trying to twist comments that Keating had made to Lt. Howard Vanick on March 19, 1982, when the two men met on the Masters' driveway after Dianne's disappearance and Keating threatened to remove Vanick from the case.

> What he's telling Vanick is good sense, the right way to do it. What he's saying is if you can't be objective, if you can't be fair, get another lieutenant who's not involved with Masters or get the Illinois Department of Law Enforcement to become involved. Common sense. They would have you believe that's a conspiracy.
>
> In this case I will submit and I believe that when the evidence is finally in, that you will see that the government has conjured up events and tried to disregard the defendant's presumption of innocence.

And Murphy launched what was the first of many attacks by the defense attorneys on Dianne's character. It appeared that she was as much on trial as the men accused of killing her. "Alan Masters had the misfortune to be married to a woman who had love affairs and made him a cuckold, consistently cheated on him" said Murphy. "There was a divorce imminent. They wanted Alan Masters from the beginning. So to do this, to support their convoluted theory, they have had to concoct a racketeering case."

Corbitt's attorney, Dennis Berkson, a former public defender with a pockmarked face and curly hair, began his presentation after the lunch break. He seized on Scorza's analogy in his opening remarks about the curtain coming down on a play. Scorza's two-hour opening remarks had been a "myth, a fairy tale."

Berkson argued that Corbitt had nothing to do with any conspiracy.

> What we have here is a murder case, pure and simple. That's what it is. That's what this is all about. And I'm going to tell you right now, the theory that they have on the murder is ridiculous. They say there's an agreement between Corbitt, Keating and Masters. Nobody is going to take that witness stand and say to you that they ever saw those three individuals do anything, particularly anything illegal, in this indictment.
>
> Ladies and gentlemen, my client is on no tape recordings. My client is on no video recordings. They say there is an agreement between these three men, and I will submit to you when the evidence is all in, you will wonder if Mr. Corbitt and Mr. Keating even knew each other.

He contended that there was no evidence that would link Corbitt to the murder of Dianne Masters.

> Mr. Scorza stood up in opening argument and said that my client put two bullets in that woman's head. And I'm going to tell you right now there will be no testimony that that happened. Because it didn't happen. The government would like you to guess that it happened.
>
> You are not going to hear anybody take that witness stand

> and say to you that they saw my client, Michael Corbitt, with Dianne Masters' Cadillac on March 18th, 19th, or 20th. No one's going to tell you that they saw my client push anything into the canal in Willow Springs on March 18th, 19th, or 20th.

And then the audience heard from the other attorney they had been waiting for. Patrick Tuite spoke to the jurors:

> I sat here this morning and it was scary. It was really scary because here's a gentleman who speaks very well and wove what we have talked to you and Mr. Berkson and Mr. Murphy talked to you about—a fantasy, a fairy tale. But it's scary because unfortunately Allen Funt isn't going to come through the door and say: "Smile. You're on Candid Camera." I thought I saw Angela Lansbury there, Mrs. Fletcher, back there writing her fiction, "Murder She Wrote," by Mr. Scorza.
>
> But that's all it is. But it's scary because a citizen's life and future is at stake here. When I say life, I don't mean the death penalty is involved, but his whole life, his whole future is at stake here. This case is as phony as a three dollar bill. This is unbelievable.

Tuite told the jury how Alan had kissed his wife good-bye the night she went to the board meeting and then discovered the next morning that she had not come home. Alan Masters, he said, had been nothing but a concerned husband when he contacted Jim Keating about his wife's failure to return home. Tuite said that Alan had even asked someone to call one of Dianne's best friends, who was on an overseas trip, to see if perhaps Dianne had joined her.

Tuite traced the path Dianne drove the night she disappeared and was followed by Genevieve Capstaff. Next door to the Masters' home, he told the jurors, the Masters' neighbors were waiting up for their daughter to come home from a date.

> The Vacis will testify that they heard a dog bark and it woke them up about 12:30 in the morning. Because their daughter wasn't home yet from her date, they stayed up and they sat in the kitchen, which faces the Masters' driveway, waiting

> for the daughter. They told police and the FBI that nobody pulled into the driveway after 12:30. The fact is anybody coming in the Masters' driveway, their headlights would hit the Vacis' house. Nobody pulled into that driveway. And they stayed up until their daughter got home about 1:30.
>
> The other thing is that the housekeeper got there at 7:30 in the morning. She said there was nothing upset in the house. There was no blood. There was no damage. There was no evidence of somebody having cleaned the house because her job was to clean the house.
>
> Their third theory is that somehow she got home, took off her underwear and was struck by Alan Masters. This is what I heard here today. Now their theory is that somebody who was stalking her, I suppose, was waiting at Artie G's for her to show up there. Well, then how does the person who was waiting get the call to come over?

It was left to Tuite to begin the attack on Ted Nykaza's credibility. "Mr. Scorza told you that Mr. Nykaza had a drinking problem. That's sort of like saying that the Hunchback of Notre Dame had a little posture problem. This man was a drunk."

He told the jurors of Nykaza's repeated hospitalization for alcoholism. "You have to take that into consideration because he's going to testify about things he heard that people who were present said they didn't hear." Tuite also noted that Nykaza had an underwear fetish, a point he would belabor in the ensuing days.

The defense attorney claimed that it had been Nykaza's idea to tap the telephones in the Masters house.

> There was no question Alan Masters was extremely upset about his wife's infidelity. He was extremely upset that she was going to leave him for another man. He was upset that she was going to put him in a divorce custody battle over the child. He wasn't worried about the outcome. He had evidence that she was sleeping around, had been sleeping around for years, and he felt he had a good chance of getting custody of that child. He asked a judge to intercede to reconcile.
>
> There's no question Ted Nykaza tapped Dianne Masters' phone. He [Alan] didn't tell him to.

Tuite said that when Alan heard the tape, he cried. He was very upset.

> He did not say, "That's it. I'm going to kill her. It's going to look like a home invasion."
>
> You decide whether that was said because they feel that is it. That's the linchpin. That's the pin that holds it together. I submit that it's more like a diaper pin holding the diaper together.
>
> When you hear all of this evidence, we ask you to use logic, common sense.
>
> We are going to produce some very important evidence to you that will establish Alan Masters didn't have anything to do with his wife's death, nor did Mr. Corbitt and Mr. Keating.
>
> And after all of that, I think it will be so clear that you will find the defendant not guilty.

Chapter Twenty-Seven

May 25, 1989

JACK Reed drove the short distance from his home to Ted Nykaza's. The Cook County Sheriff's Police sergeant had secured a promise from Nykaza that he would refrain from drinking heavily the night before his scheduled testimony. Reed hoped that he had kept his word.

It was 6 A.M. when he reached the house. Reed had to rouse the private detective from bed, and he made some coffee for Nykaza to consume before leaving the house. Reed had never seen him so nervous. He looked as if he were ready to jump out of his skin, and he was a little wobbly.

Nykaza, who had donned a bluish gray suit, was going to be the star witness that morning. Since the start of the trial, Scorza and Foley had paraded sixteen witnesses before the jury.

Reed drove into the city at the height of rush hour. Scorza had wanted Nykaza there in the early morning to review his testimony once again and to judge his demeanor before putting him on the stand. They had been over and over it before, but Scorza was a perfectionist. Nykaza knew the kinds of questions the prosecutor would ask. There would be no coddling of this witness. Almost every foible in Nykaza's character would be scrutinized by Scorza in a gut-wrenching direct examination.

Reed parked his squad car some distance away from the federal building and the two men took the subway there. Like courthouses around the country, federal marshals in Chicago screen each person entering the courtroom, checking for guns, knives, and other weapons. Reed and Nykaza started to check their firearms when one marshal, a former Chicago policeman like Nykaza, recognized him.

"You're Ted Nykaza," said the marshal. "I remember you from the police academy."

Nykaza got a blank look on his face and didn't respond to the greeting. Reed thought Nykaza was just startled that the guy had recognized him. Instead Nykaza was having a seizure, a serious one. He started to pass out. Reed caught him so that he wouldn't fall, and he took his gun away.

Oh, shit, thought the sergeant. "Nykaza was backing out," Reed recalls. "He was a key witness. Without him, the whole thing kind of fell apart. As bad as he was, as much problems as we had with him, he kind of pulled it all together. And he knew he was going to take a beating on the stand."

Nykaza had appeared numerous times before the grand jury and endured all of Scorza's questioning. Now it seemed that he might never testify at the trial.

FBI agent Harris, who was called in his office, rushed downstairs with Scorza. They discovered that Nykaza was a basket case. "I didn't know at that point whether he was going to get on the stand or not," the agent would say later. "I didn't know if that was his way to back out of this or if this was just one of those unfortunate matters that happen."

Nykaza was jittery but sober. That might have been part of the problem. Also, he had refused to eat anything that morning. When the paramedics arrived to treat him, it became clear that Nykaza was very ill. He apparently was dehydrated and his blood pressure dropped drastically. The paramedics opted to transport him to a local hospital.

Scorza went before the judge twenty minutes later and reported Nykaza's hospitalization.

During the past few days, the testimony had focused on the various racketeering acts that didn't involve Dianne's murder. Larry Damron, the undercover FBI agent who had tape recorded Alan and Keating in 1981, had been the major government witness. He had been on the stand for a day and a half testifying about $5,000 in bribes he had paid Keating, his calls to Alan, and his dealings with Corbitt.

But slowly, Scorza and Foley were calling the witnesses whose testimonies related to the murder. They had tried to set the stage for Nykaza's appearance with the testimony of Herman Pastori, the police chief of Willow Springs who suddenly had retired just before the trial. Pastori, who admitted accepting cash from Alan for referring cases, said that he had seen Alan at the airport just weeks before Dianne disappeared, and he had asked if Alan and Dianne were still having marital problems.

Alan had replied, "Yes, serious problems."

Alan looked horrible that day, Pastori related. He appeared completely run-down and very depressed. Thinking that Alan might be suicidal, Pastori asked him, "Alan, you won't do anything drastic, will you?"

"I won't, but I'll have someone else do it," Alan responded.

Instead of Ted Nykaza, Joe Hein took the stand on May 25, 1989. He had been a sheriff's deputy for twenty-two years. In 1973, he had taken a year's leave of absence to work for the Willow Springs Police Department and Chief Michael Corbitt, his onetime friend. And he had been a groomsman at one of Corbitt's weddings.

Hein had been introduced to Alan in the later part of 1974. He had wanted Alan to handle a worker's injury case for him. Alan also had represented him on some post-divorce matters. Sometimes Alan charged him a legal fee; on other occasions, he did the work gratis.

The forty-seven-year-old sergeant had been in Ireland from March 10 to March 20 in 1982. It was an alibi that had been scrutinized by authorities.

Scorza was in an awkward situation with Hein. Although Hein was his witness, he believed that Hein had not been truthful when he testified before the grand jury. Scorza was convinced that Hein had tried to protect Alan and had given false statements. In fact, Hein had failed a polygraph examination.

However, Hein was the one person who had verified Nykaza's story about the existence of the tape recording. Scorza needed Hein to repeat to the jury as many details as he could to bolster Nykaza's credibility.

As Scorza cross-examined the policeman for the next twenty

minutes, Hein recalled few details of the incident. He remembered that he, Alan, and Nykaza had stood in the kitchen area, they had gone to the basement, and Nykaza had retrieved two tapes from a tape recorder by standing on a stepladder. Hein could not remember what was being said during this time or how the subject of the tape recording had come up.

After Hein testified that not once during the replay of the tape-recorded conversations did Alan ever threaten to kill his wife, Scorza asked to present a matter to the judge outside the presence of the jury. Citing Hein's untruthfulness, he asked Judge Zagel to allow him to question Hein as an adverse witness, a highly unusual maneuver considering that Scorza had called him on the government's behalf.

Tuite exploded. "You cannot put a witness on the stand that you think is lying," he said. "You think this man is lying and you put him on the stand in front of this jury."

But Zagel overruled Tuite's objection.

The prosecutor hammered Hein about his failure to report the fact that Alan was tape recording Dianne's conversations illegally, especially after her body was found.

Hein, a veteran police officer, had investigated homicide cases. He knew the relevance of such a taped conversation to a murder case. Yet he never had come forward. And Hein had acknowledged to Sgt. Reed that he had heard the tapes only after Hein suspected that the federal government had obtained a recording of him listening to the tape.

"As an investigator in a murder case, wouldn't a husband listening to that kind of tape be a matter of interest?"

"Yes, sir."

"But you never told anybody about it, right?"

"That's correct, sir."

"And you're pleased with that, aren't you?" Scorza asked sarcastically.

Tuite spent just a few minutes cross-examining Hein, eliciting from the detective that Nykaza often was drunk. It was evident that Tuite did not think that Hein had tainted his client.

The defense corps were more concerned about the witness who would testify after lunch. If Scorza and Foley had a surprise witness, Diane Economou was it. Somehow they had managed to keep her name secret from the press. Because of discovery rules, her statements to authorities had been turned over to the defense attorneys prior to the trial, so basically, they knew what she would say on the stand. But to those jamming the courtroom, the testimony of Economou, a lawyer who shared offices with Alan, would cause a stir.

Economou gave the prosecutors the opportunity to present to the jury evidence about Alan's infidelity. Foley questioned her about an event she had attended: a De Paul Law School reunion held at a hotel in October 1981. Alan, a 1958 graduate, did not bring Dianne to the reunion. Instead he was accompanied by Sheila, the secretary in his office who later married Nykaza. Alan begged Economou not to mention to his wife that he had brought Sheila. He had told Dianne that he had stopped dating his onetime employee.

Later that month, when Sheila held a Halloween party at her house—the one Alan had helped make the down payment on—he and Economou were among the guests. Again he asked his associate not to reveal to his wife that he had attended the festivities.

Economou told the jury how Dianne and Alan's marriage had begun to fall apart in January 1982. She said that Alan had become so distressed, he gave her one of his cases because he just couldn't handle it. He told his associate that he was seeing a doctor and was taking medication.

On the first Friday night in February 1982, Alan had called Economou at her condominium in a fashionable west suburb of Chicago. Alan was at the law office and had Anndra with him. He and Dianne had had an argument over the pending divorce and Dianne was going to leave him, he told Economou. Economou suggested that he drive to her house and use one of her spare bedrooms.

When Alan arrived with Anndra, Economou left for the store to get some food. She found Alan in the kitchen by the bay window when she returned. He sat at the table, crying. He had taken all of Dianne's jewelry from the home. In front of him, there were necklaces, pins, a ring, some bracelets, and a pouch. Between sobs, he babbled, "Look what I have done for her. Look at what I have done for Dianne. Look at all I've given her and she's gonna leave me. And she's gonna take Anndra from me."

Economou's voice was cracking with emotion as she tried to choke back tears. A despondent Alan had called the operator and placed a telephone call to his home. He wanted Dianne to think that he had fled the state with Anndra, Economou said. Then, when he came into the living room, Alan rambled on almost incoherently. "Look what all I've done for her. I've made her. She came from nothing and I made her into everything she is."

In late February 1982, Economou had been in the law offices talking with Nykaza. The private detective was discussing the infamous tape recording. A few days later, on the weekend, she and Nykaza chatted again. He told her that if she found out who Dianne's boyfriend was she should not tell Alan. Unexpectedly, Alan then joined them.

"He walked in when I was talking to Nykaza and he just sat down there on the side chair, and he was crying," described Economou. "I don't even know if he knew he was talking to anybody. And he said that he was going to go to a restaurant and he was going to meet Jim Keating and they were going to talk about having Dianne murdered."

"Objection," Murphy cried out.

"And make it look like an accident," said Economou, finishing the sentence.

Economou's statement was the bombshell the defense attorneys had known was coming. As part of an agreement between the prosecutors and the defense attorneys, Zagel gave an instruction to the jury. He told them that Alan's statement to Economou "does not contain an assertion by Masters about what he actually did. It contains only a statement of what he planned or intended to do."

"After Mr. Masters said this to you and Mr. Nykaza, what did he do?" asked Foley.

"He just . . . He sat there. And I said to him, 'Don't even think such crazy thoughts.' "

In the first part of March, she said, she and Alan had been driving to downtown Chicago. That was when he told her about the tape recorded conversation between Dianne and Jim about the bottle of wine. She then identified Jim Keating, saying that he had stopped by the office periodically over the years. But just prior to Dianne's disappearance, for about a week, he was there on a daily basis.

Economou's testimony was perhaps the most damaging the government would produce. She did not come to the courtroom with the baggage of Nykaza's alcoholism or Bachman's corruption. She was Alan's friend and associate. And she had just confirmed the statements of the other government witnesses concerning the existence of the tape recording and Alan's plan to murder Dianne.

Foley ended his direct examination with a flourish. He asked Economou when it was that she first informed the government about her conversation with Alan regarding his decision to meet with Keating to plot Dianne's death.

"In 1988."

"And was there some reason why you waited until 1988 to advise the government of that?"

"I was afraid," she responded.

CHAPTER TWENTY-EIGHT

May 26, 1989

KATHY Turner's parents had become such fixtures in the courtroom that the court buffs were now saving them seats. It had become a necessity. The trial was attracting a throng of onlookers. There were a number of noteworthy events playing in the city that week, including the Bolshoi Ballet, but the reporter for the *Chicago Sun-Times* described the trial as being the hottest show in town. Office workers in the Loop were attending the proceedings on their coffee breaks. One suburban housewife, who drove more than forty miles to hear the testimonies, characterized the trial as being as much fun as "L.A. Law."

Bystanders waited eagerly for the next episode in this suddenly popular melodrama. Jim Koscielniak was going to take the stand and he was expected to reveal tantalizing details of his affair with Dianne. Much to the dismay of many women in the courtroom, neither Jim nor Alan was the heart-stopping Adonis type. Some of the crowd expressed surprise at Dianne's taste in men. "Neither one of those guys would ever stir my dandruff," one secretary told the *Sun-Times*.

Scorza and Foley's two chief witnesses on May 26 would be Jim and Jack Bachman. Jim would retell the jury how he and Dianne had met, fallen in love, and begun having an affair. Bachman would describe how for more than a decade, he had been paid bribes by Alan, and he would detail how Keating had solicited him to murder Dianne for Alan.

Jim Koscielniak's appearance on the stand provided the de-
nse attorneys with a unique opportunity. Ironically, they
uld use him to bolster Alan's image in the eyes of the jurors.
Vith Tuite's line of questioning, he would counter the prosecu-
on's portrayal of Alan as an evil and corrupt lawyer. He would
e made to look as though he were the perfect, doting father
nd devoted husband, while Dianne was painted as a scarlet
oman. In a circumstantial case such as the one Scorza was
resenting, the jurors' impressions of the defendant were some-
mes just as important as the testimony.

Bachman, on the other hand, presented Alan and Keating's
wyers with a problem. If he came across to the jury as a
redible witness, it would hurt the defense tremendously. The
lan was to depict Bachman as a crooked cop who would
urn in his closest friends and say anything to avoid going to
ail.

Jim appeared brash, sometimes cocky, during his testimony.
omehow due to his nervousness that day and the methodical
uestioning by Scorza, his true affection for Dianne became
bscured. It was as if their relationship had been nothing more
han an unromantic series of shack-ups. Even his testimony
bout the wine bottle came across as antiseptically sterile sex.

"And when you were [at the motel], did you essentially
ollow the directions of the Greeley article?"

"Yes," Jim replied.

"And again, Mr. Koscielniak, not to pry, but to be specific,
what did you and Dianne Masters do?"

"With reference to the second full paragraph on the right-
hand column, I poured wine on Dianne's vagina and had oral
sex with her."

As he testified, the spectators watched as Alan furiously
scribbled notes on a yellow legal pad, never once glancing up
at his wife's lover.

Jim endured an hour of brutal character assassination by
Tuite. His cross-examination showed the lawyer at his best. It
was the reason his clients paid him six-figure fees.

Tuite came out swinging. He asked Jim how long he had
been a teacher and if he had taught at more than one college.

When Jim replied that he was teaching at two colleges, Tuite intoned, "I take it from your testimony you weren't teaching morals." Tuite asked if perhaps Jim was teaching sex education.

Next he asked why Jim had cut out Greeley's article in 198[illegible] and saved it in a file and whether he had been planning to use the article in a class. When the professor replied that he had, Tuite retorted, "You were going to teach various different ways of using wine?"

The defense attorney then honed in on February 24, the night of the incident with the wine bottle.

"Did you tell her we're going to go to a motel and do something with some wine?" he asked.

"I don't think so."

"Did you tell her tonight we're going to have a biblical evening?"

"I don't remember her saying that—me saying that, no," replied a flustered Jim.

"Was it usual that when you went to motels you took wine with you?"

"Yes."

"That was part of your ritual to have some wine?"

"Yes."

"And so that night you brought the wine?"

"Right."

"No crackers and cheese, right?"

"There were times when we had crackers and cheese. I don't remember."

"Sometimes you even had crackers and cheese. Just like the opening of an art gallery, right?" Tuite asked. "A little wine and cheese and adultery always goes good, right? Tell me, sir, does white wine or red wine go better with adultery?"

Scorza objected, but it didn't stop Tuite.

"Did you, following Father Greeley's article, take out the Bible in the motel room and read it along, or didn't that motel room have Bibles?" When Jim said he had saved the original article in one of his files, Tuite asked, "Would you tell us what other articles of sexual perversion you kept in that file?"

At each opportunity, Tuite portrayed Dianne and Jim as unrepentant sinners, with Alan, the doting father, at home caring for the couple's daughter. It was effective rhetoric and it was making an impression on the jurors.

"When you went out to the motels on various nights with Mrs. Masters having sex with her, the husband was home with the baby, right?" Tuite asked.

"I wouldn't know."

"Well, you ever ask her: 'Where's your husband tonight?' "

"No," Jim replied stoically.

Tuite's attack reached a crescendo when it came to Jim's last visit with Dianne in the La Grange Motel. "Let me just ask you this: after she showed you the picture of her husband and child, you then had sex with her, right?"

"Yes, a little later, yes," Jim said.

"Did you prop up the picture on the pillow for a remembrance? That was kinky enough for you?" Tuite asked.

Scorza leaped to his feet. "Objection, Judge. This man's not on trial."

"The objection is sustained. Mr. Tuite, cease," Judge Zagel ordered.

Tuite knew he had to depict Jim Koscielniak as depraved. Through his cross-examination, he had successfully conveyed to the jury the image of Alan as a loving husband who stayed at home while his wife cheated on him. The carefully woven defense strategy, however, would unravel with the government's next witness, Jack Bachman.

Jack Bachman now drove over-the-road trucks for a living. His twenty-two-year career with the Cook County Sheriff's Department had ended when he pled guilty to two criminal charges: income tax fraud and racketeering. He was facing a possible twenty-three-year prison term, but the government prosecutors had promised that they would tell his sentencing judge of his extensive cooperation and urge an appropriate sentence. Sheldon Zenner, the former assistant, had warned him that if he ever lied on the stand, the U.S. Attorney's Office would come down on him like a ton of bricks.

As Bachman sat in the witness box, Scorza recounted to the

jurors the guilty plea he had entered and his corruption-filled years as a sheriff's deputy. The ex-Marine and black belt in one of the martial arts was uncharacteristically demure. Scorza kept telling him to speak louder so that the jurors could hear him. There was surrender in his voice each time he answered "yes, sir" to the questions being posed.

Yes, he was a crooked cop, he told the jurors. In the spring of 1972, he had gone on the take after learning that his supervisor, Jim Keating, was taking money to protect four gambling locations in Cicero, the western suburb made infamous by gangster Alphonso Capone. He started receiving $50 a month just for looking the other way. Then the amount grew, and he and Keating split the $300 a month that the gambling operators were paying them through their attorney, Alan Masters.

When Keating left for advance police schooling, Bachman picked up the cash from Alan directly or got an envelope filled with the greenbacks from a mail slot at Alan's office in Summit. It was always there waiting for him around the first of each month.

In 1980 or 1981, Alan cut himself in. Bachman got the envelope, but it contained just $200 and a note from Alan saying he was keeping $100. Bachman and Keating stopped taking the payoffs in 1984, when FBI agents interviewed Keating, then a target of Operation Safebet, the federal investigation of corruption in the sheriff's department.

There were other instances where he had accepted bribes, too. He even had taken money from Mike Corbitt once for a case involving a businessman in the south suburbs.

"Mr. Bachman, besides these receipts of money by you as a police officer, did you have any business connection with a vice business?"

"Yes, sir, I did."

"What type of vice business?" Scorza asked.

"It was a whorehouse."

"Who were you partners in that business with?"

"Alan Masters and Clarke Buckendahl."

With Bachman's response, Judge Zagel ordered a lunch break. The timing was perfect for the government; while the jurors ate their meal, Bachman's last words would be what they remembered. Alan Masters owned a whorehouse.

Bachman already had managed to undo the damage done by Tuite's cross-examination of Jim Koscielniak. It didn't matter that Bachman was a crooked cop. His testimony had credibility.

After the recess, Bachman explained how he had first met Dianne when she was his real estate agent on the purchase of a home. He had known Alan since the 1960s through Alan's work in the local courthouses. He had been among the policemen invited to the Masters' homes and he once had repaired a hole in the roof of the Palos Park house.

He also had been privy to their spats. The first time was in 1975 or 1976. Alan thought Dianne was having an affair with a maintenance man at their Naperville house. When Bachman was assigned to Forest Park, Alan once called him from his car phone. Bachman said that Alan was screaming in a high-pitched voice that he had just beaten Dianne up and he felt great about it.

In February 1982, Bachman learned through Vanick that Dianne had been spotted with Jim Koscielniak at a restaurant. Vanick had told him to make sure that Alan got the license number information and to be sure that Alan knew it had come from Howard Vanick.

A few weeks later, he was in Jim Keating's office. Keating had just hung up the telephone after a conversation with Alan and he looked worried. Keating told Bachman that Alan had heard the taped conversation between Dianne and Jim. Keating described the tape in some detail for Bachman.

Scorza kept urging his witness to speak up. He needed Bachman to emphasize those statements to the jury.

"Did you go to Mr. Keating's office again around the latter part of February 1982?" the prosecutor asked.

"Yes," Bachman replied.

"And what happened as you entered the office?"

"Again, Keating was hanging up the phone. He looked worried. He was hanging up the phone as I walked in."

"As best you remember, what did you say and what did Keating say in that conversation?"

"I asked, 'What's going on?' And he said that Alan was going off the deep end. Dianne was having an affair and Alan wanted to have her killed."

"And when he said Alan wanted to have her killed, what did you say?" Scorza asked, again coaxing his witness to speak louder.

"I said: 'That's crazy. He's been mad at her before. Go buy him coffee and talk to him.' He [Keating] said: 'No. He wants to have the dog whacked, the maid whacked and make it look like a home invasion.' He said that Alan was offering $25,000 to have her—whoever killed her and wanted to know if I was interested."

"And what did you tell him?" Scorza asked Bachman.

"I made some joke and said I've got $25,000."

"Did Mr. Keating mention any other name in this conversation?"

"He said that Michael Corbitt would get rid of the body for whoever agreed to kill the woman."

A few weeks later, Bachman asked Keating if Alan had calmed down, and Keating replied that Alan was still ranting and raving. And as Bachman left the office, Keating told him to make sure he was with his wife that night. Bachman took the comment as a warning to have an alibi because Dianne was to be murdered that evening. The next day, however, Keating told Bachman that something had gone wrong. "Keating said that whoever was waiting for her, the guy chickened out. She didn't show up. And it was cold out that night."

Under questioning by Scorza, Bachman admitted that he never had tried to warn Dianne and that for years, he never had told anyone about Keating's comments.

For the next hour or so, the three defense attorneys attacked the credibility of the former policeman. But unlike Tuite's examination of Jim Koscielniak earlier that day, they had little success.

Scorza frequently objected to the form of questioning by the attorneys. And there were many sidebars with the judge, where they huddled to discuss the case out of earshot of the jury and the spectators.

In those meetings, the defense attorneys were revealing for

the first time their main strategy in refuting the charges. They were going to try to make Ted Nykaza look much more repugnant than a drunk. They were going to accuse Ted Nykaza of killing Dianne Masters.

The prosecution was amazed at their opponents' theory. It was Memorial Day weekend. Scorza had three days to think about whether he should call Nykaza to testify.

Chapter Twenty-Nine

May 30, 1989

TED Anthony Nykaza took the stand on Tuesday afternoon, May 30, 1989. The government had made sure that the private detective was healthy and ready to testify. He had been in the federal building most of the day, with Jack Reed serving as his bodyguard, protecting him from the bottle and other demons.

Scorza and the defense attorneys approached the bench for a sidebar with Judge Zagel before Nykaza began testifying. The prosecutor was appalled that the defense was going to brand Nykaza as the person who had killed Dianne.

''We know of no evidence tying Mr. Nykaza to the murder of Dianne Masters,'' he told the judge. ''I don't believe there's a good faith basis for that theory.''

The defense lawyers had been busy compiling a dossier on Nykaza. In their version of the events, Nykaza was more than a drunk. He was a sex pervert with a fetish for women's underwear.

One of Nykaza's ex-wives, Sheila—Alan's former lover—had been helpful to the attorneys. She had told them about Nykaza's fetish and how he had collected women's panties and stored them in bags in the attic of their home. She also noted that Nykaza liked to wear women's underwear during sex when they were married.

They also had learned that he would take a camera equipped with a special infrared-type lens to shopping malls, where he would photograph women to view their undergarments.

But Nykaza's fetish was far more serious, they would try to argue, which was why Dianne Masters' panties had been missing when she was found. Nykaza had stolen them after he killed her, perhaps after she resisted his sexual advances, they contended.

And there had been an incident when Nykaza was treated in an emergency room. During his treatment, a nurse noticed that he was wearing women's underwear. The defense would call her as one of their first witnesses.

Scorza was afraid that on cross-examination, Nykaza would be questioned unmercifully about whether he killed Dianne as well as about his sexual habits. "What I am trying to avoid is that the man is simply being the subject of a mudslinging attack here or the equivalent of: Isn't it true that you beat your wife questions," Scorza told the judge. "The man is going to be severely cross-examined on the basis of a whole host of problems that he's got, including his alcoholism, prior inconsistent statements, and so on. The jury is going to see this man attacked, but this is supposed to be a fair trial; and I don't believe attacking him on the basis of allegations that he was involved in the murder have any good faith basis and also allegations about things like his sexual conduct."

Scorza had plotted his direct examination of Nykaza weeks earlier. It would be like precision surgery. He would open up Nykaza, highlight his character flaws, and expose them to the jury. Make sure they understand the government knew fully well that Ted Nykaza was a drunk, but convince the jurors that he was telling the truth. Scorza had rehearsed it with Nykaza several times. The private detective knew exactly the line of questioning the prosecutor would pursue.

Nykaza, a decorated cop, had been on the witness stand dozens of times, so he anticipated a grueling examination. Nothing could prepare him, however, for the extremely painful operation Scorza was going to perform on his psyche. Nykaza was one of the heroes of the case, but he also would become one of its victims.

"During your twelve years as a Chicago policeman, did you have some disciplinary problems?" Scorza asked after a brief review of Nykaza's personal history.

"Yes," Nykaza replied.

"Were there occasions where you didn't come to work because you had been drunk the night before?"

"Yes."

"Have you, in fact, had a drinking problem, Mr. Nykaza?"

"Yes."

"When did you first have a drinking problem?"

"I believe it began in high school."

"And do you continue to have a problem with alcoholism today?"

"Yes."

"Have you been drinking in the recent couple of days?"

"Yes."

"Did you drink a lot or in moderation?"

"A lot."

"How about just today? Are you drunk today?"

"No, sir."

"Mr. Nykaza, is it difficult for you not to drink?"

"Yes."

"And have you received treatment from doctors about your drinking?"

"Yes."

"Have you ever gone into a hospital specifically to be treated for alcoholism problems?"

"Yes."

"Approximately how many occasions?"

"Just a guess, I believe three times."

"And besides going into a hospital for drinking-related problems, have you ever had to go into a hospital because of injuries that came from being drunk?"

"Yes."

Two years earlier, an intoxicated Nykaza had been out driving and had shot his finger with his own derringer. Twice he had been ticketed for drunk driving. He also had fallen down the stairs and required hospitalization. In 1981, he had been arrested for trying to shoot a chain off a driveway at a local monastery because he wanted to see if there were ghosts on the grounds. He also had torched his car and filed a phony insurance claim.

"Mr. Nykaza, it would be fair to say that all of these problems indicate that in the ordinary language you are a drunk; is that correct?"

"That's correct."

The surgery completed, Scorza concentrated on the evidence. Nykaza described one telephone call he had overheard between Dianne and Alan in mid-1981. He was at his desk in the Summit office when a tearful Alan pleadingly asked, "Dianne why are you doing this to me?"

He recalled a day that same year when he and Diane Economou had been talking in the law office and Alan had entered, complaining about Dianne and how she wanted to leave him.

"Alan, don't you think it might be a part of your screwing around with other women, too?" Nykaza suggested to Alan.

"That has nothing to do with it," Alan retorted in a loud voice.

Later Alan asked Nykaza to bug his two home telephone lines, saying he wanted to find out the identity of Dianne's boyfriend. Nykaza complied, knowing it was illegal. Alan agreed to pay for the devices and Nykaza had kept the receipts for the purchases as well as the express mailing of the packages by a freight company. The recorders arrived in January of 1982 and Nykaza installed them on about January 25, 1982.

Alan bungled trying to play back the tapes, and Nykaza went to Alan's home once to make emergency phone repairs. Alan wanted him to buy two more of the special recorders so that Alan could play back the tapes without having to disconnect the two machines that Nykaza had installed above a furnace vent in the basement. The new machines arrived on about February 14.

Several days later, Nykaza was at the law office when Alan summoned him to the house. Sgt. Joe Hein, of the Cook County Sheriff's Department, who was working for Nykaza's private detective agency, accompanied Nykaza. Nykaza said he hadn't been drinking, and he drove. He brought along the new equipment so that he could play the tapes from the hidden recorders. Nykaza went down to the basement alone, got a small stool or ladder to reach above the furnace duct, and retrieved the two tapes. He brought them upstairs to the kitchen.

With Alan to his left and Hein to his right, Nykaza played the tapes several times. Hein remained in the room and the trio overheard Dianne and her boyfriend discussing their lovemaking and the wine bottle incident. Alan seemed to be getting more angry each time he heard the conversation.

"Again, as best you can remember, can you tell the ladies and gentlemen of the jury what this comment was that Mr. Masters made," said Scorza.

"I'll kill that motherfucker."

"Anything besides that?"

"Then he talked about having a home invasion where the dogs will go, the cats will go, everything will go, including Dianne. Dianne will be there, but he and Anndra will not be there. Those two phrases highlight in my mind and I won't forget that."

"And where in the house did those statements take place?"

"In the kitchen cooking area, not at the seating area, but by the sink," Nykaza replied. Alan was sitting on the countertop.

Nykaza said he had brought the tapes home and played them for his wife Sheryl while they were in bed together. In the early part of March, Alan told him to destroy the tapes. His stepson, Joseph Danzl, helped him break apart the cassettes in the basement office of his home. He subsequently went and removed the tape recorders from the Masters' home, although at this point he couldn't remember when he had done so.

He said that twice during a three-week span in March, he had been called by Alan and warned to make sure he had an alibi for the upcoming day.

Nykaza admitted that after Dianne had disappeared, he kept the secret of the tapes. And he said he had shared it only with Reed, during one of his drunks when he rambled on. He told the jurors that he doubted he had been sober any of the times Reed visited him. It was a period when he was drinking very heavily. Some of the things he had told Reed were lies.

Nykaza had ended his relationship with Alan in July 1987, at which point he already was cooperating with the federal government's investigation. He had gone to the office one day and found a note from Alan asking him to leave. Nykaza removed his belongings from the premises the following day.

The trial adjourned until the following morning. Reed was assigned the task of keeping Nykaza sober.

Tuite started his cross-examination by asking Nykaza if he knew what fraud was. He accused him of torching not one car, but two, including a 1983 Camaro that had been a lemon, which Nykaza denied. He accused Nykaza of taking his Camaro, which had problems with the catalytic converter, pushing it down somewhere on a cul-de-sac near his home, and setting fire to it. Then Nykaza went home and wrote "You'll be next" on his garage.

"No, sir," Nykaza replied, admitting he had, however, scribbled that on his garage. He explained that he and his wife Sheryl had been having a bitter argument. "I was trying to get a thought through her head, thinking that since Dianne Masters was murdered, possibly she would be murdered also. I was trying to scare her because it was a bitter argument, a verbal fight we had."

It was exactly the kind of response Tuite had hoped for. He would craft his questions carefully over the ensuing minutes to place doubts in the minds of the jurors. Did Nykaza have a violent nature? Was he capable of murder? Could he be Dianne's killer?

Tuite segued to the shooting incident at the monastery. With his questions, he noted that Nykaza had emptied his pistol violently at the lock. "You blew off the head of the lock?" he asked.

"Correct," responded Nykaza.

"How many shots did it take to blow the head off the lock?" he asked, emphasizing again "the head of the lock."

Nykaza admitted to Tuite that when he had shot himself, he actually had accused Alan of the shooting. He had gone to Alan's house and awakened him in the middle of the night. Under the emotionally exhausting cross-examination, Tuite also elicited from Nykaza that the private detective usually carried a gun and wasn't adverse to using it.

Tuite asked whether Nykaza had ever told anyone he had killed people as a Chicago policeman. The defense lawyer reviewed a number of shootings that Nykaza had bragged about, even after Nykaza said he had never shot anyone. Tuite then had Nykaza tell the jurors about his boasts that he kept a morgue photo at his home.

"Have you ever, to your knowledge when at home, sat there and talking to yourself said: 'I can't kill again. I can't kill anymore.' Have you ever said that talking to yourself at home?" Tuite asked.

Scorza objected. Tuite had found this statement in a police interview of Nykaza's ex-wife. And he wanted to question Nykaza further about it and in a sidebar, he presented a persuasive argument.

"The purpose is that this man says he had never killed anyone. It is our theory that he was responsible for the death of Dianne Masters," said Tuite. "If he didn't commit these killings, it's our theory that he was involved in Dianne Masters' killing."

"We have a right, Judge, to raise doubts as to the guilt of the defendant. And one of the ways you can do it is to show that someone else could have committed the offense. We don't have to prove it beyond a reasonable doubt. But we have a witness that the man says: 'I can't kill again. I can't do it again.' Now, this is after Dianne Masters is dead. He's referring to some killing. We have got evidence that Dianne was on that road that night not only was she heading toward her house, but in the direction of Nykaza's house. We have this statement of him. We have him carrying guns and shooting the guns at various times." Judge Zagel permitted him to ask whether Nykaza had sat at home by himself and said aloud: "I can't kill anymore" or "I can't kill again."

Nykaza replied that he did not recall having made such a statement, but that it was possible.

"Have you ever either in a drunken or sober state told anyone that little voices tell you to kill?" Tuite asked.

"No, that's ridiculous."

"Will you tell us, Mr. Nykaza, where you were at about 1:15 in the morning, early morning hours of March 19, 1982?"

"To be honest with you sir, I couldn't tell you where I was last week. I don't keep track of every minute."

"The point is that when you found out that Mrs. Masters had disappeared and you found out the date she disappeared, did you think back to where you were the night she disappeared?''

''No. I had no reason to.''

As the questioning continued, Nykaza and Tuite became bitter enemies. It was now clear in Nykaza's mind that Tuite was trying to implicate him in the murder. Every time Nykaza made a slip of the tongue, Tuite seized the opportunity.

Tuite accused Nykaza of trying to blackmail Alan over the incident when Nykaza had shot himself accidentally with his own derringer. Tuite contended that Nykaza was aware then that Alan was being investigated for Dianne's murder by the federal government.

''That's ridiculous,'' responded Nykaza.

''But you took the time to go to his house with a bloody or taped up finger and tell him to his face that he shot you when you knew he didn't?''

''I'm sober now, and I'll say this to you. It was drunken behavior. Maybe it was intoxicated thinking that I was going to create a diversion, that he wouldn't know that I was already talking to the government, that I was talking to the police. There's a lot of things that alcohol could have done to me. I don't know the exact reason. A sober reason I could give you, but I wasn't sober at the time.''

The rhetoric kept escalating and the tempers flared. Finally Tuite scored his point.

''Nykaza,''—Tuite had dropped the ''mister'' now—''you can't tell us whether you were at home or on the road between your house and the Masters' house on the 19th, the early morning hours of March 19th?''

''No, sir, I could not.''

''Nykaza, that evening, March 19th, as a favor to a friend, did you stop and abduct Dianne Masters?''

''Are you serious?'' Nykaza replied.

''Yes, I am serious, sir. This is not a joke, sir. Maybe it is to you, but it's not a joke.''

Scorza tried to halt the cross-examination. In a sidebar before Judge Zagel, he argued again that there was no evidence to support their claim that Nykaza had been involved in Dianne's disappearance.

"We think that he saw her, that he did something with her, that he killed her," Tuite countered. "I think that's reasonable because we have a witness who says that this man, who says he never killed anybody, was sitting in his room saying: 'I can't kill again. I can't kill again.'

"I think that the evidence will establish he has guns. He shoots at people.

"We have very definite strong evidence that this man wears and collects women's underwear. We have hospital personnel that when he went into the hospital, he wears women's underwear. We have testimony that he wears women's underwear. I think that is a very strong fact, one that would explain that there's a reasonable basis that someone else took [Dianne's] underwear and she did not get home."

"If you want to ask this individual whether or not he killed Dianne Masters, you can do that," Judge Zagel told Tuite.

"Mr. Nykaza, on the early morning hours of March 19, 1982, did you beat, shoot, and kill Dianne Masters?"

"No, sir," Nykaza responded.

"Did you, sir, take off her underwear?"

Scorza leaped up from his seat to object. Zagel ordered Nykaza not to answer.

"Mr. Nykaza, isn't it a fact that in March of 1982 you wore women's underwear as a regular matter?" Tuite asked.

Scorza objected before the defense attorney could finish his question.

The two legal adversaries squared off in another sidebar. Judge Zagel told Tuite that he could ask Nykaza if he had worn women's underwear or if he had seen Dianne that night. "And then let's stop the show."

Nykaza swore he had not seen Dianne the night she disappeared.

"Did you in March of 1982 sometime before and sometime after that wear women's underwear?"

"In sexual games my wife and I played, it's very possible I did at that time," Nykaza responded.

"Did you continue to wear women's underwear not in sexual games with your wife?" Tuite asked.

"No."

Tuite's next question drew a series of objections from Scorza. The defense attorney, though, ignored the shouts of his opposition, knowing that the judge was not likely to let Nykaza answer. Nevertheless, Tuite wanted the jury to hear the question.

"Did you . . . during that period of time have on you or in your collection . . . shiny . . . lacy, feminine women's underwear?"

His scathing cross-examination now finished, Tuite looked smug. He had destroyed Nykaza's reputation and possibly the detective's livelihood.

Alan could not have been happier with the way the trial was progressing. He was overheard saying in a conversation recorded by the government that he was convinced he would be found innocent of the charges.

Feeling self-confident, he was taking jabs at the men who had conducted the investigation. Right before court resumed in the afternoon, Alan approached Jack Reed, the sheriff's deputy, in the hallway.

"Jack, did you read *Time* magazine this week?" he asked. "They are no longer using white mice and rats for cancer research. They have switched over from rats to detective police sergeants, for three reasons. Detective police sergeants are more plentiful than rats. The lab people do not get as attached to the detective sergeants as they did to the rats. And there are some things that rats will not do that police sergeants will. That's my little joke for you. You can apply it to anyone."

Jack Reed is a massive man whose frame is anchored firmly by feet the size of a professional basketball player. Alan noticed their size. "Boy, do you have big feet," he told Reed. "The next size—the shoe box." Then he touched the sergeant on the right forearm and asked him about his weight. The perpetually dieting Alan wanted to know, "Are you putting on weight or taking it off?"

A few days later, Reed would be the brunt of Alan's jests once again. He approached Reed outside the courtroom. "I know you have a good sense of humor, John. This is the way to slap someone in the face without actually hitting them,'' Alan said, moving his right hand as if he was preparing to hit the detective.

Then Alan told Reed another joke: ''A lawyer was calling another lawyer every reprehensible name in the book except one. I would call you a cocksucker, but I know you are trying to stop.''

Jack Reed hoped he would have the last laugh.

Chapter Thirty

June 1, 1989

Tom Scorza didn't just *think* Mike Corbitt had dumped Dianne Masters' Cadillac into the canal in March of 1982, he *knew* it. In fact, Corbitt himself had told the federal prosecutor. Corbitt and his attorney had sat down with Scorza and the FBI agents and had made a proffer, which the government could not use against him unless he took the stand in his own defense and contradicted his statement.

The proffer was part of the negotiations of a possible plea bargain by Corbitt. Three months' incarceration in Chicago's federal jail, where he had been sentenced following his conviction on corruption charges, had made him more open-minded. But the deal had fallen apart, because the federal agents didn't believe Corbitt was telling the whole truth. His version of dumping the car into the canal differed sharply from the prosecutor's.

Corbitt said he had dumped the car into the canal in the middle of the night, not twenty-two hours later. He picked the car up at the Blue Front Lounge and drove it to the canal by himself. After he deep-sixed the vehicle, he walked back to his squad car, which was parked at the tavern. A witness, however, placed Corbitt at another bar, In First Place, at around 11 P.M. on the night Dianne disappeared.

More important, in Corbitt's rendition, no gunshots had been fired at the shore of the canal. No one had pulled the trigger and put two bullets into Dianne's head while she lay unconscious in the trunk of her car. No one had murdered Dianne after her beating. In fact, Corbitt claimed he had not even known that Dianne was inside the trunk.

He did admit, however, that once he had agreed to kill Dianne for Alan and that he even had accepted a set of house keys from Alan so that he could enter the home. But he had chickened out and given the keys back to Alan. The police chief had thought he was doing Alan a favor by disposing of the car, enabling Alan to report the Cadillac as stolen and file an insurance claim. Besides, Alan had paid him about $8,000 to dump the vehicle.

The question facing Scorza on June 1, 1989, was whether he could prove that Corbitt had disposed of the car. His two key witnesses were former Willow Springs patrolman Robert Olson and George Witzel. Scorza was hoping that their testimony would provide the circumstantial evidence necessary for the jury to convict Corbitt for his role in the murder scheme. The prosecutor was relying on them and the records of the Willow Springs Police Department to place Mike Corbitt at the canal immediately after gunshots were heard coming from the waterway, in exactly the spot where Dianne's car was jettisoned.

The job for Dennis Berkson, Corbitt's lawyer, was obvious. He needed to cast some doubt on the credibility of the two witnesses. And it was imperative that he emphasize to the jury that not one soul had seen Mike Corbitt either dumping Dianne's Cadillac or firing any shots that night.

Over the years, Olson had given numerous statements to the authorities. Luckily for Corbitt, there were huge discrepancies in his statements. Olson was not the one to blame. David Parker, the FBI agent who had taken Olson's original statement, had been unclear in his report in relating exactly what Olson had told him.

Former Willow Springs patrolman George Witzel was the first to testify. His five years in the corrupt Willow Springs Police Department had ended when Ross was named police chief in 1982. After being fired in Willow Springs, he got a position on another force in a rural community in the far-west suburbs. He later was terminated from his job on departmental charges of submitting a false application for employment, in which he had stated that he never had been arrested. In fact, he had been booked for fighting outside a restaurant, but the charges were later dropped.

Jack Reed and Bob Colby had interviewed Witzel, who was now a truck driver, in October 1987. Witzel had told the investigators that he had left a $31,000 job as an over-the-road trucker to take the Willow Springs opening. When he started on October 12, 1977, he made just $3.15 per hour. The former patrolman had bragged that he had made the most DUI arrests in Willow Springs and had received just $10 per court date from the department. He claimed he had been an honest cop. "I just did my job. I was just a part-timer who arrested the bad guys and put them in jail," he had told Reed and Colby. "What they did in the back room was none of my business. I figured that's how Corbitt lined his pockets."

Witzel was thirty-eight years old. He was being asked by Scorza to recall events from seven years ago. With the help of some coaching from the FBI agents who had gone over the details repeatedly, he was doing quite well.

At 10:47 P.M. on March 19, 1982, Witzel had driven his squad car to the now-defunct In First Place lounge, where Mike Corbitt supposedly was helping someone who'd locked himself out of his car. The two-story tavern was a unique old structure. On the first floor was a bar and banquet hall. On the second floor, a live band performed. In the basement, there was a garage, a garage where, Scorza believed, Dianne's Cadillac had been stored until it could be disposed of safely.

Witzel described how he had spotted Corbitt's unmarked squad car in the tavern's parking lot. Corbitt was pulling away just as Witzel drove up to the bar. He pulled his squad car next to the driver's side of Corbitt's car, so both men were facing each other. In the car with Mike Corbitt was a male companion whom he couldn't identify, but he had a dark complexion and was wearing a shiny-type jacket, a leather jacket or a windbreaker.

Corbitt told him that he had handled the lockout and didn't need any assistance. Corbitt's passenger, who was sitting in the front seat, never spoke to Witzel and kept looking out the passenger window toward the bar. Witzel was ordered by Corbitt to go clear out the canal before he went off duty. A few seconds later, Witzel was at the exact spot where Dianne's car was later found. He beamed his spotlight from his squad car in the direction of the canal. There were no cars. The teenagers who sometimes drank beer under the bridge were not there that night.

It had taken Witzel just four minutes to meet Corbitt at the tavern, check out the canal, and radio back to the police station that he was going off duty. Given the town's geography, this was entirely conceivable. Willow Springs was an old river town, and Archer Avenue was its main thoroughfare and, essentially, its southern border. The canal where Dianne's car was found was the northern border. At some points, the distance between the two was less than the length of a football field. Tiny streets less than three-hundred feet long intersected with Archer Avenue, and it was possible to drive from one of the bars that lined Archer Avenue to the canal and back toward the police station in mere seconds.

Inside the police station, Witzel accumulated some overtime by completing some reports. Over his hand-held police radio, he heard the radio operator broadcast the reports of "shots fired."

In cross-examination, Berkson tried to show that it was routine for patrolmen to clear out the canal and that shots frequently were fired from the nearby forest preserves, where hunters frequently poached deer.

Like Witzel, Robert Olson, who took the stand next, had also been one of the police officers under Michael Corbitt. Scorza had been painting a picture for the jurors of a department rife with corruption, but he needed a choirboy to testify. He didn't need a former cop from Willow Springs, so in the first few minutes of his direct examination, he would depict Olson to the jury as just that—a choirboy—or a reasonable facsimile.

Scorza made sure the jurors knew that Olson was married with children and that he was just thirty years old, but responsible. He was the corporate loss prevention manager for Montgomery Ward, a step up from security manager.

"Oh, and do you also have another profession?" Scorza asked.

"Yes," Olson replied, "I am a licensed attorney."

"And where did you go to law school?"

"John Marshall."

"Did you go to law school while you were working for Montgomery Ward?"

"Yes, I did."

"And how did you manage that?"

"It was rough."

"Did you go the night hours?"

"Yes, I did."

He even had done some legal work that morning before coming to court. A product of one of the blue-collar suburbs, he'd spent his whole life in the area, working and achieving his goals. At one point, he had considered the priesthood.

"Did you continue on the path of the priesthood?"

"No, I didn't," Olson replied. Scorza wasn't quite that lucky.

After graduating from college, the industrious Olson had joined the Willow Springs Police Department as a part-time patrolman. At the same time, he was both attending law school and working as a security manager.

The night after Dianne's disappearance, Olson was standing on the steps of the police department shortly after Witzel had ended his shift when he heard two shots fired in rapid succession. He recalled that there had been two other policemen on the steps, but he couldn't remember their names. The shots sounded like they had come from west of the station.

Olson told his two colleagues that he would go toward the canal. He jumped in his squad car, drove the few hundred yards to Market Street, and turned right. The road curved left toward the bridge, and then he made a right-hand turn on a roadway leading to the area beneath the Willow Springs bridge. He arrived at the bridge within approximately thirty to sixty seconds after hearing the blasts. He stopped the car on the railroad tracks that ran parallel to the canal.

"The reason I had stopped there is because all of a sudden I saw lights come on. It scared me," he told Scorza.

"Did you draw your weapon at that time?"

"I unstrapped it."

"And when you say you saw lights, where did you first see these lights? Where did you first see them?"

"Coming from the area back here," Olson said, referring to the gravel-and-dirt section that surrounds the bridge abutments. Olson switched on his spotlight and pointed it at the vehicle that was now moving toward him. "I saw a vehicle coming toward me with I believe the license plate was a 9989 or something to that effect, which I recognized to be the chief's vehicle."

Corbitt's car pulled up next to his squad car. Corbitt was driving and a second man, a white male with a dark complexion and wearing a leather jacket, sat in the passenger seat. Olson and Corbitt then began a short conversation. Corbitt had told him that he already had checked out the area and that everything was OK. So Olson turned around and left.

Berkson's cross-examination would not be as vitriolic as Tuite's questioning of Jim Koscielniak, yet when he was through, it would plant some uncertainty in the jurors' minds.

Berkson noted that several Willow Springs police officers had responded to the calls of shots being fired that night. Among those who radioed in and indicated that they would investigate was none other than Michael Corbitt.

The department's radio log indicated that between 11:16 and 11:21 P.M., Olson had stopped a red Mustang for a traffic violation just one block west of the canal before he had reviewed the traffic log, Olson had indicated to Reed and Sabin that first he had made the traffic stop that night and then he had spotted Corbitt at the canal—just one of the discrepancies Berkson highlighted.

Then Berkson concentrated on the report by FBI agent David Parker of his interview with Olson. It was Berkson's view that Olson had repeatedly changed his story. He noted that Parker had reported that Olson had told the FBI agent that he had been walking out of the Willow Springs Police Department at the beginning of the shift when he heard two shots fired. When Berkson asked whether Olson had made such a statement to Parker, Olson said he had not.

Berkson continued to attack the inconsistencies in Olson's

statements. And hadn't Olson told Parker that he, Michael Corbitt, and another office had gone in different directions in their squad cars? Again Olson denied it.

"Was Parker lying when he wrote that down?" Berkson asked. Scorza objected and Olson wasn't permitted to answer.

Berkson was successful at implying that Olson had gotten his job back as a Willow Springs policeman after he talked to the FBI and made statements against Corbitt. He also established that not only had Olson gotten his job back, but he later had become an investigator, a coveted position in the department.

Berkson returned to the night that Dianne had disappeared. He asked Olson whether he had seen Michael Corbitt at about eleven o'clock with a female. Olson said he had not. Berkson then established that Olson had not seen Michael Corbitt out of his automobile at any time that night; nor had he seen Michael Corbitt in a yellow-over-white Cadillac that night. The only car Olson had seen Michael Corbitt in was Corbitt's own vehicle.

Equally important to Berkson's case was the fact that Olson said he had not seen Michael Corbitt push anything into the sanitary and ship canal on March 19; nor had he seen the police chief with a gun.

Berkson then focused on the unidentified passenger in Corbitt's car. Olson said he had not seen the other individual with a gun and he had not seen him discharge a weapon. Nor had he seen the individual push anything into the canal.

The defense attorney then went on to prove that Olson had noticed nothing unusual about Corbitt's demeanor the night of Dianne's disappearance. Olson told the jurors that the police chief had looked calm and had not acted surprised to see him when they met. Nor had he been advised by Corbitt not to go down by the waterway.

Berkson also got Olson to admit that he never had made a written report of the incident at the canal. Olson pointed out that Corbitt had never asked him not to; Corbitt never had requested that he keep their meeting a secret.

On redirect, Scorza was brief. He elicited from Olson that

the FBI had not helped him get back his job on the force. He again asked who Olson had seen at the canal and Olson reiterated that he had met Corbitt.

"How many times in your career as a police officer in Willow Springs did you hear two shots at the beginning of your tour of duty, did you drive to the canal and then you ran into Michael Corbitt. How many times did that happen?"

"Just the once that I remember."

Scorza's choirboy had hit every note.

Chapter Thirty-One

June 6, 1989

SGT. John Reed was acting as a gofer now. If Scorza needed a document, he sent the sheriff's deputy for it. If a witness needed a ride home, Reed played chauffeur. Because he was going to testify, he was barred from attending the trial. His reports on how the case was progressing came from the news media and the various witnesses he escorted.

He was convinced that Nykaza and Bachman had provided the key testimony that would convict Alan, Keating, and Corbitt. But there was a nagging doubt in the back of his mind. Alan was too confident that he would be acquitted. Reed had learned through the grapevine that the attorney was planning a victory party. Alan believed that he never would be convicted based on the evidence that had been presented.

The defense began its case on Tuesday, June 6, 1989. Reed wondered what Scorza thought the chances were of Alan testifying in his own behalf. Having been involved in numerous trials, Reed was aware that almost any time a defendant took the stand, it made a significant impression on the jury.

Reed was helping the prosecutors push one of the carts loaded with their case files. The policeman turned to Scorza and asked whether he envisioned Alan taking the stand.

"The baloney is always afraid of the meat grinder," Scorza replied, then marched down the hall and into the courtroom without saying another word.

The defense was confident. The lawyers believed in the

concept of presumption of innocence and they believed that Scorza and Foley's case was weak and circumstantial.

Tuite planned to present two witnesses who he hoped would sway the jury into believing that Nykaza might have been the person who killed Dianne—the nurse who had spotted Nykaza wearing women's underwear, and Nykaza's ex-wife. Most of his remaining witnesses were being called to try to bolster the defense's contention that Dianne had not come home that night and that Alan never had taken any steps to conceal the homicide.

A final witness, a policeman, would say that several weeks before Dianne was murdered, he had spotted Dianne necking in her car in a parking lot at the canal. And the man she was with did not match Jim Koscielniak's description. If the jury wouldn't buy the defense's theory that Nykaza was the killer, maybe they would believe that this mystery man might have murdered her. It was another attempt to raise in the jurors' minds reasonable doubt that someone other than Alan was the killer.

Lisa Borowiak, Tuite's first witness, was a nurse in one of the south suburban hospitals. She had been on duty in the emergency room one night in December 1988, the night Ted Nykaza was brought to the hospital.

Borowiak had been on the stand less than a minute before Scorza objected to Tuite's line of questioning. In a sidebar, Tuite told Judge Zagel that the witness was going to testify that during the course of Nykaza's treatment, she had undressed the private detective and discovered that he was wearing ladies' panties. Tuite believed that there was evidence that Dianne might have seen Nykaza the night she disappeared and that Nykaza's fetish might have been the reason Dianne was found without her underwear.

Scorza demanded that Tuite's tactic was blatant character assassination. After lengthy arguing, Judge Zagel, whose rulings consistently had favored the government, once again sided with the prosecutors and prevented Tuite from questioning the nurse about the incident.

The defense attorney then excused the nurse. The jury

learned only that she once had treated Ted Nykaza in an emergency room.

Donna Davis, the former housekeeper for the Masters, was called to the stand next. Now a factory worker making pantyhose in Tennessee, she had been the first person at the house on March 19, the day Alan had reported Dianne missing. Tuite wanted her to describe the condition of the house when she arrived the morning after Dianne's disappearance. Her testimony would prove that Dianne had not been murdered on the premises.

Davis said that there had been no signs of struggle anywhere in the house. Nor had she seen blood or any indication that someone had tried to clean a rug or a spot on the floor. She had worked throughout the house that day. She had retrieved cat food from the garage and fed the pets. Because it was raining, she had gone into the basement and mopped up some water on the basement rug with a Wet-vac—a duty she had performed whenever it rained, because the water would trickle into the subterranean rec room and soak the carpet. She also had gone into Dianne's bedroom to clean and had seen no evidence of blood stains on the room's light-yellow carpet.

Alan had left the house about an hour after she arrived and, throughout the morning, he had called to see if there was any news of her whereabouts. He had returned home at noon and dismissed Davis early. That day, Anndra had not gone to school.

The next two witnesses, a locksmith and the president of a company that installed alarm systems, told the jurors that despite what others had said, Alan had changed the locks in the house after Dianne's disappearance, and in fact he had installed even more security. He had purchased two remote panic buttons—devices similar to a garage door opener—so he could trip the alarm from anywhere in the house if there was a home invasion or burglary.

While Alan had changed the locks, it took him months to replace the alarm key. Dianne had possessed one of the home's alarm keys, and this key had been missing—along with her house keys—when her brass key ring was found in the ignition of her car.

Scorza, on his cross-examination of the owner of the alarm company, harped on the missing alarm key. His objective was to show that when someone loses a purse containing their keys or when their car is stolen, most people will call immediately to change their security system. But Alan Masters had waited until May 19 to order new keys.

The former Mrs. Nykaza, Sheila Mikel, was Tuite's next witness. When she was married to Nykaza, she had gone home one night after working the three-to-eleven shift as a dispatcher at a local police department. When she had gone upstairs to the bedroom, she had found Nykaza standing and talking to himself.

"I won't do it. You can't make me," she quoted Nykaza as saying. "I will not kill anyone again. That's it. I won't do it."

"Had he been drinking?" Tuite asked.

"That was one of the few rare times that I don't think he was drinking that night. I didn't smell anything on him. And he drank to such a severe degree, there was maybe only one day of every week to ten days that he didn't drink. He drank scotch and it has a very strong smell. And that night when I entered the room, I don't remember smelling any alcohol."

Since Scorza had told Zagel in a sidebar he intended to question Mikel about her affair with Alan in order to show her bias, Tuite was forced to bring out her relationship with his client on direct examination.

She admitted having had sex with Alan during their relationship, which started in about 1978. The affair had lasted almost three years, ending in the middle of 1981, she said. On various occasions, Alan had given her money, and he had loaned her $5,000 for the purchase of a house. But the home was now on the market and she intended to pay him back shortly.

Tuite was eager to present the private detective's unusual sexual proclivities to the jury. Outside the presence of the jurors, Tuite told Judge Zagel that during their brief marriage, Sheila had noticed Nykaza wearing women's underwear. When she moved out of the house, she found a garbage bag in the attic stuffed with panties that did not belong to her. Also, one of Nykaza's possessions was a picture of a dead woman, naked, lying facedown on a bed. But Zagel would not permit such testimony.

Tuite's sixth witness was the owner of the towing operation that had been involved in pulling the cars from the canal. Tuite's sole purpose for calling him to the stand was to emphasize to the jury that Alan, who was a friend of the towing operator, never had asked the man to stop searching for cars in the canal.

As the prosecutors feared, Dennis Berkson, Corbitt's attorney, called FBI agent David Parker to testify. Berkson hammered at the inconsistencies in Parker's interview of Olson, the Willow Springs officer who had spotted Corbitt at the canal. Berkson was particularly interested in one point that could provide his client with an alibi. Parker reiterated that Olson had said that Corbitt was standing with him on the steps of the Willow Springs Police Department when shots were heard coming from the canal. Under oath, Olson had denied, though, making the statement to Parker.

Former Cook County Sheriff's deputy Paul Sabin was also questioned about the discrepancy between his report and Olson's testimony. He said that when Olson was first interrogated, Olson was unable to recall whether he heard the shots fired in March or April of 1982. Olson later reviewed police logs to pinpoint the exact date for the investigators.

The last defense witness was Willow Springs policeman Charles "Sonny" Fisher, a close friend of Corbitt's who had been before the grand jury on two occasions. According to Fisher, it had been the policy of the police department to allow the town's youth to congregate underneath the bridge. They would light bonfires, drink, and play their boom boxes. The citizens approved, because it kept the kids out of their businesses. The spot was also a popular lovers' lane.

Fisher told the jurors that several weeks before Dianne had disappeared, he'd been patrolling the area near the canal. There was a small forest preserve parking lot nearby, and in it, he spotted the yellow-and-white Cadillac at about 10 P.M. As he approached the car, it started driving away. He stopped it by shining a spotlight on the windshield and drove up to the driver's side.

The driver was a male, between thirty-five and forty years old, with brown hair, slim build, and a razor-cut mustache, trimmed on both the top and the bottom. The passenger in the car was a nice-looking blond woman about the same age as her companion. Fisher noted that months later, he had reported the incident to Willow Springs Police Chief James Ross, saying he believed the occupant to be Dianne Masters.

He told the jurors that the day the car was pulled from the canal, the bridge's abutments were filled with graffiti. Among them were three sayings about Dianne. One stated: D.M. IS, followed by a long arrow pointing to the canal, and then 26 FEET DOWN STUPID. And he had seen the writing prior to the day Dianne's car was recovered.

Fisher's testimony made Scorza livid. During cross-examination, he deftly exposed the contradictions in Fisher's story and showed that there was nothing to substantiate his claims.

The policeman admitted that he had never volunteered any of this information when he went before the grand jury, which he had done on two separate occasions. Fisher also admitted that no report had been made about these events in the course of the Willow Springs investigation of Dianne Masters' murder. Nor did he have the log recording his report to the radio dispatcher that he was about to approach a car with the license plate DGM 19.

Fisher claimed that he had told FBI agent Ivan Harris about seeing the Cadillac down at the canal a few weeks before Dianne disappeared, but later, Scorza put Harris on the stand, and he testified that Fisher never had made any such statement.

With Sonny Fisher's testimony, the defense rested. It had called just twelve witnesses. The government's case had taken weeks; the defense had presented its evidence in just a day and a half.

Outside the presence of the jury, Judge Zagel questioned each of the defendant's about his decision not to take the stand. Each responded as Alan did.

"Mr. Masters, I'm sure you understand that you have a right

to testify in your own behalf if you so choose; is that correct? You understand that?''

''Yes, sir, I do,'' Alan replied.

''Your attorney has rested his case without calling you to the witness stand and I wish to inquire as to whether your decision not to testify was made by you?''

''Yes, sir,'' said Alan.

''And you understand that if at this very moment you should decide to change your mind, I would happily reopen the case and permit you to testify? Do you understand that?''

''Yes, I do.''

''And do you still wish to waive your right to testify?''

''That's correct.''

Scorza had been right. The baloney was always afraid of the meat grinder.

Chapter Thirty-Two

June 8, 1989

ANGER still consumed Randy regarding his sister's murder. It wasn't a menacing kind of hatred, but it was always there, smoldering beneath the surface. His family had been taken from him. His father and mother were dead and so was his only sister. Not only did he want justice; he wanted revenge.

Barred from the courtroom during the trial, he visited the graves of his sister and parents. The barren cemetery disturbed him. He bought flowers and laid them at the headstones, praying that the jurors would find Alan and his cohorts guilty. At Dianne's grave, he told her he hoped that the long ordeal would be over soon.

Days later, he called Scorza. With the case nearing an end, he pleaded with the prosecutor to let him attend the trial. Scorza reiterated that he was not permitted to be there until the closing remarks.

It was June 8 when Randy first walked inside the federal building. As he and Laurie Willcoxon, Dianne's aunt and godmother, got off the elevator, they ran into Alan. It was the first time they had seen him in the seven years since Dianne's funeral service. Randy glared at Alan. No words were spoken.

The court buffs were upset because Rick and Virginia Hawley, Kathy's parents, had saved extra seats in the second-to-last row of the courtroom. They complained that such a practice was forbidden, but when they learned that Dianne's brother would be making his first appearance at the trial, they apologized. Across the courtroom, the regulars whispered that Dianne's brother was in the audience.

Just as Randy felt disdain for Alan, Alan and some of his family found Randy equally contemptible. Were it not for Randy and his persistence, Alan would not be on trial, they believed. It was Randy's public statements that had cast suspicion on the attorney.

One of Alan son's, Steven, was sitting behind his father and turned around and stared coldly at Randy, refusing to remove his eyes from his nemesis. Like Alan, Steven was a lawyer, but there was no resemblance between the men. Steven was thin, about five feet ten, medium built, with dark-brown hair. Steven's piercing scrutiny continued for several minutes. Randy was taken aback by his juvenile behavior and was tempted to ask what was bothering him, but he refrained. Instead, Virginia, Kathy's mother, mouthed the words, "What's the matter with you?" Steven did not reply, but the glowers stopped.

The summations would last two days. Pat Foley would review the government's case and Keating's attorney, William P. Murphy, would lead off for the defense.

Foley's was the painstaking task, going through each count of the indictment and recalling the crucial testimony of each witness who supported the charge. It took two and a half hours. And he did something that no one else had done during the trial: he defended Dianne. How was it that the victim had been forgotten? he asked. The defense consistently had portrayed Dianne throughout the trial as a floozy. They had relished the depiction, in fact. Just hours earlier, Sonny Fisher's testimony had placed her necking in the car with a man other than Jim Koscielniak.

"Let me tell you a little bit about Dianne Masters," Foley told the jurors. "She would have been 43 this month." He recalled how Dianne had met Alan, who was handling her divorce. She was impressionable, vulnerable. And Alan lavished gifts upon her—jewelry, leather suits, and furs. He paid for her apartment. He paid her bills. Foley continued:

> Mr. Tuite will tell you that this is a generous man and kind man, Alan Masters.
>
> What he is, ladies and gentlemen, is a man who knows nothing but paying bribes; a man who knows nothing but graft, corruption; a man who buys things that suit and serve his purpose.
>
> While there may have been some love, while there may have been some affection, Alan Masters, the man who buys what serves his ego, had a pretty woman on his arm; the man who bought the judges; the man who bought the cops; the man who bought Dianne.

Alan sucked her into a relationship, said Foley. She found herself a man who could provide her with material things, but there was a big price to pay. Alan had an uncontrollable temper and he beat her. And his rage led to Dianne's murder.

Dianne did make it home that night, he told the jurors. And Alan, the man who could not handle his rage, knew what was at stake. He was going to lose his daughter and lose the woman he had bought. The blows to the head showed that she probably was attacked right in the house. It was obvious that Alan Masters had struck Dianne.

Foley argued that Mike Corbitt had shot Dianne to further conceal the murder. And setting the clock in her Cadillac and her wristwatch to stop at about the same time, the prosecutor said, was something only someone in law enforcement would think of.

Of the defense attorneys, Murphy was in the worst spot. Keating was on tape laughing about Dianne's demise. Keating was the one Diane Economou had said Alan was going to meet to plot Dianne's murder. And because of Bachman's testimony, Keating was linked to the conspiracy directly by having offered Bachman $25,000 to kill Dianne.

Murphy returned to the analogy Scorza had used in his opening statement: the curtain had fallen on the drama when Dianne Masters left the restaurant that morning. The government never had proven what happened after she left. He noted that the government's case was circumstantial and that the prosecutors hoped that the jurors would ignore any reasonable hypothesis of innocence that the testimony had presented.

Murphy quickly honed in on the government's reliance on the testimony of Jack Bachman. He contended that by lying, Bachman had more to gain than any other witness who had testified: his freedom. Murphy reemphasized Bachman's lack of credibility. He had lied under oath before, and as a policeman who had sworn to serve and protect the public, he had accepted payoffs. Bachman, the vice cop, was the owner of a brothel. And he never had reported—until he was about to be indicted—that he had any knowledge of Dianne's murder.

"When you go into the jury room, ladies and gentlemen, examine what the government put on and examine the things they didn't put on; the things that were behind that curtain that never came up.

"You can find Mr. Keating not guilty, ladies and gentlemen, and you can walk out of this courtroom just the way you came in, as proud Americans."

Judge Zagel then adjourned the proceedings until the following day.

The next morning, Anndra came to court. It was a shock for Randy, who hadn't seen his niece in seven years, and he was overcome by emotion. She was a month shy of her twelfth birthday. And there was a striking resemblance between mother and daughter. Anndra had Dianne's face and fragile bone structure but had inherited Alan's brown hair and hazel eyes. She sat in the second row behind the defendants with Jan, Keating's girlfriend, and Corbitt's wife and son Joey. Randy was angry that Alan had brought her to court. "That was really sick. It kind of sums up everything wrong with Alan Masters. It summed up everything we had gone through."

Aunt Laurie, who had accompanied Randy, waved to her niece and Anndra waved back. Jan quickly turned Anndra around in her seat.

Later, at one of the breaks, Laurie approached a group of women who were surrounding the young girl. "Would it be all right if I just say hi?" she asked sweetly.

Alan came charging over. "Get away from her," he screamed. "I don't want you saying anything to her."

"Daddy, can't I just say hi?" Anndra pleaded before being whisked off.

Laurie was distraught and astonished that Alan would not allow her to speak to Anndra. Laurie located the closest washroom and cried for her niece, who, like her mother, was lost to her forever.

Mike Corbitt's attorney, Dennis Berkson, opened the morning session. He was at his best since the trial began.

> Four weeks ago, we came here and I told you that you would be entertained, that you would hear a story that was more incredible, that was more entertaining, that was more ridiculous than anything you would ever see on television, than any soap opera you could ever imagine, than any video you would ever see.
>
> You heard about sex. You heard about adultery. You heard about infidelity. You heard about new and innovative ways for the use of wine bottles. You have heard all these things and you have heard about murder.
>
> But, ladies and gentlemen, let me tell you something. Like any piece of fiction, like any soap opera, like any book by Father Greeley, there was one thing that was always consistent. Whether this is short fiction, good fiction, bad fiction . . . it was the figment of someone's imagination.

Berkson pointed out to the jurors that over the previous four weeks, the government had paraded forty-eight people before them in "a dog and pony show." Despite the number of witnesses the government called, not one of them said they had seen the murder of Dianne Masters, Berkson said. "Reasonable doubt, ladies and gentlemen. That's what we're here for. Not for you to critique their fantasies. Not for you to say, that was a good show."

None of the witnesses testified that they had seen Alan, Corbitt, and Keating together. "Isn't that reasonable doubt?" the attorney asked. "And none of the witnesses testified that they'd heard Alan and Corbitt talking together about anything, criminal or otherwise," said Berkson, pointing to the defendants.

He argued that the government had to prove that these men had agreed to commit crimes, but no evidence was presented that showed the defendants agreeing to do anything with one another.

Berkson noted that FBI agent Larry Damron had met with Corbitt only once and that had been only a ten-minute conversation. And during all of the wiretapped conversations, virtually no one had mentioned Michael Corbitt's name other than to talk about his job prospects for another police chief's job.

The prosecution had spun a fantasy that became the ultimate fairy tale, Berkson said of the murder conspiracy charge facing his client. The prosecution was asking the jurors to don thinking caps and magic 3-D guessing glasses and look behind the curtain that came down on the scene, he contended.

Berkson ridiculed the government's theory that Corbitt had changed the clock on the car, and he began a minute-by-minute account of the night after Dianne had disappeared, when Corbitt supposedly was dumping the car into the canal. Using the contradictions between Olson's earlier statements to the authorities and Parker's testimony, he attacked Olson's credibility. "Here's where the fantasy really begins," he told the jurors.

Berkson branded Olson a liar and accused him of fabricating a story to comply with the government's version of events. The prosecution wanted the jury to believe that the statement he had made to federal authorities was now the truth. Despite the fact that Olson had given three different accounts of the same night, the jury was being asked to convict Corbitt.

Berkson posed the issue of timing. "How could Corbitt fire the fatal shots, close the lid of the car, change the clock and dump the car in the canal and then sweep up the site after he was done, and be sitting in his car when Olson spots him?" he asked the jurors.

Like Murphy the day before, Berkson attacked Bachman's credibility as well. His testimony was the only way the government could prove that Michael Corbitt had known about Dianne Masters' murder.

"Well, I would submit to you I can't tell you who killed her. It could be Nykaza. It could be anybody. And I'll tell you one thing. It's not my client. But you've got to guess. And they want you to convict my client on a guess. And nobody gets convicted on a guess, not in this country."

Berkson's closing remarks made Randy nervous. He hadn't heard the evidence, but he was concerned about Berkson's impact on the jury.

Tuite's final address would do nothing to allay Randy's fears. He took the jury through each charge, providing the defense's view of the evidence and pointing out the contradictions.

"So now we get to why we're here. The disappearance and the murder of Dianne Masters. The weakest homicide case you'll ever see if you sat in the state criminal court from now until the year 2000.

"It's human nature to presume someone guilty," Tuite said. "A woman is missing and people conclude that her husband is responsible. This is not a newspaper. This is not gossip. This is not rumor. You heard the facts. And there is no evidence," he said.

"I'm not here to condemn. It's not surprising she got herself a boyfriend. I said to Alan once before and I'll say it again. He's got a weight problem. He's got a hair problem. He snores. Works hard. So she found someone else."

Tuite claimed that Alan had suffered a broken heart. He was a loving husband. Hadn't Diane Economou testified about how Alan had cried over losing Dianne? Tuite reminded the jurors that Alan had called people, pleading with them to help him and Dianne reconcile.

Alan knew Dianne was going to leave him. Because he practices in Cook County, that's where he wanted the divorce to take place, he told the jurors. He filed first, in fact. He wasn't afraid of a divorce. "They say he's powerful. He's influential. Then he had no reason to kill her," Tuite emphasized.

As a lawyer involved in a custody battle for his own child, Alan knew it was prudent to gather evidence of his wife's affair, Tuite said. Alan did not deny that a tape recording had been made of a phone call. With evidence of Dianne's infidelity, Alan wasn't worried about losing Anndra. Nor was he worried about the divorce.

Tuite accused the government of continually refreshing the minds of their witnesses. "I have the greatest cure for Alzheimer's disease for the world. Send them to the federal government. I wish my poor mother was alive. She'd remember me."

Pointing to Fisher's testimony about seeing Dianne at the canal just weeks before she disappeared, Tuite suggested that perhaps the man in the car was the murderer. But then, once again, he focused on Nykaza as the chief suspect in the murder. Didn't you hear testimony that Nykaza had an automatic weapon like the kind used to kill Dianne? Isn't it interesting that Nykaza spray painted his garage and there was similar graffiti at the canal? Who is the graffiti artist in this case? Ted Nykaza.

Tuite focused in on the fact that Dianne's underwear had been missing. He told the jurors that that was the reason the defense had brought out the fact that Nykaza had worn women's underwear. "It's going to be very difficult for me from now on, maybe for you too, that everytime I see those little short lingerie items called teddies that I won't think of Nykaza.

"Who had a perverse interest in death? Teddy Nykaza.

"Who kept a picture of a dead body around his house?

"Who told people that he [had] killed people when he said he didn't?"

Tuite noted that the prosecutors had put on the stand two neighbors who said they never had seen Dianne come home that night. And he urged the jurors to recall the testimony of Donna Davis, the housekeeper, who said there had been no signs of a struggle in the house. Then, turning to Anndra sitting in the second row and pointing her out to the jury, he said, "I'm sorry, Anndra."

"Where's the blood? They would have you believe that she didn't bleed at all. Just miraculous. Yellow carpeting. And then she's removed." Tuite recalled for the jurors that it wasn't just Donna Davis who said she had seen nothing amiss in the house that day. A policeman had gone through that house too, and he had seen nothing unusual.

But more than anything else, timing exonerated Alan, declared Tuite. He asked the jury why Corbitt would have fixed the clock at 1:50, the time period when something drastic allegedly happened at the house. Why not make it later, much later?

Alan had reported her missing at 2:30 in the afternoon. If he was involved with the killer and the people dumping the body, if some problem had arisen concerning the disposal of the corpse on the night or the early morning hours of the nineteenth, it would have been logical for him to receive a phone call. He'd have been told not to report Dianne's disappearance yet because the job wasn't done, theorized Tuite. He concluded:

> Justice cries out in this case for a not guilty. That's the lady with the blindfold and the scales and the sword. And our only hope is that when this is over that you will listen to the evidence and you will talk about reasonable doubts and whether its been all tied together. And that lady with the scales and the sword will be smiling.
>
> Let's hope that she doesn't have to cry under that blindfold because justice demands, justice cries out, for not guilty.

Tuite had planned the summations so that the jury would be hungry if the prosecutor went into a lengthy rebuttal that extended into the lunch hour. If this occurred, the jurors' attention would be on food—not Scorza's remarks.

And Tuite's rhetoric had shaken Randy. There was a ten-minute break and he went in search of Scorza. He found Scorza and Foley in the washroom. Scorza was eating a Snickers candy bar and talking over last-minute decisions with his cocounsel. Randy wondered what Scorza thought. Had Tuite been successful in his arguments? Had he won the jury over? Scorza sensed that Dianne's brother needed reassurance. "Don't worry, you ain't seen nothing yet," he told Randy.

"My adrenaline was flowing," Scorza recalled later. "You eat one of these Snickers and you get enough sugar to really get going. I could have not eaten for six days and still been all right. I had given the rebuttal argument in that case in my mind sixty times."

Scorza's rebuttal lasted more than two hours. It was spontaneous and conversational. He talked to the jurors as if they were his next door neighbors. At one point, he even told them about a recent movie he had seen and how it had given him an idea about the murder.

Scorza's main goal was to defend his witnesses—even the most problematic ones—and that's what he intended to accomplish.

> I could probably get away with telling you a clever little argument like this: Ladies and gentlemen, subtract out Ted Nykaza and we still can convict these guys beyond a reasonable doubt. Because the tape is confirmed by Hein. Even though Ted Nykaza's rendition of what Masters said would be out the window, we still have the same exact statement coming out of Masters from Keating to Bachman.
>
> We could probably take Nykaza out and I could still say to you, ladies and gentlemen, we still got them. But I'm not going to do that.

Scorza went on to explain how Ted Nykaza and Jack Bachman had become witnesses for the government. Because Alan Masters had picked Ted Nykaza as his private eye to do his dirty work, actually it was Alan who had picked Nykaza as a witness. Jack Bachman had been picked by the crooked Keating, who had brought Bachman into the bookmaking deal he had with Alan.

> The reason that Ted Nykaza and Jack Bachman have so many fleas is they spent so many years laying down with dogs. And everything you want to think badly of them before they came over to us, go right ahead. We cheer you on. Jack Bachman was a crooked cop. He stood up here telling you he's a crooked cop. Nykaza was a drunk. He told you he was a drunk. He's a weird guy. You will never have the desire to invite Ted Nykaza to Thanksgiving dinner and neither will anybody else here.
>
> The question that you have to ask, the question you have to ask is: Did they tell you the truth about the important things in this case, the material things in this case? That's the question.

Scorza told the jury that, like them, he had been skeptical when Reed brought Nykaza into the office and he talked about the tape recordings and Alan's declaration that he would kill Dianne. How could the government believe Nykaza? he asked rhetorically. Because Joe Hein was there, too.

The government had relied on the testimony of admitted chop shop operators and others with legal problems to prove some of the minor racketeering charges. Scorza explained that crooked cops are unlikely to prey on individuals who are upstanding citizens in the community. They aren't the ones who are vulnerable. "You can't shake down Cardinal Bernardin," he declared.

To counter the defense argument that Corbitt had not had enough time to dispose of the car, Scorza told the jurors to look at the radio logs from the department and compare it to the testimony.

Scorza also began an attack on the character of the three defendants, especially Alan and Corbitt. Alan was not the doting father who stayed home to babysit his child. Alan Masters is the guy who owns a brothel and brags about it. He's the guy who brags that he has the cops and the judges in his pocket. "The true Alan Masters was an Alan Masters who thought people would think well of him because he was a pimp," said Scorza.

Scorza reiterated how Keating had depicted Alan in his conversations with undercover agent Larry Damron: "I know a guy who's the biggest fixer in the world. He pays everybody referral fees. I know a guy who does all of that, the master fixer, Alan Masters."

Calling Corbitt a policeman whose motto was "to serve and collect," Scorza reminded the jurors that they knew that Corbitt was down at the canal when the shots were fired. The reason they knew, was because Olson had seen Mike Corbitt coming up from under the bridge under the canal following those two shots. It was devastating to Corbitt's claim of innocence. And, he said, there was no question that there had been sufficient time for Corbitt to transport Dianne's car from its hiding place to the waterway.

Because of the shift change, there had been twice the usual

number of cops in Willows Springs. But they were all in the station. Nobody was near the canal.

Scorza asked the jurors to remember what Corbitt had said to Olson when the patrolman, who responded to the reports of shots fired, spotted Corbitt at the canal. "I took care of it," Corbitt had told Olson. "What the heck did he take care of?" Scorza asked the jurors.

Unbeknownst to Dianne, she had thwarted the killers' original plan by not going to Artie G's, the college board's usual hangout, or meeting Jim that night.

Scorza admitted that the government didn't know where Dianne was killed, but he told the jurors to remember one thing. She had come home that night. "What's definite is, and it's very simple, this woman made it home.

"She was going home, not to Nykaza's house. This woman wasn't somebody who was voluntarily hanging around with a guy like Nykaza, a drunk, an associate of her husband. She had business in the morning. Her daughter was there."

Her missing underwear, he said, showed that she was attacked after she started to undress in the house. Then Scorza explained how he had arrived at the conclusion. He was watching the movie *Broadcast News*, featuring Holly Hunter as a television news producer and William Hurt as an anchorman. In the movie, the couple came home from a frustrating date and Hunter said good-night. When she closed the door, she reached under her skirt, pulled down her pantyhose, and took off her shoes.

"I'm sitting in the movie theater and saying: Holy Mackerel. She's dressed right there on the screen right now the way Dianne Masters was found. I took a poll of women that I knew. Saying like I take off my tie sometimes when I get home. Excuse me, do you ever take off your pantyhose first? I'm glad Mr. Tuite didn't hear about it. He'd be in here telling you I did the murder."

"You didn't collect them," Tuite interrupted.

"It's one explanation," replied Scorza.

After Dianne was attacked and her head bashed in, something else obviously went wrong, continued the prosecutor. Whether it was a flat tire, dawn approaching, or a logistics problem involving the person responsible for disposing of the car, it's clear that throwing the car into the canal had to be an alternate plan.

Scorza reminded the jurors how senseless it was to shoot Dianne. Her head was bashed in. Her car was being dumped into the canal, where she certainly would drown if she still was alive. Why shoot her? Because the shooting, he said, was part of the coverup. It made it appear as if she had been abducted, not killed in her own home.

Why did Dianne's body end up in the canal? Perhaps it was a mistake, offered Scorza. Perhaps the original plan was to take her car and body to a junkyard, where the car would be turned into scrap. Or perhaps they simply were confident that Mike Corbitt would remain the police chief and that their secret would remain underwater for eternity.

Scorza told the jurors that they never would worry about making the right decision. In fact, they would be proud of what they did in this case. They would tell their loved ones, their children, and their grandchildren about their decision in the case.

> When Dianne Masters could not point to those who plotted and carried out and covered up her murder, when she couldn't speak, you spoke for her. And you will beg your loved ones to understand that although you could not bring Dianne Masters back to life, you're the ones who breathed new life into the principle that in the end, right makes might. In the end, justice triumphs over those who would abuse the power that society gives them.

The jury met briefly, elected a foreman, and then decided to begin their deliberation on Monday. It would be a long weekend for both the Turners and the Masters.

Chapter Thirty-Three

June 12, 1989

WAITING was the hardest part for the Turners. They expected that the jury would be out for some time, so they spent the weekend as they always did, consumed by their sons' Little League games. Randy was the manager of eight-year-old son Austin's team and the coach of nine-year-old Sean's team. There were two games on Saturday and then the usual Sunday dinner at a relative's home.

Meanwhile, on Saturday, Alan and Jan celebrated her twenty-fifth birthday with Pat Tuite and his wife by going out to dinner. The Masters remained optimistic about hosting a victory party after the trial. A throng of their friends and relatives were going to be invited and Alan was going to announce that he and Jan had wed.

At about 2:30 P.M on Monday, June 13, the jury announced that it had reached a verdict. They had deliberated for roughly five hours. It was 3 P.M. by the time the attorneys, defendants, reporters, and court buffs assembled to hear the jury's findings. A feeling of apprehension swept through the courtroom, and within seconds, conversations ceased or became whispered exchanges.

Alan had witnessed similar scenes many times in his legal career, but never had the stakes been so high for him. He knew it was not a good sign that the jurors had been out for only a few hours, yet he appeared composed.

Tuite and the other defense attorneys offered encouragement

to their clients as they waited for the jury to return. At the prosecutors' table sat a calm Scorza, while Foley fidgeted.

As soon as the audience spotted the jurors entering the courtroom, silence fell. After they took their seats, the foreman, Richard Hendren, a computer supervisor from the south suburbs, handed the jury's verdict to the clerk. The clerk announced the verdict, declaring that Alan was guilty of two counts in the indictment.

His demeanor immediately changed, reflecting his disbelief. His face flushed and he nervously began stroking his mustache. Alan turned around and looked at Jan, who was dressed in a royal blue suit and sitting two rows behind him. She, too, was shocked. She started to cry.

Alan had been convicted of two racketeering counts that charged that he had fixed court cases, bribed police officers, and conspired to murder Dianne. The jury found him innocent of mail fraud charges stemming from the money he had received as the beneficiary of Dianne's $100,000 life insurance policy.

Like Alan, Keating was found guilty of two racketeering counts that charged that he had accepted bribes from Alan and solicited Bachman to kill Dianne in return for $25,000. Corbitt was convicted on one count that charged that he had dumped Dianne's car into the canal and accepted bribes from Alan.

Each juror was polled. Each replied that this was, indeed, his or her verdict.

Scorza moved to revoke Alan's bond. He said that Alan posed a danger to the community and was very likely to flee now that he had been convicted of planning and soliciting the murder of his wife. That was a heinous crime in itself, but he also had used his police buddies to help him conceal the homicide for seven years.

So why would Alan cease his criminal activities at this point, when he realized that he was going to jail? the prosecutor argued. He was likely to harm himself or others and Scorza was concerned about the safety of the witnesses who had testified against Alan. "Here's a man who lived in riot, in violation of the law, corrupting judges, corrupting police officers, corrupting an entire court system."

Scorza said that Alan already had demonstrated his disregard for the law. There was no reason to think he suddenly would respect it and comply with the terms of a bond.

Tuite argued vehemently that Alan should remain free. He still was practicing as an attorney and would need time to transfer cases and notify clients. Alan was not a flight risk, Tuite contended. He had neither a passport nor the inclination to use it. No witness need fear Alan Masters, he told the judge. Not once had Nykaza, Bachman, or any other witness received any kind of threat against them, even though Alan knew they were cooperating.

And there was the issue of Anndra. Alan had not explained to her that he was facing imprisonment. "He obviously has not gotten his daughter ready for this and I think it is something he should discuss with her, what's going to happen to him, what their life is going to be, what her life is going to be. And I think it is not unreasonable that he be allowed to do that face to face, not over some telephone. He shouldn't have to bring an 11-year-old into the federal jail."

Tuite pleaded with Judge Zagel on Anndra's behalf. "I mean here's an 11-year-old girl who doesn't have a mother and now will not have a father." It was an argument tinged with irony, considering that her father had just been convicted of planning her mother's murder.

Judge Zagel's ruling followed the law rather than the heart. The statute, he noted, virtually required incarceration unless it was clear that the person was not likely to flee. The judge also commented on the swiftness of the jury's verdict, saying it was apparent that they had accepted the government's version of the case.

He compared the prosecutors' case to a mosaic, in which tiles had been added until the picture had become clear and convincing. In Zagel's opinion, the government's presentation had exceeded the criteria of proof beyond a reasonable doubt.

As a lawyer well versed in criminal law, Alan must have known that his chances of remaining free on appeal were slight, and Zagel viewed Alan not only as a flight risk but also as a potential danger to the community and to witnesses.

The judge, however, sympathized with Tuite's plea that Alan

be given a chance to talk to his daughter. He told Tuite that he would arrange for Anndra to meet with her father in a courtroom or another room in the building to allow him to tell her that he was going to jail and to say good-bye.

As the hearing came to a close, Jan could not control her tears. She hadn't expected Alan to be taken into custody immediately. "It seemed like a nightmare. It couldn't be real," she would say later. But she had to say good-bye. Jan stood next to Alan, sobbing as he pulled his wallet, comb, and keys from his gray-and-white pinstriped suit and handed them to her.

"I love you and I'm sorry," he told her as he was led away. Jan could not stop crying and had run out of tissues. No one had a handkerchief for her.

Meanwhile, Tuite claimed that the verdict was a partial victory. "If this case had been tried in the state courts, I'm sure it never would have gotten past a directed verdict for acquittal."

What the jury had concluded was that there was sufficient evidence to find that Alan had planned and solicited the murder of Dianne G. Masters, as the indictment had charged, and that Corbitt and Keating had aided and abetted the solicitation and planning of the murder.

The men were acquitted of the allegations that Masters had conspired with others to commit the murder and aided and abetted in the murder. They also were acquitted of concealing Dianne's death.

Outside the courtroom, foreman Hendren explained the verdict to the press. The jury was sure that Alan had planned the murder and called on others for help. But the jurors could not find enough evidence to prove that the trio actually had committed the murder. "The only thing we had a problem with was the actual murder. I am sure they did it, but there was no way to prove it," Hendren said.

Randy was in his office when someone telephoned to say that the jury was returning with a verdict. He turned to the local news radio station to try to ascertain how the jury had voted. When he learned the jury's verdict, Randy was thrilled. "We rejoiced. It was a bittersweet victory because of Anndra, but we rejoiced."

But Randy was confused by Tuite's claim of a partial victory.

How could he claim a victory? His client was facing a lengthy prison term. Randy tried to reach Scorza to find out what Tuite had meant.

Scorza and Foley, though, were celebrating at a pub near the federal building. U.S. Attorney Anton Valukas was buying his prosecutors, along with Jack Reed and FBI agents Ivan Harris and Roger Griggs, beer and pizza.

In Northbrook, Aunt Laurie told the media that the family was just glad that Alan had been convicted. "I'm buying a big bouquet of flowers and going to the cemetery. I'm telling Dianne to rest and go to sleep. It sounds funny, but I always felt she couldn't rest. Her soul couldn't sleep. I want to tell her it is over."

Chapter Thirty-Four

August 24, 1989

It was the day of reckoning for Alan Masters, James Keating, and Michael Corbitt, and Randy was nervous as he sat in the courtroom waiting for the sentencing hearing to begin. He chatted with the Hawleys, who had accompanied him, but his mind was elsewhere. All he could think about was the punishment that Alan would receive. Randy desperately wanted Judge Zagel to impose a harsh prison term—the longer the better. He still worried that someday, when his former brother-in-law was free again, he might seek retribution against Randy and his family.

The proceedings began at 2:15 P.M. on August 24, 1989. Alan, dressed in a gray business suit, had spent eleven weeks in the federal jail and the experience had diminished his bravado. He no longer exuded confidence. He was fifty-four years old and looking at a sentence that could mean he might well die in prison. His future rested in the hands of Pat Tuite, his lawyer.

Corbitt and Keating, who were serving terms for their earlier convictions, sat in navy blue prison jump suits. There were signs of perspiration under their arms.

The trio appeared resigned to their fate. It was just a matter of how much time Zagel, who had a reputation among the defense bar as a hanging judge, would hand down. Already they were anticipating their appeals.

There had been a huge outpouring of support from friends, relatives, judges, and other officials who touted the virtues of the defendants in hopes of convincing Zagel to be lenient when he sentenced the men.

Alan's submissions contained mostly personal letters from attorneys and a couple from judges. Others detailed his performance and general reputation as an attorney. His supporters included an Illinois Appellate Court judge, who had written that all of Alan's colleagues had considered him a lawyer of integrity. In another missive, he was called ethical. Still another called him honest. And one writer urged a suspended sentence for Alan. Scorza was aghast at how far the letters had gone.

Judge Zagel also had reviewed a videotape from Anndra that had been made at Tuite's behest. Giggling throughout the film, the twelve year old talked about her wonderful, loving father, not the man who was to be sentenced for plotting her mother's murder. She told the judge how she already had picked out the college she hoped to attend, Cornell University, and that she wanted to be either a certified public accountant or an interior decorator.

In urging leniency, the defense attorneys would begin a systematic attack on the government's theory as to how Dianne was killed. And they would characterize their clients as simple sinners who had engaged in some wrongdoing but never had murdered anyone.

Scorza had saved his best oratory for this day, and his best-kept secret. He would publicly disclose for the first time that the government had obtained proffers from both Corbitt and Keating prior to the trial that implicated Alan in the murder of Dianne and partly revealed their roles in the conspiracy. The proffers could not be introduced in court unless the defendants had taken the stand and contradicted those statements.

Dennis Berkson began by noting that Corbitt's six-year-old son Joey was afflicted with Down's syndrome and that Corbitt was a devoted father. Corbitt's wife needed him, too, Berkson said. In his view, there had not been one scintilla of evidence that Corbitt ever had received any money from Alan. Admittedly, Corbitt had referred cases to the lawyer. But Corbitt had never received a bribe, fixed a case, or done anything to violate the public trust when he was the Willow Springs police chief.

Berkson acknowledged that the jury believed that Corbitt

had, in fact, conspired in the planning of the homicide. But he insisted that Michael Corbitt had not killed Dianne:

> My client is not a murderer. Mr. Scorza stood up during the trial and he said in opening argument that he would prove not beyond a reasonable doubt, but beyond all doubt that Michael Corbitt, and he pointed to him, put two bullets into Dianne Masters' head and he killed her.
>
> And the jury did not believe that. The jury did not believe that that man killed her. The jury did not believe he concealed the homicide. They do believe that in some way he planned or conspired to plan her murder. Well, I would submit to Your Honor that my client wants me to tell you, and I will tell you, my client did not murder this woman.

Corbitt's meeting with Larry Damron had been crucial to his convictions in Corbitt's earlier corruption case and in the Masters case. Berkson argued that Corbitt had been convicted twice for the same crime—his meeting with Larry Damron. He said that the forty-five-year-old Corbitt was serving time for that already.

"My client did not murder anybody. Temper the sentence with mercy and give my client some remaining respect of his life. And when he gets out, allow him to live with his family and help his child," Berkson concluded.

Using the same strategy as Berkson, William Murphy, Keating's defense lawyer, also emphasized that much of the evidence that had been used to convict Keating in the Masters case had come from his previous conviction in the federal investigation of corruption in the sheriff's department.

Murphy told Judge Zagel that his sentence in the previous case was three times that received by others convicted in the investigation. "He is doing 15 years, which is a harsh, harsh sentence especially for a man 52-years-old."

While Murphy acknowledged that in his statement to federal prosecutors, Keating had admitted having had some information about the crime, neither Keating's nor Corbitt's statement had indicated that Keating was involved in the actual murder of Dianne.

Murphy also discussed Keating's personality. Like most who

knew him, the lawyer had discovered that he was humorous and personable. "He's a friendly, gregarious guy. He likes to help everybody. He's loyal to his friends. And as you can see, Judge, it got him in a great deal of trouble," Murphy noted.

He told Judge Zagel how Keating had done everything he could to support his former wife and their two children. He had given his sheriff's department's pension to her so that she could support the family. Murphy noted that Keating's daughter had written a letter on behalf of her father to the judge. In it, she said that her father had thought about everyone else before he thought about himself.

"I am not here to beg. Mr. Keating didn't want me to beg for mercy for him. But when he was a police officer, he did good things. You know, even the FBI has given him commendations for the work he did then. He is a kind and generous man. I think he's a decent man, Your Honor. And I think that he got in over his head in this case."

Murphy asked Zagel to make any sentence that he handed down concurrent with the fifteen-year term that Keating was serving, so that he would have the opportunity to return to society.

Tuite's spiel to Judge Zagel had a more onerous tone. He wasn't seeking pity for his client. Instead Tuite said he was still seeking justice. "I have been practicing in this building for over 20 years. And when I leave this building with clients, win or lose, it's important that they feel they were treated fairly.

"And respectfully, Mr. Masters and I do not believe he's been treated fairly in this case. And we hope and we pray that we will be treated fairly today."

At the onset of the trial, Tuite had objected to Judge Zagel presiding over the case. Prior to being appointed to the federal bench, the judge had been the head of the Illinois State Police, which had investigated Dianne's murder following the discovery of her body. The defense attorney raised the issue again at the hearing.

He said that because Judge Zagel had been the director of the state police and he had refused to step down from hearing the case, Alan felt that Zagel was biased.

Tuite also criticized Zagel's handling of the trial, especially his rulings.

> Heresay came into the trial. It flowed like water. I will not say it flowed like wine, but it flowed like water. And yet, when we tried to bring out hearsay from the lips of Dianne Masters, objections to that were sustained. There were instances where the defendant has offered, and I hope you take into consideration what you didn't consider during the trial, a reward for the arrest and apprehension and conviction of his wife's killer. That was kept out for evidentiary reasons.

The defense also had tried to show the importance of Nykaza's penchant for ladies' underwear to the case. But that, too, had been kept from the jury.

Tuite downplayed Alan's payment of referral fees to policemen like Corbitt and Pastori, and he glossed over Alan's acceptance of bribe money to protect the Cicero gambling dens. He noted that the jury could not conclude who actually had killed Dianne and he implied that Alan was simply an innocent victim. He acknowledged that Alan was angry at Dianne and that there had been infidelity. And he contended that sometimes, angry people make statements like "I'll kill that person" out of frustration.

Tuite asked Judge Zagel to reject Scorza's request for a forty-year sentence, saying that had the case been tried in state court with the same outcome, Alan would not be considered for such a lengthy term.

He described Alan as one of the most generous men whom he had ever met. He cited a letter written on Alan's behalf that said that on Sundays, Alan went to a nursing home where he had elderly parents. When he visited, he would bring ice cream, and the patients had dubbed him the ice-cream man.

Tuite said that Alan had connections at the Mayo Clinic, where there were sometimes long waits for admittance. Alan could get people in on a moment's notice. Although it probably had slipped Tuite's mind, Alan's connection to the Mayo Clinic had been through the late Charlie Nicosia, a First Ward businessman known for his ties to organized crime, his illicit relationship with judges, and his alleged operation of a prostitution ring called Charlie's Angels. Police believe that Nicosia had supplied doctors visiting Chicago with free escorts during their weekend stays in the city.

Finally Tuite noted the impact Alan's imprisonment would have on Anndra. "One of the most tragic things in this whole case is Anndra Masters," he said. For Anndra sake, Tuite said, Alan had maintained the home almost as a shrine to Dianne. Her pictures were still on the wall. In the bedroom, there were family photos of the three of them. And her mother's pictures still were displayed in a place of prominence.

Tuite acknowledged that the authorities had conducted an investigation of Alan after someone had reported that he might be abusing his daughter. Friends of Dianne's told the police that they suspected that Alan showed an unhealthy interest in Anndra's body, spending hours bathing her. But Tuite noted that Alan had been cleared of any wrongdoing. In fact, the caseworker who conducted the investigation had been so amazed at Anndra's loving environment that she teasingly had asked when she could bring over her own children.

So Tuite begged for mercy on Anndra's behalf, urging the judge to sentence Alan to less than ten years. Anndra was going to need her father as she grew up. And a lenient sentence also would mean that Alan, now fifty-four, might again have a life.

Then it was Scorza's turn. He requested Judge Zagel to tailor the sentences to the men who were before him. "Who is the real Michael Corbitt? Who is the real James Keating? Who is the real Alan Masters who should be sentenced here?" he asked rhetorically.

Scorza started his review with the forty-five-year-old Corbitt. Referring to Corbitt's sentencing in his earlier case, he pointed out that he had called Corbitt nothing more than a prostitute with a badge. Corbitt, he said, was a man who was willing to sell his office as often as possible and at whatever price was offered.

Corbitt had preyed on men like owners of the chop shops and taverns. These kinds of individuals are weak and will submit to shakedowns and plundering.

The government was convinced, he said, that the real

Michael Corbitt was the man who shot Dianne Masters in the head that night as she lay in the trunk of her car with a crushed skull.

> Shooting her in the head was, if not an act of outright blood lust, if not an act of just a showoff, an act to help cover up that crime. So when I ask the court to look at Michael Corbitt, I say we look at the Michael Corbitt who stood at the banks of the Willow Springs Canal at 11 o'clock on March 19, 1982, and did what he did. That was a man who knew no restraint, who knew no decency. He deserves no mercy from this Court.

For the affable Keating, Scorza had nothing but contempt. "In an unspeakably corrupt police department, Keating was one of the kings. And, in fact, his rank somewhat understates his influence in that department. He was one of the highest officers; in fact, one of the most powerful officers. He was thoroughly corrupt."

Keating was portraying himself before the court as harshly treated, said the prosecutor. But actually, Keating's fifteen-year prison term was inadequate considering how he had abused the power and the office entrusted to him. Scorza characterized Keating as the extortionist behind the shakedowns and the protector of the bookmakers.

Scorza reminded Judge Zagel that Keating had been seeking a hit man for Alan to kill Dianne at the same time he was a lieutenant in the Cook County Sheriff's Police Department. That fact by itself was sufficient for Keating to receive the maximum penalty, Scorza argued.

The real James Keating, Scorza told Zagel, was the individual who once bragged to undercover agent Larry Damron about Dianne's timely disappearance. Keating had found it humorous. The real James Keating was the man who had orchestrated the sheriff's department's coverup. Said Scorza, "The real James Keating is the man who is proud of his relationship with Alan Masters, who bragged about it to Larry Damron, and the James Keating who was only too happy to help Alan Masters solicit and arrange the murder of Dianne Masters."

It was Alan Masters, however, who was the target of Scorza's harshest invective. He called Tuite's depiction of Alan obscene, saying that Tuite had made it sound like Alan was running for the U.S. Senate. "Alan Masters was the most notoriously corrupt attorney in the south suburbs. He defiled every courtroom that he ever slithered into." The case was not just about Dianne's murder, said Scorza, it was also about how Alan Masters and two high-ranking corrupt police officers had corrupted an entire system of justice.

Scorza said he was saddened by the depiction of Dianne during the trial and amazed that Alan had contended in a presentence report that he still loved his dead wife. That had not been the defense's position during the trial, he noted, when they ridiculed her memory, depicting her in the most offensive way possible.

Dianne Masters, Scorza reminded the judge, was simply a woman who wanted to be loved. When she didn't receive it at home, she sought love elsewhere. Scorza continued:

> I can't believe that a just and merciful God turns his back on Dianne Masters, and I personally—although I'm not a pious man—I see a lot of things that make me think that this case turned out the way it did as a way of signaling to us that Dianne Masters was not the human being portrayed by the defense at trial.
>
> Alan Masters no doubt loves his daughter the way a father would love his daughter. But we can't forget he killed her mother in 1982.

Then he lambasted the trio for bringing their family members into the courtroom. Scorza quoted a passage in the Apology of Socrates, where the philosopher said bringing children into court was a way of receiving compassion—not justice. And that was just what the defendants had done. They had used their families as shields, as their last refuge, said the prosecutor.

"Judge, there is a big mystery in my case for me, and the mystery is how a just God allows people like Masters and Corbitt and Keating to crawl on the face of the earth. I think it's to test our mettle. I think it's to test to see what we will do when faced with them, to see if we will flinch."

After Alan, Keating, and Corbitt all declined to speak on their behalf, an undercurrent of tension pervaded the courtroom. There would be no outbursts from the defendants or their families. When the judge began his pronouncements, Randy grew apprehensive. He concentrated on listening solely for Alan's name.

Michael Corbitt: twenty years, to run concurrent with the six-year sentence he was serving already.

James Keating: twenty years, to run concurrent with the fifteen-year prison term he was serving already.

Alan Masters: forty years and a $250,000 fine.

Randy felt jubilant. "Once Alan got that many years, I was tickled," he would say later. "I felt real good about it."

He had anticipated post-sentencing interviews and had worn a black pinstriped suit, white shirt, and polka-dot tie to court. In the federal building's lobby, members of the media awaited him. The major television stations had their crews in place, and as soon as Randy emerged from the elevator, cameras and lights were flashing and microphones were shoved in front of him.

He told the reporters that he was elated at Alan's lengthy sentence. But given the heinous nature of the crime, it wasn't enough. He hoped the state attorney would press forward with the case and file charges against Dianne's killers.

For Randy never would rest until Alan actually was convicted of his sister's murder.

Chapter Thirty-Five

March 19, 1982

As Dianne Masters emerged from the Village Courtyard restaurant with her three companions from the college, she was surprised by the change in the weather. The springlike temperatures of earlier that day had vanished; the mercury had dropped to near freezing. She shivered in her dark-blue raincoat, inadequate against the chilling dampness that now permeated the air. The sky was overcast, threatening rain.

It was 1:10 A.M. when she and one of her colleagues, who had walked her to her yellow-and-white Cadillac, which was parked in front of the restaurant, exchanged good-byes. He watched as Dianne started the engine and backed out of the space.

Condensation had formed on the car's windows and she immediately turned on the windshield wipers to clean off the glass. She turned left out of the parking lot and began her eight-minute journey home, heading west on 123d Street. The two-lane highway was a darkened thoroughfare, and at that hour, there was virtually no traffic.

Dianne was thankful that the evening had ended earlier than most of the post-board meeting sessions. The three glasses of Chablis had calmed her jittery nerves and she was anxious to get home, curl up in bed with her animals and a snack, and write Jim a note.

She missed him dreadfully. She hadn't seen him in nearly three days and they had no plans for the weekend. When the divorce papers were filed on Monday, they would start a normal relationship. They would have time. The time to be together whenever they chose. And free of the duplicity she had been forced to resort to: using friends to lie for her. How she hated it.

Monday seemed like an eternity away. At least she was seeing Randy and his family for dinner on Sunday. Talking to her brother and sister-in-law helped tremendously.

Just three days to go and it would all be over, Dianne thought as she pushed the accelerator, quickly exceeding 123d Street's forty-miles-per-hour speed limit. She was unaware that Genevieve Capstaff, the inquisitive humanities professor, was following her. Dianne reached the stop sign at Wolf Road and then turned left toward her home, which was about a hundred yards away.

Dianne drove into her winding driveway and turned off the ignition. She grabbed her purse and opened the door of the Cadillac, leaving her satchel filled with papers from the board meeting in the car.

What happened during the next few minutes at the Masters' sprawling ranch home may never be revealed. Clearly, Dianne died a horrible, violent death, ending the life of a young woman whose future promised happiness. She finally had resolved who she was, and independence was within her grasp. And after years of searching for love, she had attained a fulfilling, nurturing relationship.

Dianne's murderer took much more, though, than just one life that night. He not only deprived Anndra of a mother, but also robbed her of a normal childhood. Every day, she has had to confront the memory that her father was accused of killing her mother.

The authorities have yet to discover what actually occurred after Dianne arrived home. They have only theories. Among the unresolved issues is the possibility that Alan and his hired killer were waiting at the house for Dianne to return. Because of the previous foul-ups in trying to track her after the board meetings, they had decided simply to lay in wait at the location where they knew she eventually would appear—her home.

When they heard Dianne pull into the driveway, Alan and a Cook County sheriff's deputy, who was a family friend, walked to the car. Corbitt told prosecutors that the deputy fired one shot into Dianne's skull as she got out of the Cadillac. When she fell to the ground, she began to moan and Alan fired a second shot.

Corbitt's version of the events was based on conversations he reportedly had with Alan discussing details of the crime, but investigators give little weight to his statements. The neighbors probably would have heard a gunshot, unless the weapon had been equipped with a silencer. But it was the shell casing that investigators discovered in the sleeve of Dianne's raincoat that chiefly discounted the theory. There was virtually no way that the casing could have gotten into her sleeve if she had been shot on the driveway. That evidence suggests that Dianne was already inside the trunk of her car when the two shots were fired.

Keating said that Alan had told him that the hired killer had struck Dianne in the head when she returned home that evening. The authorities, though, suspect that Dianne once again had eluded Alan's hired killer. When she arrived home, Alan was surprised. Enraged by her presence, he assaulted Dianne himself.

Another possibility is that the plan from the onset was for Alan and his accomplice to murder Dianne inside the house when she returned from the board meeting. The authorities believe that Dianne might have been lured to the basement after she had gone to her bedroom and taken off her pantyhose and shoes. She came downstairs wearing her brown suit, brown silk blouse, and all of her jewelry, including her Baume and Mercier watch.

Perhaps Alan used the ruse that he had to discuss the divorce papers her attorney was filing on Monday or the issue of custody of their daughter. They would not have talked upstairs, for fear of waking Anndra.

The basement was decorated in rust and navy blue tones and there was an L-shaped sofa near the fireplace. Alan's weapon of choice may have been one of the nearby fireplace tools.

When he struck Dianne, she fell to the floor and lay dying on the rust-colored carpeting. When the maid arrived the next morning and found the carpet wet, she vacuumed it.

If Alan was alone in the house, investigators are puzzled about how he might have obtained help to dispose of Dianne's corpse. There are four alternatives: (1) he called from a telephone at home; (2) he went to a nearby pay phone; (3) his hired killer called to report that he was unable to find Dianne; (4) or, by sheer luck, the assassin arrived unexpectedly at the house.

The Masters home is literally miles away from any pay phone. The prospect of Alan murdering his wife and calmly plotting his next steps didn't seem logical, given Alan's propensity to panic during any emergency. He wasn't likely to leave the house, especially with Anndra sleeping upstairs and the possibility that she might awaken and discover her mother's body.

Alan was a shrewd criminal attorney who might have known there was no way that police could trace his local telephone calls. Or he simply might have taken the chance and called for help from his home, figuring that he could account for the late-night telephone calls if questioned by the police.

Undoubtedly, someone assisted Alan in removing Dianne's body from the house and transporting it to Willow Springs, which was a ten-minute drive. Some authorities surmise that Alan and his hired assassin placed Dianne's body in the back of a jeeplike vehicle that was driven by the accomplice. Alan followed in Dianne's Cadillac. He had to chance leaving Anndra alone in the house, hoping she would not awaken while he was gone.

Alan drove the Cadillac for two reasons. Should he be stopped by the police, there would be no questions asked about the ownership of the vehicle. And most of the police who patrolled the area would recognize him by sight.

Once in Willow Springs, they drove to the back of a tavern parking lot, far away from the quiet street, and transferred Dianne's body from the truck to the trunk of her Cadillac. Alan already had made room for the body weeks earlier, when he had borrowed Dianne's car for the day and removed the spare tire. Alan's accomplice took Dianne's satchel from the car. Later he would burn it.

When Willow Springs Police Chief Michael Corbitt arrived, the Cadillac was sitting exactly where he had told Alan to put it. Corbitt told the authorities that he opened the door of the Caddy, adjusted the seat, and reached under the floor mat to retrieve the key ring with the two car keys on it—just where Alan had told him the key ring would be. He started the car and was just driving away when he noticed that the car was making a noise, as if it had a flat tire.

While it was only a few blocks to the canal, Corbitt couldn't risk driving with a flat, investigators believed. Instead he was forced to store the Caddy overnight in the tavern's underground garage. He would get the tire repaired the next day.

At 10:32 P.M. on March 19, Corbitt hatched his scheme. He announced on the police radio that he was assisting a citizen who was locked out of his vehicle at the In First Place lounge. It was a ploy to move the Cadillac, under Corbitt's police escort. Shortly before the police changed shifts at 11 P.M., Corbitt and an accomplice went into the garage and changed the clock on the car to read 1:50 A.M. He set Dianne's watch for a few minutes later. Alan had told him that day that the police had suspected that Dianne had left the restaurant at 1:10 A.M. Corbitt was hoping that if the clock and wristwatch stopped when the car was dumped into the canal, if the car ever was retrieved, it would lead investigators to conclude that Dianne never had arrived home that night, that she had been abducted and killed enroute.

Corbitt's accomplice jumped inside Dianne's Cadillac and backed it up the driveway from the underground garage. With Corbitt following as his escort, he drove the vehicle to the canal.

The waterway was pitch-black, and high overhead on the Willow Springs bridge, there was virtually no traffic at that hour. At the edge of the canal, Corbitt's accomplice rolled down the window of the Cadillac, stepped outside, and quietly closed the driver's side door of the still-idling vehicle.

Then they opened the trunk, where Dianne Masters was almost certainly dead. They left her wearing her blue raincoat.

But they almost completely unbuttoned her blouse, removed her panties, and pushed her white slip and skirt above her navel to give the impression that she may have been sexually molested. Then one of them shot her twice in the head with a .22-caliber automatic, to make it appear that she had been killed by an abductor, not by a violent husband. One of the shells from the weapon ejected into the sleeve of her raincoat.

When the shots rang out, Corbitt ran to the car door, reached through the open window and quickly pulled down the gearshift from park into drive. The men watched as the car slowly drove over the limestone edge, its metal frame scraping the quarry and leaving a telltale mark. As the Cadillac bobbed for a minute or so as the water filled the interior, Corbitt jumped into his own vehicle and announced on the car radio that he was investigating reports of shots fired at the canal. As the yellow roof of the Caddy disappeared, bubbles erupted on the water and the car began its gradual, twenty-five-foot descent to the bottom of the canal.

Dianne Masters had vanished.

Epilogue

AFTER the trial, Randy and Kathy Turner tried to convince Janet that Anndra needed to become acquainted with her family. Despite what had happened, they wanted the youngster to know that they still loved her, that she was very important to them. A concerted effort was made by a handful of relatives who called Janet to try to persuade her to share Anndra with the Turners.

Shortly before either Thanksgiving or Christmas, Randy phoned and was permitted to talk to his niece. He told her he had three boys, all younger than she, who were her cousins whom she had not seen for years. They wanted to meet her, he said. He asked if she would come over to their house and visit.

About a week later, Anndra called one night asking for Randy. He was out of town on a sales trip, but when he returned the following evening, he phoned her, hoping that she was going to accept their invitation.

"I talked to Jan for a few minutes and then Jan said, 'Anndra has something to say to you,' " Randy recalls.

"I don't want to talk to you anymore because you are the person who put my daddy in jail," Anndra told Randy.

He tried to explain. "Anndra I didn't do anything. I am not a policeman. I am not a lawyer. The law and those people put him in jail. I didn't do any of that Anndra. You can't blame me."

"Well, I still don't want to talk to you," she replied, and she hung up the phone.

That was the last time that Randy or Kathy Turner ever talked to their niece.

Randy concluded that Jan had urged Anndra to tell her uncle that she never wanted to hear from him again. He thought Jan's machinations were due, in part, to a phone call she had received from one of his relatives, an attempt to reconcile the two families. During the conversation, Jan maintains that the person insinuated that she was a prostitute, or words to that affect.

Months passed before Randy and Jan talked again. Later she gave the Turners some memorabilia that Dianne had collected through the years—treasures such as baptismal cards and family photos. For Randy, they were a connection to his beloved sister and he was thrilled to have them. He picked them up at the Palos Park home when Anndra wasn't present and was allowed inside. He was unprepared for the sight that greeted him, never expecting to see so many of Dianne's possessions still hanging on the walls and displayed on shelves.

But the troubles between Randy and Jan had started before the trial, when he had made the mistake of hiring the city's top attorney in preparation for a custody battle for Anndra. It had been a disaster from the beginning and it had left behind deep emotional scars that contributed to Anndra's refusal to see Randy as well as a big legal debt for him.

Convinced that he needed someone with impeccable credentials to challenge Alan, he had chosen Dan Webb, the former U.S. attorney in Chicago. Boyish looking but tough as nails, he was picked by the U.S. Justice Department as the special prosecutor of former National Security Adviser John Poindexter in the Iran-contra trials.

Webb works for Winston and Strawn, one of the city's most elite law firms. His services aren't cheap; he can charge as much as $300 an hour. Randy, who had lengthy conversations with Webb and his associates, eventually received a bill for $27,995. He paid slightly over $16,000, most of his life savings.

Yet he thought he got very little in the way of legal services for his money. Webb and his associates originally had two ideas. One was to file a lawsuit against the Cook County Sheriff's Department and others for the coverup of Dianne's murder. Webb said that it would be best if Dianne's estate filed the suit on behalf of Anndra. To do so, the lawyers would seek to wrest control of the estate from Alan, the sole heir and executor.

Removing Alan as executor of the estate and substituting Anndra as the sole heir was tricky. Illinois law provides that a person who is convicted of the murder of another shall not inherit from the murdered person any interest in the estate of the descendent by reason of the death.

But Alan was not convicted of the murder of Dianne, and as a result, the case law in Illinois did not clearly favor Randy. The lawyers filed briefs seeking to reopen Dianne's estate and to have Anndra named the sole qualified heir, but because of a dispute with Randy over legal fees, the issue never was resolved by a judge.

Nor were the attorneys anxious to enter into such a court battle, because Dianne's estate had few assets. All Anndra could gain from Randy's intervention in the probate case was several thousand dollars in cash and Dianne's expensive jewelry, unless a lawsuit was filed against the Cook County Sheriff's Department.

Although Alan had received the proceeds of the $100,000 life insurance policy, that was not part of the estate. Nor were the couple's marital home and their Florida condominium, because the property had been in both of their names. However, under Illinois law, Alan's right to retain the $100,000 and the homes also could have been challenged because of his federal court conviction. But once again, the litigation would have been costly.

Second, Randy wanted the firm to seek custody of Anndra for him. The attorneys assured him that because Alan would be going to prison and Randy was the sole surviving relative, he probably could get custody of Anndra. What the lawyers did not figure into the equation was Alan's secret marriage to Jan, which virtually precluded any chance of Randy obtaining custody of his niece.

Webb also called in the state authorities, the Illinois Department of Children and Family Services, asking them to review, after the trial, Anndra's home life to see if it was a proper family situation. More than anything else, the state investigation was the primary reason for the schism between the Turners and Jan Masters.

The letter Webb wrote to Gordon Johnson, the head of the agency, chiefly cited Dianne's brutal murder and her husband's pending criminal charges as the reason that an investigation was warranted. Webb expressed concern about Anndra's environment saying it could affect her mentally and morally. He also raised the possibility that Anndra could be in jeopardy.

Because of Webb's political ties, it was a complaint that the agency took seriously. They sent out an investigator, but as Tuite noted to Judge Zagel, the state agency concluded that Anndra was in a safe and loving environment.

Randy believed that he had been taken advantage of by the law firm. He insisted that there had been a verbal agreement to take the case for a $10,000 retainer and that he would be billed only for the expenses that the firm incurred for such items as filing court documents.

Webb, in a letter to the Turners, contended that there had been a misunderstanding. The law firm would continue to represent him only if he paid the outstanding balance, about $13,000 of the $27,995 bill. He explained that he had tried to minimize the fees. Webb related that he had reduced his hourly rate, and he did not charge Randy for all the time he had devoted to the case. Wherever possible, he had used other employees, whose hourly fees were lower, to do the work.

Webb agreed to write off the balance due, and the law firm withdrew from the case.

Every April, Randy visits the grave of his sister and parents. The one thing he still prays for is that someday, Alan Masters will be charged with Dianne's murder. The federal trial was only a partial victory. "It wasn't everything we wanted. We still to this day want murder one charges. It still scares me with politics and everything that someday, somehow, Alan is going to go free. Alan and Tuite are going to find some way to overturn this thing."

The Turners and their relatives periodically call the Cook County State Attorney's Office asking them to review their file against Alan to see whether murder charges could be brought forth. The state attorney has taken no action, though.

Randy has come to the painful realization that until Anndra is independent and can make her own decisions, she never will be part of his family. But he continues to love and worry about his only niece—Dianne's daughter.

Anndra Masters currently attends Morgan Park Academy, a private school in Chicago that is considered among the best in the city. An honor roll student, she plays the flute and piano. She loves to swim, ride her bicycle, and read, and she is very interested in acting. In accordance with Alan's wishes, she is being raised in the Jewish faith and was bat mitzvahed.

"Anndra is kind of quiet. Serious," notes Jan. "But when she is with her friends, she laughs and has a good time."

On several occasions, some of her classmates have been cruel, taunting Anndra about her mother's death and her father's role in it. "She gets back at them. She won't let them get her down," declares Jan. "We're survivors or we wouldn't have made it this long. From being with me so long, she has the attitude that I have. Worrying about it isn't going to change it."

Providing her adopted daughter with stability and a haven from the outside world is her primary concern. "Right now, I'm the person she's known the longest and the most stable. I want to make sure that she's OK and that people aren't bothering her. I want her to move forward with her life instead of the past being thrown up."

Anndra refers to Jan as her mother. There is only thirteen years difference between them, and they do everything together, which enhances and strengthens their relationship. They are very close.

They have always spent many hours talking about the typical things that interest girls as well as the unusual circumstances surrounding Anndra's life: the murder; whether Anndra's father is going to come home; the possibility of moving; her plans for the future. And when Anndra asks questions about her parents,

Jan answers them as best she can. "I tell her that there could have been a lot of things that happened to Mommy. I told her Dianne was having an affair and things weren't good. We sit and talk about all that."

On July 20, 1995, Anndra will turn eighteen. On that day, she will have access to $194,000 in investment funds that Alan established for his daughter in 1985. The funds stem from an August 1982 traffic accident that Alan had in Florida while driving a rental car.

A month after Alan was incarcerated, Jan's father was killed in a farm accident. Ironically, he had become an intimate of the Masters family. Alan's representation of Jan's ex-mother had produced bitter feelings. "Dad, through the divorce, got the short end of the stick," Jan explains. "They ended up being very good friends."

Shortly after the trial, she realized that she was being followed by federal agents, and possibly by someone else. When she and a friend went out to lunch, the person following her would sit at a nearby table and observe them.

Alan instructed her to find out who was shadowing her and to get his license plate number. But Jan chooses not to worry about her safety. Her attitude is that you can only die once.

She and Anndra live in the Palos Park home, and she admits that sometimes it feels strange to be living in the house where Dianne might have been murdered. She also thinks that it's eerie that Dianne got to the driveway before she was killed, which contradicts Tuite's contention throughout the trial that Dianne never arrived home.

"It was obvious she didn't expect to die then," says Jan who has read Dianne's diary. "She wrote up until she disappeared. It was basically about Alan; his good and bad aspects as well as her past affairs. It talked about how much she loved Alan. Dianne was insecure. She had changed a lot over the years. She had gone back to her religion. She finally found that she was a good person. . . . I think I would have liked her. She sure must have been a complicated person."

Obviously Jan thinks about what *really* happened. But she won't divulge her thoughts on the matter. She does note, however, that from the onset of her relationship with Alan, she told him that as long as he was nice to her and they got along, she would stay with him. And Alan has been very good to her. She also emphasizes that she is totally different from Dianne. She never would behave as Dianne did; nor would she insult or criticize Alan as Dianne did.

Trying to understand why Dianne didn't flee if she so feared for her life remains an enigma to Jan. She has concluded that Dianne was a good mother, but when she puts herself in Dianne's place, she says she would have left and come back for Anndra later if she believed that her life really was in jeopardy. Or Dianne could have taken Anndra with her.

People often ask Jan when she is going to crack from stress. Her outlet is to cry a lot. But she also has a supportive family and wonderful friends. Her one luxury is a weekly manicure. Jan's days remain busy. She works as a demonstrator for perfume and makeup companies in local department stores. And during the tax season, she continues to operate Tax Masters.

She is uncertain, however, as to what her future holds. "It can't keep being heartaches and hard times. There's got to be something good coming for me one of these days. I'd like to have all this over with. The things I really want aren't going to happen."

Jan fears that this book will depict Alan "as a really terrible, ruthless guy. He's not like that. He's a very wonderful, warm person. Alan's very friendly. He loves to tell jokes and he's one of those people who can tell them well, too."

Initially, Alan was incarcerated at the federal penitentiary in Oxford, Wisconsin, where he worked eight hours a day as a clerk in the library. To keep busy, he also walked on the track, read, played cards, wrote letters.

Because of a heart ailment, he was then transferred to a facility in Springfield, Missouri, which is equipped to deal with inmates' medical problems.

Michael Corbitt is in the federal penitentiary at La Tuna, Texas, a small town outside of El Paso that straddles the borders of New Mexico, Texas, and Mexico.

The desert climate is a boon for Corbitt, who once suffered

from emphysema and obesity. Chicago, as his fellow inmates supposedly call him, reportedly trains daily. The former Willow Springs police chief walks twenty miles each day in the unbearable heat. At the medium-security prison, which is filled with drug dealers, he is in charge of scheduling the other prisoners' use of the phones.

In June 1990, a jury convicted Corbitt for the third time. Scorza had indicted him again, this time accusing him of obstruction of justice for trying to falsify an alibi in the 1987 racketeering and extortion case to which he had pleaded guilty.

James Keating is in the federal detention center in Oakdale, Louisiana. Those who have seen him say that he is a truly beaten individual. The once-affable Keating now is subservient to the system.

Keating presently works in the prison earning $200 a month. His attorney asked that Judge Zagel consider resentencing Keating to a lesser prison term, contending that he has been cooperating with authorities in a criminal investigation. However, those who interviewed Keating refused to comment on whether he was helpful.

On February 6, 1991, the U.S. Court of Appeals denied the appeal of Alan, Corbitt, and Keating. In handing down their decision, the judges referred to the defendants as "the miniature suburban Mafia" and called the facts in the case "a lurid mixture of corruption and murder."

On August 2, 1991, Alan was resentenced by Zagel. Ironically, his lawyers had raised an issue on appeal that led to a longer prison term. Tuite had argued that Zagel had erred by failing to apply 1987 sentencing guidelines to his conviction on the conspiracy count. The appellate court ordered that Alan be resentenced.

It was a legal blunder by the defense. Under these more stringent guidelines, Alan's prison term was almost certain to increase. At the resentencing hearing, Zagel again sentenced him to a total of forty years.

Originally, Alan would have served a term ranging between ten and twenty-three years. Now he must be incarcerated at least twenty-four years and a maximum of thirty years. Under the guidelines, Zagel also returned a judicial finding concluding Alan was responsible for the murder of Dianne.

Alan's only victory, of sorts, was Zagel's reduction of his $250,000 fine to just $1,700. Tuite claimed that Alan had only $1,700 in assets. Under a 1988 prenuptial agreement, Alan agreed to give Jan the Palos Park house, the Summit law-office building, a lot in Galena, and his interest in Domes America.

Under the appellate court ruling, however, Alan must still forfeit $42,000, part of the bribes and fees he received.

Tuite also revealed that the Internal Revenue Service had placed a lien for back taxes totaling $250,000 against Alan's only known source of income—fees that he was receiving from a law firm as part of a prior business arrangement.

Jack Bachman continues to cooperate with the federal prosecutors and has assisted them in a long-running investigation into organized crime's control of judges and politicians in Chicago.

His four-year prison sentence was one of the stiffest handed out to the corrupt sheriff's deputies who agreed to cooperate with the government. The judge also ordered that he serve one thousand hours of community service and complete five years of probation.

Lt. Howard Vanick, who had headed the sheriff's department's investigation into Dianne's disappearance, remains on the force. He was suspended initially, though, because of trial testimony showing that he had supplied Jim Koscielniak's license plate number to Alan's associates.

It was odd that Vanick would be considered a hero in the Masters case. Yet that is precisely how he was portrayed later by the FBI. Days before Vanick was to appear before a panel and face the departmental charges against him, the FBI came to his rescue. James D. McKenzie, the special agent in charge of the Chicago office, told Vanick's bosses that Vanick had made unique and significant contributions to the Masters case that were not known to the sheriff's department's internal investigators.

Three FBI agents maintained that shortly after Dianne's disappearance in 1982, Vanick had approached them and reported his suspicions in the case. It was through Vanick's efforts, they said, that the FBI had unofficially entered the investigation. According to the FBI agents, Vanick had demanded that they never reveal his role, because he feared retaliation from Keating.

Vanick's twenty-six-year career in the department was saved. Then Sheriff James O'Grady said that he secretly had learned from the FBI in 1988 of Vanick's cooperation but had pledged not to disclose it even to members of his own department. "I'm just a cop trying to do a good job," said Vanick upon hearing the news.

His heroics and courage later were touted in a *Chicago Tribune* editorial. A national television show contacted him about doing a dramatization of his exploits.

Then, two months later, the *Tribune*, in another story, basically rescinded its adulation. Quoting sources, the newspaper reported that Vanick's friends in the FBI had exaggerated his importance in the case to help him keep his job. Yet that wasn't the only incident of individuals erroneously being credited for their role in the Dianne Masters investigation. Sheriff James O'Grady even got into the act by having the Chicago Police Department give one of his partners at Special Operations Associates a special award for having solved the case.

Nowhere in SOA's own reports did it ever reveal any evidence that came close to determining what had happened to Dianne. The agency also continues to take credit for finding Genevieve Capstaff, the woman who had followed Dianne the night she left the restaurant, even though Jim Koscielniak and Randy had given SOA her name.

Sgt. Clarke Buckendahl now operates a video store. He was suspended from the sheriff's department and later resigned. Under a grant of immunity from criminal prosecution, he had testified about his and Alan's ownership of a whorehouse.

Sgt. Joe Hein, the twenty-two-year veteran and former head of the security detail for the state attorney, is no longer a Cook County sheriff's deputy. He resigned shortly after he was suspended, admitting that he had not informed his superiors that Alan had illegally tape-recorded his wife's phone calls.

In November 1989, U.S. Attorney Richard Thornburgh cited John Reed as the one individual who had solved the Dianne Masters case.

"There was something wrong going on in the sheriff's office. You are the one officer involved in this case who most deserves this," said Chicago's U.S. attorney at the time, Anton Valukas.

Subsequently, Reed received a department commendation from O'Grady. The commendation noted that his work was under the direction of the esteemed sheriff.

For Reed, the award was the culmination of the kind of investigation that homicide detectives dream of. For twenty-two months, he was assigned primarily to one case. He and his partners, Sabin and Colby, recorded literally hundreds of interviews and compiled more than a thousand pages of reports.

"I think the thing I liked the most about this was getting a letter from Thornburgh. That meant more to me than any backhanded compliments from Mr. O'Grady."

Most investigators who solve big murder cases get rewarded in their careers. That, however, was not the case with Reed.

"I couldn't say they punished me. I am working four to twelve in an investigative section. I am buried, but I couldn't say I was punished. I don't think Mr. O'Grady knows what to do with somebody who has an ounce of integrity or an ounce of character and who is not a lackey or a boot kisser. All he wants around him are lackeys and yes-men. And I am not that type of person."

Despite the revelations about corruption among the sheriff's police, little changed after the trial. The department's top brass blamed the problem on O'Grady's predecessor, Richard J. Elrod, and ignored the allegations that surfaced.

Reed said, "It was a bad dream. Something that happened on another planet, in another time warp or dimension. It had nothing to do with us. It was like this strange foreign power came here and kidnapped Jim Keating and Clarke Buckendahl. It had nothing to do with what was going on."

For Reed, the investigation helped him decide what kind of police officers his brethren were. The honest ones never were angry about what he was doing. The crooked ones told him he should not be investigating a colleague.

"To me it was a delineator. A way of separating the good from the bad. The good guys knew it had to be done. That these guys were a cancer on our department. A big wart. And someone should excise it. It wasn't me. It was the federal government."

Reed wasn't the only one who lacked respect for O'Grady. On November 6, 1990, the voters of Cook County ousted him from office after serving just one four-year term.

Despite his campaign promises, the corruption remained and the department became even more political during his tenure. O'Grady had vowed to halt fund-raising in the sheriff's office. Instead he gave sensitive jobs to his cronies and muscled the department's employees for contributions to his campaign war chest. He had promised to get tough on organized crime, but vice arrests plummeted under his administration.

O'Grady arranged the selection of James Dvorak, his second-in-command at the sheriff's office and one of his business partners in the detective agency, as the chairman of the Cook County Republican Organization. Dvorak proved an embarrassing appointment when authorities acknowledged that he was the target of a federal investigation. The disclosures by the U.S. Attorney's Office followed the release of secretly made tape recordings of Chicago organized crime figures bragging about their influence with Dvorak.

He eventually resigned from both his sheriff's post and the party chairmanship. As yet, no criminal charges have been filed.

Following reports in the *Chicago Tribune*, O'Grady's private detective agency, SOA, also became a target of the federal grand jury. Because of severe overcrowding at the Cook County Jail, O'Grady was forced by the federal courts to start releasing inmates charged with less serious crimes. He instituted a program where inmates would be confined to their homes and wear an electronic bracelet that allowed the department to monitor their whereabouts. Part of the contracts for the program were doled out to a former attorney in O'Grady's detective agency. And Tom Scorza conducted an investigation to determine whether criminal laws were violated.

On August 1, 1991, U.S. attorney Fred Foreman and Scorza announced the indictment of Daniel M. Davis, O'Grady's partner in SOA. Davis was charged with obstruction of justice for thwarting the grand jury's investigation. The indictment alleged that Davis had provided a $138,000 loan to a woman who was the chief executive of the firm that received the electronic monitoring contract. In addition, there was a purported written agreement that Davis failed to provide to the grand jury under which Davis and another SOA employee would be entitled to purchase all of the firm's stock at a prearranged price.

The grand jury is continuing its investigation and looking at possible wrongdoing by O'Grady and Dvorak, according to Foreman and Scorza.

The voters' collective memories about Richard J. Elrod and his operation of the sheriff's department were short. In a recent election, he was an easy winner over his Republican rival for a circuit court judgeship.

Tom Scorza remains the deputy chief of the organized crime and drug enforcement task force in Chicago's U.S. Attorney's Office. His trial partner, Pat Foley, is in private practice.

For Ted Nykaza, the trial was even more destructive. Although Tuite had tried to brand Nykaza a suspect in Dianne's murder, there was never any evidence presented linking Nykaza to the crime. His private detective business plummeted and he eventually lost his home in foreclosure proceedings. He moved away from the Chicago area and reportedly now lives in a trailer.

In a letter to Reed, which he received during the final days of the trial, Nykaza blasted his treatment in the courtroom at the hands of Tuite, saying that he had been the victim of character assassination. While he admitted he had a drinking problem, the defense attorney's other accusations were totally false, he told Reed.

Nykaza discussed his future. His intention was to eventually restore his agency to its glory days, when he was making thousands of dollars.

As far as he was concerned, he was convinced that he had acted morally. Nykaza only asked that Reed remain his friend.

Diane Economou, another of the government's chief witnesses, continues to practice law in the south suburbs of Chicago. She is the past president of the Crisis Center for South Suburbia, the group Dianne founded to assist battered women.

Economou had aspirations to sit on the bench. In 1983, she was one of the candidates for an associate judgeship in Cook County. Those with some political clout usually get such appointments. That year, she was asking Alan to call his friends on her behalf.

Despite defeat, she again sought election as an associate judge and later ran unsuccessfully for a full circuit judgeship.

Jim Koscielniak still teaches economics at Moraine Valley Community College.

One question remains unanswered. It is the question that haunts Randy Turner. The question to which Jack Reed can't provide the answer. The question Tom Scorza couldn't resolve at the trial. The nagging question there still wasn't sufficient evidence to answer: *Who killed Dianne Masters*?

Keating had said that she was killed by Alan on the driveway. Corbitt had said that she was shot on the driveway by Alan. During Reed's investigation, he had theorized that as many as eleven different individuals might be the mysterious killer hired by Alan.

A twelfth person, someone whose name surfaced only briefly in the investigation, should now be added to Reed's list. Jack Bachman mentioned him to Reed during their first meeting.

He may be the mystery person whose vehicle Corbitt mentioned in his proffer to authorities. Perhaps he was the person who drove Dianne's Cadillac from the house, delivered it to Corbitt, then left. No one carefully checked the license plate information that Corbitt had given them in his proffer.

The authorities have since run a license plate check. The father of the man Bachman had mentioned to Reed did, in fact, have a vehicle with a license plate that is very similar to the one that Corbitt had told the authorities he spotted on two occasions when he went to pick up Dianne's Cadillac for disposal.

Federal investigative files indicate that the individual Bachman mentioned was dealing narcotics, although the charges were later dropped. One police agency that was conducting an investigation of the man said he hadn't paid state income taxes for three years.

His phone number was in Dianne's address and telephone book. He was a former client of Alan Masters and had been a policeman in the west suburbs.

Nine years later, the policeman and his wife filed for divorce. One of Alan's close friends, an attorney who had handled Alan's own divorce, represented the officer at first, but then withdrew.

His wife was a bookkeeper. He ran a small store, the court records show. Surprisingly, they were immensely wealthy. There were $90,000 in pure silver in a safe deposit box, a small plane in a hangar somewhere near Chicago, several luxury cars, and two expensive boats. He was giving his wife $1,000 a week for grocery money. Yet all of his property was in other people's names—the store that he ran, his summer home, and his $120,000 bomb shelter.

Two years after she had filed for divorce, the case was heard by Judge Daniel Ryan. In a February 4, 1986, hearing, the policeman's wife was asked about her husband's business.

"Your husband has been engaged in various business activities that have generated enormous amounts of cash; isn't that correct?" her attorney asked.

"Yes, he has," she replied.

"Tell the court, madam, the occasion of the safe in the basement, the story."

"We had a flood in our basement and everything got wet. He didn't shut the flood control valve. We had an enormous safe in our basement that contained all of our currency. It got wet. We had to blow dry the money. There was $500,000 in a safe, and we had to blow dry it with hair dryers because it was getting moldy. And I counted it all personally with my older daughter and packaged it up and put it back in the safe. It was $500,000 at that time."

"Do you have any idea where it came from?" asked Judge Ryan.

"From his various business activities," her attorney replied. "She has been kept in the dark, Your Honor, as to exactly what her husband does."

"Are you sure you are getting enough out of this?" the judge asked.

"She wants out," answered her attorney.

According to the lawyer, at one point during the divorce proceedings, the husband uttered this threat: "I am going to take care of you like Dianne Masters."

Here is an excerpt from *Fair Game*—a startling tale of serial murder by Bernard DuClos, coming from St. Martin's Paperbacks:

On Sunday night, the bars on Fourth and Fifth Avenue were quiet. In the midst of single-story, box-like buildings that formed the "tenderloin strip" in downtown Anchorage, Alaska, business wasn't as brisk as the midnight air. Nineteen-year-old Cindy Paulson stood on the corner of Fifth and Denali with a lot of territory to herself.

Cindy spotted a car passing the Mackay Building. When it headed toward her, she postured her five-six frame, cocked her chin, and put a sensual bend into one of her legs. She was "doin' business." As the car approached and slowed down, Cindy recognized the green Buick Century. It was the John who had stood her up last night, so the price tonight would be higher.

Cindy Paulson stepped to the curb, bent down and rested her forearms on the opened front passenger window. "Well, Mr. 'Day-Late,' you're in luck, I'm here! What's it gonna be?"

Robert Hansen sat at the wheel in jeans, a brown shirt and green down jacket, wearing a bright green baseball cap. Staring through his glasses with a half-smile on his 44-year-old pockmarked face, he told her what he wanted.

They worked out a price and Cindy got in the car. Suddenly, she found the barrel of a .357 Magnum sticking in her face. From behind the cold blue barrel she heard a snarling, deliberate voice. "All right, now you'll do exactly what I say. I know what I'm doing . . . I've done this before. So just sit and stay still."

In the slow motion of terror, Cindy complied. Her captor reached under the seat, came up with a pair of handcuffs and grinned. "We're going to my house."

Hansen cuffed Cindy and put the gun to her face. He clicked the action. "Now remember, don't move . . . be quiet." The gun on his lap, he readjusted the seat, started the car, and drove out of the lot and turned north.

After a few minutes, the car slowed down, and Cindy saw a blue-gray ranch nestled in a quiet stand of pines. When Hansen made a right turn into its driveway, she noticed an expansive rack of caribou antlers above the doors of its two-car garage.

"Here we are." Hansen dragged his captive into the house. His grip tightened on her arm as he led her down some steps and into a dark room.

The frightened woman saw brown carpet at her feet when a light went on. Her gaze came up and she was confronted with a menagerie of icy stares. The walls around a couch were covered with stuffed trophy mounts—fish, Dall Sheep, mountain goats, a grizzly bear and game birds. A black bear rug was in front of the couch, and behind it was a tiled area containing a pool table.

Hansen handcuffed Cindy to a support beam, then wrapped a chain around her neck, attaching the chain to a metal ring on the pillar.

After he was finished assaulting her from this position, Hansen unchained her, but left the handcuffs on. He started bragging about his hunting—a world record Dall Sheep—and showed his captive a trophy plaque.

It was different than the name he'd used to make an appointment with Cindy for Saturday night. She figured that since he let her know his real name, he'd probably decided to kill her. *She would have to escape if she was going to survive!*

But Robert Hansen wasn't finished with his prey. "You're so good," he said, "I'm going to fly you to a cabin for a few days." He led her, cuffed, upstairs and out to the Buick. Forcing her into the floor of the back seat, he covered her with an Army blanket.

Cindy heard the back door close and the driver's door open and shut as Hansen got in. The engine started and the car pulled out of the drive; Cindy sensed they were back-tracking the route they'd taken earlier.

Hansen drove down the Glenn Highway, heading for Merrill Field.

Cindy felt the car turn left and continue at a much slower speed. It came to a halt and the engine died. She heard her captor shift in the driver's seat, then his voice overhead.

"I'm gonna load my plane. Stay down and don't move . . . if you try anything, I'll kill you!"

Cindy felt Hansen get out and heard him go around and get something out of the trunk. When she heard his footsteps trail away, she pushed off the blanket and crawled up to the window to see where he'd gone.

As her eyes adjusted to the light, she could see a sign for Airparts Inc., and, between her and the sign, a row of bushplanes. She saw Hansen loading something into a blue-and-white airplane. *Now was her chance!*

Cindy turned and lunged to the driver's seat, threw open the door, and stumbled out barefoot into the roadway. She ran north toward Fifth Avenue, not yielding to the stabs of pain in her feet.

"Stop, you bitch . . . Stop or I'll kill you!" roared Hansen's voice from behind. He started out after her.

Cindy never looked back; she ran onto Fifth and headed west. . . .

Fair Game—coming in February
From St. Martin's Paperbacks

Newlyweds Pam and Gregg Smart seemed like the perfect American couple. He was an up-and-coming young insurance executive, she the beautiful former cheerleader who now worked in the administration of the local school.

But on May 1, 1990, their idyllic life was shattered when Gregg was murdered in the couple's upscale Derry, New Hampshire townhouse—a single shot to his head. Three months later, the grieving widow was arrested and charged with the brutal crime.

In the dramatic trial that followed, a dark portrait of Pam Smart emerged—one of a cold manipulator who seduced a high school student with a striptease and then had a wild affair with him—until he was so involved with her that he was willing to do anything for her...even murder...

DEADLY LESSONS

BY EDGAR AWARD NOMINEE

KEN ENGLADE

DEADLY LESSONS
Ken Englade
_____ 92761-4 $4.99 U.S./$5.99 Can.

Publishers Book and Audio Mailing Service
P.O. Box 120159, Staten Island, NY 10312-0004
Please send me the book(s) I have checked above. I am enclosing $______ (please add $1.50 for the first book, and $.50 for each additional book to cover postage and handling. Send check or money order only—no CODs) or charge my VISA, MASTERCARD or AMERICAN EXPRESS card.

Card number ________________________

Expiration date ____________ Signature ____________

Name ________________________

Address ________________________

City ____________ State/Zip ____________

Please allow six weeks for delivery. Prices subject to change without notice. Payment in U.S. funds only. New York residents add applicable sales tax.

When the sheriff of East Chatham, N.Y. first described the bloody scene—"Worse than anything I ever saw in Korea"—he was reduced to tears. Four people—a popular local businessman, his live-in girlfriend, his nineteen-year-old son, and his three-year-old orphaned nephew—had been brutally murdered in an isolated country cabin.

By the next day, a stunned community learned that the dead man's seventeen-year-old son, Wyley Gates—vice-president of his class and voted "most likely to succeed"—had allegedly confessed to the murders. What could possibly be the motive for such a grisly crime—and how could such an upright teenage boy explode with such lethal fury?

MOST LIKELY TO SUCCEED

ALAN GELB

MOST LIKELY TO SUCCEED
Alan Gelb
_____ 92566-2 $5.99 U.S./$6.99 Can.

Publishers Book and Audio Mailing Service
P.O. Box 120159, Staten Island, NY 10312-0004
Please send me the book(s) I have checked above. I am enclosing $ _______ (please add $1.50 for the first book, and $.50 for each additional book to cover postage and handling. Send check or money order only—no CODs) or charge my VISA, MASTERCARD or AMERICAN EXPRESS card.

Card number ____

Expiration date ____________________ Signature ____________________

Name ____

Address ____

City ____________________ State/Zip ____________________

Please allow six weeks for delivery. Prices subject to change without notice. Payment in U.S. funds only. New York residents add applicable sales tax.

MLS 11/91

Bob Evans. Legendary producer of megahit movies like *Chinatown* and *The Godfather*, he was now on the verge of his biggest blockbuster ever. All he needed was one more investor...

Roy Radin. A flashy New York entrepreneur, he tried to make it big in Hollywood—until his bullet-riddled body turned up in a dry desert creek...

Laney Jacobs. Beautiful, glamorous, seductive, she clawed her way to the top of Miami's fast-living super-rich. Now, she wanted a piece of Hollywood—and it seemed as if no price would be too high to pay for it...

From the sprawling mansions of Long Island to the tantalizing glitz of the Sunset Strip, this is the startling truth behind the sensational "Cotton Club" murder—a story more shocking than any Hollywood script!

COMPANY

by Pulitzer Prize-Winning Author

STEVE WICK

"A mean tale of unspeakable deeds."
—Dominick Dunne, author of *People Like Us*

BAD COMPANY
Steve Wick
_____ 92517-4 $5.99 U.S./$6.99 Can.

Publishers Book and Audio Mailing Service
P.O. Box 120159, Staten Island, NY 10312-0004
Please send me the book(s) I have checked above. I am enclosing $ _______ (please add $1.50 for the first book, and $.50 for each additional book to cover postage and handling. Send check or money order only—no CODs) or charge my VISA, MASTERCARD or AMERICAN EXPRESS card.

Card number ______________________________

Expiration date ______________ Signature ______________

Name ______________________________

Address ______________________________

City ______________ State/Zip ______________

Please allow six weeks for delivery. Prices subject to change without notice. Payment in U.S. funds only. New York residents add applicable sales tax.

BC 11/91

True Crime From St. Martin's Paperbacks!

ULTERIOR MOTIVES
by Suzanne Finstad
When Flamboyant tycoon Henry Kyle was found murdered in 1983, it was only the beginning...
______ 91185-8 $4.50 U.S. ______ 91186-6 $5.50 Can.

DEADLY BLESSING
by Steve Salerno
The tragic consequences of a marriage between a wealthy young power broker and a local waitress.
______ 92804-1 $4.99 U.S./$5.99 Can.

THE SERPENT'S TOOTH
by Christopher P. Anderson
The story of an extremely rich family destroyed by greed...and murder.
______ 90541-6 $3.95 U.S. ______ 90542-4 $4.95 Can.

CELLAR OF HORROR
by Ken Englade
What police found in Gary Heidnik's basement went beyond mere horror...
______ 90959-4 $4.50 U.S. ______ 90960-8 $5.50 Can.

Publishers Book and Audio Mailing Service
P.O. Box 120159, Staten Island, NY 10312-0004
Please send me the book(s) I have checked above. I am enclosing $ ______ (please add $1.50 for the first book, and $.50 for each additional book to cover postage and handling. Send check or money order only—no CODs) or charge my VISA, MASTERCARD or AMERICAN EXPRESS card.

Card number ______

Expiration date ______ Signature ______

Name ______

Address ______

City ______ State/Zip ______

Please allow six weeks for delivery. Prices subject to change without notice. Payment in U.S. funds only. New York residents add applicable sales tax.

WTC 9/91